# RUN, BROTHER, RUN

~

*A Memoir of a Murder in My Family*

# DAVID BERG

SCRIBNER

*New York  London  Toronto  Sydney  New Delhi*

SCRIBNER
A Division of Simon & Schuster, Inc.
1230 Avenue of the Americas
New York, NY 10020

First Scribner hardcover edition June 2013

SCRIBNER and design are registered trademarks of The Gale Group, Inc.,
used under license by Simon & Schuster, Inc., the publisher of this work.

For information about special discounts for bulk purchases,
please contact Simon & Schuster Special Sales at 1-866-506-1949 or
business@simonandschuster.com.

The Simon & Schuster Speakers Bureau can bring authors to your
live event. For more information or to book an event contact the
Simon & Schuster Speakers Bureau at 1-866-248-3049 or
visit our website at www.simonspeakers.com.

Manufactured in the United States of America

1   3   5   7   9   10   8   6   4   2

ISBN 978-1-4767-1563-6
ISBN 978-1-4767-1679-4 (ebook)

For A H B

H ouston is a cruel and crazy town on a filthy river in East Texas with no zoning laws and a culture of sex, money and violence. It's a shabby sprawling metropolis ruled by brazen women, crooked cops and super-rich pansexual cowboys who live by the code of the West—which can mean just about anything you need it to mean, in a pinch.

—DR. HUNTER S. THOMPSON

# PROLOGUE

I owe my legal career to two men and three aphorisms. The first man is my brother. He was smart, funny, irreverent, and I idolized him. He was also almost six years older, and, from my end of that gap, seemed to be everything that I wanted to be, and little that I was. But that didn't stop him from having confidence in me. "Kid," he said, "you're a person who has to excel," a word that did not seem to belong in my universe. When, in return, I gave him a profoundly skeptical look, he added even greater assurance. "Relax, kid," he said, "even Queen Elizabeth breaks wind."

The second man is Richard "Racehorse" Haynes, his nickname coined by a high school football coach unimpressed by the young Haynes's speed. When Racehorse later became a criminal lawyer and won a string of seemingly unwinnable cases, the nickname took on metaphorical significance: no one could keep up with Race in a courtroom. One day soon, Race would become the most famous criminal lawyer of his generation, but even before that and certainly by 1964, when I entered the University of Houston Law School, he was already our most renowned alumnus, the one my classmates and I would gather in the student lounge to talk about almost reverentially. ("The Horse made twenty-five thousand last year, Bubba, I shit you not!")

After I opened my own law offices in 1968, I used to position myself in the criminal courthouse's green-tiled basement cafeteria just to "bump into" Haynes. Soon I was drinking Teddy Roosevelt quantities of coffee with the Great Man and other young lawyers eager to soak up his insights and axioms, some of which ought to be chiseled into marble above the courthouse steps. Of course, many fine and noble sentiments about the law are inscribed up there, but it would be far more practical if lawyers could look up and be reminded, "Never put a woman on the jury with lips the size of a chicken's asshole."

Race had one rule that remains for me first among equals: "All knowledge is useful in a courtroom," he would say, "and nothing is more important than knowing your client." It took a few trials, but I soon learned how to humanize the person I represented—to establish not only the facts of his case but also of his life, so that the twelve strangers in the box could not judge him without knowing him—as a husband and father, fellow worker and friend. And that's when I started winning, too.

Consider the case of *The State of Texas v. Diana B.*

In the summer of 1979, I was sitting with a cup of coffee and a newspaper in the Avalon Diner & Drug Store near the Houston neighborhood of River Oaks. I'd been reading about a young woman named Diana B., who was being held on charges of murdering her husband. The headlines were gruesome: after shooting and killing him, she had used a chain saw to dismember his body. When the blade broke, instead of calling it a day, she drove to the hardware store and bought a new one. Once her husband's body lay in five parts, Diana stuffed them into five garbage bags and loaded them into the trunk of her car. Three days later, at her family's ranch in San Bernardino, California, she confessed to her parents, asked for their help in disposing of the body, and when they refused, slashed her wrists and ran into a field, which is where local homicide detectives found and arrested her. Doctors sewed her up, the police jailed her, and now she awaited extradition to Houston to stand trial for murder.

Everyone at the Avalon was talking about the case. We all assumed the woman was guilty. At that moment, my secretary phoned the diner to tell me that a former client was on the other line asking if I would be willing to represent a friend of his who'd landed in a bit of trouble.

His friend was Diana B. I immediately accepted.

On the Saturday morning before trial, I sat at Racehorse's kitchen table, seeking his advice. Even he was not optimistic. "People don't mind killin'," he said. "What they *don't* like is messin' with the body." He suggested I pitch the case toward convincing the jury to give Diana B. a lighter sentence. "Unless," he said, "you get lucky during voir dire."

Voir dire is another name for jury selection, when lawyers from both sides ask potential jurors about their backgrounds and beliefs in order to figure out whom they want and, even more important, *don't* want on the jury. It is also an excellent opportunity to condition panelists by the questions they ask and the answers they elicit to see the facts their way. In Diana's case I would have to persuade a jury that a wife had the right to act in self-defense—use deadly force—against her husband, which was far from a given in Texas back then. So I began voir dire by introducing my four-foot-eleven client to the jury. Then, with Diana still standing, I asked if anyone had known her deceased husband, whom I described as "a really big man, almost six four and two hundred fifty pounds." No one did, but that was not the point. That mental image was a perfect segue into my next question, which was whether anyone had reservations about following the law that allowed a woman to use every means necessary to protect herself—even if her attacker was her husband and even if protecting herself meant killing him. A hand shot up in the rear of the courtroom. A man on the aisle pointed down the row to an old woman who sat crying quietly. She was so far in the back of the panel that there was no chance she'd make it to the jury; I almost suggested that she be excused. Instead, I walked down the aisle, handed her a glass of water, and asked if she was okay. The woman took a moment to compose herself and then said, "I wish my daughter had the courage to do what she did," gesturing toward my client. "If she had, she would still be alive today."

Obviously, that woman did not make it to the jury. But before she left, she had encapsulated our defense and humanized Diana B. in a single statement. On the stand, Diana testified about her husband's abuse, including how it had once landed her in the hospital. And I introduced the pictures of her swollen face and the record of his guilty plea to misdemeanor assault—a rare admission for a man to make in those days. Then, with the jury leaning forward in their seats, I walked Diana through the events that led up to the shooting, how for three full days and nights, her husband had kept her awake, slugging her, poking her in the breasts with an ice pick, and holding a gun to her head while threatening to kill her and her two children. Finally he thrust the gun into her hands and said she didn't have the guts to kill him. He was mistaken.

I *had* gotten lucky during voir dire, but Diana hadn't even tried to retreat—an essential element of self-defense—much less hold her husband at bay with the pistol while she called the police. So how to convince the jury that she was nonetheless entitled to the defense and explain what happened after she killed him? Prior to trial, Diana told me that she had spent a year of her adolescence in a full-body cast— the victim of severe scoliosis, or curvature of the spine—and couldn't even turn over or go to the bathroom without her dad carrying her. So, the next witness I called was a psychiatrist, not to create an insanity defense, but to explain her state of mind that night. He testified that being held in confinement again, and under such extreme conditions, made Diana's response inevitable. Not only did she have to fight, she also had to flee the scene of her captivity; if that meant dismembering the body to make it possible to put it in her car, then she'd do what she had to do. It wasn't a perfect explanation—far from it—but it did demonstrate her lack of mens rea, the mind "bent on evil" required to convict someone of murder. Still, I was worried about what Race had said about "messin' with the body."

After eight days of trial, the jury went out to deliberate. The judge, a former prosecutor and defense lawyer himself, predicted that they would find Diana guilty and give her probation. But he was wrong. They returned after forty-five minutes and acquitted her.

In Diana's case, there was a plausible defense—but beyond her compelling side of the story, was justice done? To me, it is hard to argue otherwise: the jury followed the law of self-defense, Diana was exonerated, and her deceased husband—in blunt terms—got what he had coming. But what about cases where the reviled and clearly guilty defendant walks free? Has justice, nonetheless, been done? Think of O. J. Simpson, acquitted of murdering his estranged wife, Nicole. I don't know of anyone—except the members of the jury—who thinks he didn't do it, and he's all but admitted it. Did Johnnie Cochran, the lawyer who "got him off," as the public is prone to say, serve justice or thwart it? The answer is that Cochran did precisely what was required of him: he served justice by winning his case within the rules. Still, an overwhelming majority of people believe that if Simpson really did get away with murder, justice wasn't served, and on a moral or religious level, that's an unassailable conclusion. But *legal* justice, no less moral or exacting, is something else. Legal justice requires that in the presence of reasonable doubt about the defendant's guilt, he must be acquitted. That makes my responsibility as a criminal lawyer clear: I have to push the prosecution, with its vast resources and built-in credibility, to meet that standard, regardless of my client's actual guilt or innocence. Or, as Racehorse once put it, "When I hear the federal judge read, *The United States of America v. Henry Gonzalez,*' I know there's nothing standing between the United States government and Henry Gonzalez but me." Whatever Henry may have done, he still deserves to be tried according to the standards of our criminal justice system: within it, when both the defense and the prosecution have done their absolute principled best to "win," the system has been served, no matter the outcome. Justice, seldom perfect, often subjective, but in its own rough way, has been done.

Now consider another example: *The State of Texas v. Charles H.*

Alan B., a thirty-one-year-old carpet executive and father of two, with an expectant wife, disappears outside the Brass Jug, a bar in Houston. Police dismiss the matter as a "runaway husband" and refuse to open an investigation, leaving Alan's devastated father to launch one of his own.

Six months later, a private investigator locates Alan's skeletal remains in a watery ditch near Galveston.

Shortly afterward, a woman confesses to having witnessed the killing. She names the defendant as Charles H. and describes in detail how the murder occurred; she even suggests a credible motive. Her statement—typed up in a holding cell—fills twelve single-spaced pages.

On the other hand, as the defendant's attorney will argue, the "victim" was a gambler, a philanderer, and up to his ears in debt. Lots of people had reason to kill Alan B.—indeed, compelling reasons to want him dead, while the defendant had never even seen him before.

Still, the eyewitness's story is detailed and persuasive.

That is, until an alibi witness put the defendant a hundred miles away from the murder when it allegedly occurred.

Who is to be believed? What should the verdict be? What would it mean, in this case, for justice to be served? More than ever, resolution comes down to the skillfulness of the lawyers involved. Who knows his own client—*or* The Bad Guy (the other side's client)—better? Who can better use that knowledge to persuade the jury to see things his way? A trial like this is one of the reasons why I love the law: guilty or innocent, were I the lawyer defending Charles H., the man accused of murdering Alan B., and I didn't do everything in my power to win his case, *I* would be the one failing justice.

Well, not *everything* within my power, of course. One must always, *always,* play by the rules. Unfortunately, there are some lawyers—more ruthless than one would imagine—who do whatever it takes to win. They want it so badly that when they think no one is looking they put a thumb on the scales of justice, sometimes tilting them inexorably.

This last example—of the carpet executive dumped near Galveston—is the most perfect illustration of courtroom injustice I have encountered in more than forty years of trial law. Evidence was destroyed, perjury suborned, and justice defiled. But in this case I wasn't the defense attorney, trying to get his client "off." Nor was I the prosecutor, pursuing justice for the victim. Alan B. was my brother.

∾

The first autopsy report I ever read was my brother's. Even now, more than four decades later, there is rarely a day that goes by when I don't recall, unbidden, its haunting cause of death: "Gunshot wound to the head through-and-through." Since the day we buried him four decades ago, I have rarely talked about Alan and almost never about how he died. My children knew nothing of their uncle, and some of my friends were unaware that I ever had a brother, never mind that he was murdered. It wasn't that he didn't matter; I was closer to Alan than I've been to anyone. I just couldn't remember *why*. A violent death can do that: saturate your most vivid memories of the victim's life, like blood staining dirt on a deserted road.

Until finally, in 2008, I decided to write this book, to give Alan a life of sorts, and, to the extent possible, set the record straight about his murder and him, his astonishing qualities and alarming flaws included. The more I wrote, the more comfort I took in remembering him and our relationship—and the more I learned and remembered, the more I wanted to lay out in writing the injustices he suffered, not just in the tortured hours of his death or the weeks of his murderer's sordid trial but also at the hands of those of us who loved him.

And that is a story that begins a very long time ago.

# PART I

~

*Row, brothers, row, the stream runs fast,*
*The Rapids are near, and the daylight's past.*

—Thomas Moore

# 1

My earliest memory is of Alan and me jumping up and down on the bed that we shared in Kalamazoo, Michigan. Mom shouted from the living room, "Go to sleep or your father's coming in there with a strap!" We shouted back that we would, but we didn't—and Dad came rumbling down the hall like a bowling ball headed for the tenpin.

My brother and I scrambled under the cover, a prickly blue woolen blanket that would follow me halfway across America, with Alan on top of me as my shield.

Then the door flung open and there he was, as menacing as the professional wrestler Man Mountain Dean, pulling off his belt and doubling it over, snapping its sides and heading for our bed. When he got within range, he bent over and poked around until he found us. Then he hollered about putting a stop to all this horsing around and began slapping down his belt: WHAP! WHAP! WHAP!

Finally, I caught on: the belt landed only where we were not. Alan, already playing along, wailed loudly for Dad to stop, which he did. Then he plucked us out of our hiding place, lowered us one by one onto the pillow, tucked the blanket around our shoulders, and kissed us good night. Slamming the door behind him, he bellowed down the hallway: "And I'll come straight back in there if I hear another peep out of either of you!"

My brother and I giggled ourselves to sleep that night. What satisfaction, to be included in our father's elaborate deception!

And what a habit it had become for our father to deceive.

⁓

That was 1946, the year our father met Dorothy Heinrich in a Kalamazoo diner. She would one day become his wife, but for now, she was his waitress. "Dot" was five ten, with the sultriness of Rita Hayworth. Mom was four ten, with the temperament of Henry VIII—so there you have it. It wasn't the first time Mom had caught Dad cheating, but it was the last. Our parents would scream at each other for what felt like hours. Alan would cry in bed beside me, and then, to my astonishment, get up and go down the hall to intervene. Mom would shriek, *Get out of here, Mr. Buttinski, this is not your business! Get back in that bed!* To her, he had become a "hellion" she could not control.

That December, when I was four and Alan ten, our parents separated and divvied us up, my brother to Dad and me to Mom. (Mom was also pregnant with our sister, Linda.) So, from that point on, during childhoods that rarely overlapped, my brother and I were raised as only sons. Over the years, Mom offered a litany of excuses for why she left her firstborn son with "that *momser*" (Yiddish for "bastard" and all things irredeemable): a boy needs his dad, our father adored him, Alan had to finish the fifth grade—each true but none the truth. The truth was that Mom thought her little hellion would scare off eighteen-year-old Dorothy Heinrich—a serious miscalculation.

The way Alan must have seen things—the way many children see these things—was that our mother gave up on him because he was responsible for her marriage falling apart. And when I think about what went wrong for my brother, as I often do, I keep returning to the irremediable damage that our parents' separation and all its repercussions had on the way he viewed himself and the world.

Mom and I left out of Detroit on a train bound for Little Rock, where she grew up. Soon after arriving, Mom gave birth to Linda, and the three of us lived in the relative tranquility of my maternal grandparents' home. (I say "relative" because we were, after all, Jews.) The five of us shared their two-bedroom house, warmed by the hallway register in winter and serenaded by cardinals in the backyard each spring. Small though it was, I felt at home there and home felt luxurious. I certainly didn't miss my father or brother, at least not yet.

My grandmother, Momma Hattie, was the safe harbor where I docked the sundry hurts of childhood. Be it a broken tooth or a skinned knee, I could escape it easily enough by tucking myself into the folds of her skirt, often while she stood tending a sizzling stove. Momma Hattie served blackened everything, fried foods that had to be coaxed out of the skillet with a metal spatula and serious scraping. Then she poured the greasy residue into a Crisco can, where it congealed into schmaltz: a slippery mass whose consistency would hold your thumbprint until it came time to melt it down and use it again.

"Momma Hattie," I'd say, "make me a hamburger."

"I'll hamburger you," she'd respond.

Then she'd ladle out a wad of schmaltz, jerk the spoon back and forth until it unglued itself, and let it plop into the sizzling pan.

Whenever she had an extra dollar, Momma Hattie would spend it on us. After she noticed that my soles were taped to the tops of my shoes, she took me to JCPenney and bought me a pair made of shiny black material, with zippers up the front. At Woodruff Elementary School, where new shoes were rare events, anyone wearing some got to sit with his feet in the aisle all day, which I did, frequently leaning over to noisily zip and unzip them so I could catch my classmates looking.

On the other hand, my grandfather, Daddy Joe, was hardly involved in our lives at all. Sitting down to breakfast, he'd wordlessly grab his knife and fork and set about savaging his eggs into a bleeding yellow mass, then lift the plate and scoop it all into his mouth with the blunt side of his butter knife. Only then would he pick up his coffee saucer, which he did with both hands and pinkies extended, suck the coffee over a liquid bridge into his mouth, gargle, gulp it down, and belch.

Daddy Joe did smile a lot, but that had less to do with his good nature than with his Peppermint Schnapps, which he squirreled away in pint bottles and nipped at with the dawn. When I was seven, on Yom Kippur, Daddy Joe decided to break the fast early, left the synagogue shortly before services ended, and repaired himself to the family car. There he ate a Hershey bar, washed it down with a lukewarm six-pack of Schlitz, and returned to the sanctuary. To his credit, he *almost* made it back to his seat, but puked and passed out in the aisle instead. It happened right next to me, while my mother and Momma Hattie watched in horror from their segregated seats upstairs. They jumped up, ran down into the sanctuary, cordoned off the area like a crime scene, and, as the congregants filed out, loudly announced their diagnosis:

"Daddy's had a stroke!"

"Looks like a stroke to me!"

"Somebody call an ambulance. Joe's had a stroke!"

My grandfather lay there with his head cradled in my mother's arms, prostrate before the altar of God. Upon awakening, he waved off the ambulance, preferring to walk off his stroke rather than have it treated. All the way home, Momma Hattie slowly drove alongside him, occasionally barking out the window, "Polish *hundt*! Polish *hundt*!"— onomatopoetic Yiddish meaning "hound," a dog she could not abide.

"Hocus pocus/Kiss my tokas," he replied.

But he was a hard worker, my grandfather: he woke every weekday morning at five-thirty for his calisthenics, fifty jumping jacks, knee bends, and toe touches each—a routine I repeated for all my years in Little Rock—and then he'd set off for the small department store he managed for nearly three decades. There, I hesitate to say, he would stand outside and genially greet the black men who walked by, "Nigger, you need a hat." More often than you'd expect, a black man would follow him into the store, where my grandfather, with great courtesy, would sell him a hat or something else, on layaway, a dollar down, a dollar a month.

Mom's first job in Little Rock was as a secretary at a casket company. She was so terrified of the coffins that she used to walk through the showroom backward, with her eyes closed. One day, she tripped, fell into one, and quit. Her next job was at a local radio station, KLRA, first as a secretary and then, due to her skills as a copywriter and an affair with the station manager, as the host of *Homemaker's Harmony*, an afternoon talk show that soon became *Meet Millie*. It was said that Millie Berg was the first woman to host her own show in Arkansas, and she built a loyal following, interviewing the likes of Little Richard and Elvis Presley in between sharing gossip and cooking tips. After her promotion in the summer of 1949, we moved into a house Mom rented just up the block from my grandparents, with a screened-in porch where I slept and awoke each day in summer with the sun.

So I lacked for nothing, really. I had not one but two mothers, effectively: my grandmother, who was gentle and forgiving, and my mother, who was industrious and encouraging. At night, after Linda was in bed, Mom would call me into the kitchen to teach me things "you won't learn in school." She drew a keyboard on a piece of cardboard, which I sat over every night for weeks, learning to type fast and accurately. She also taught me a cardinal rule of public speaking so effective that it has given me a lifetime leg up. At the radio station, whenever anyone on air interrupted a sentence with an "uh," "um," or "er," the speaker was required to drop a quarter in the "Fluff Box," a metal can with a slot cut in the top. But *Meet Millie* was the only unscripted show, so Mom was at a disadvantage to the newsmen and announcers—and, of course, she couldn't afford too many quarters. So we developed a "gotcha" game at home, requiring each of us to catch the other doing it. Even now, if I stumble during an oral argument or cross-examination, it's an unmistakable sign I'm losing focus. When that happens, *plunk!* goes a quarter into my mental Fluff Box, and instantly I am back on track.

At my bedtime, she read the ancient myths to me and compared me favorably to the gods—the point being that despite being poor and mortal, I could become anything I wanted. In fact, she said that being poor was an advantage, something those rich kids—the ones whose fathers drove Buicks—would never have.

Money was always tight, of course. In all those years, my father sent a total of $100 in child support and not another cent. So Mom parted with a dollar like a scientist measuring out enriched uranium. She spent almost nothing on herself and stretched our weekly groceries by diluting ketchup with water and crafting sandwiches out of a single slice of bread covered with a mixture of relish, pickles, and mayonnaise. But once a month, on a Sunday, even if she had to borrow a couple bucks from Momma Hattie, Mom broiled T-bones seasoned with garlic and slathered in butter that Linda and I gnawed till they glistened like elephant tusks.

Indeed, the only problem I had in those halcyon days was a kid named Piggy Waldrip. Fat, fifteen, and mean as a snake, Piggy was among the more vocal of our neighborhood Jew-haters, and he stationed himself every day at the dreaded corner of Valmar and W. 4th, pacing back and forth across the sidewalk, blocking my way, enraged, like the three-headed dog who guards the Gates of Hell. For a brief moment we'd have something like a standoff, and then, as I darted past him, he'd slug me in the pit of the back. Sometimes he would follow it up with theological justification: "Daddy says the Joooos killed Jesus!" No number of Daddy Joe's jumping jacks was going to help me hold my own against Piggy. He was just too big.

Where were my father and brother now?

~

Alan reentered my life in 1952, when I was ten and he was sixteen. Dad and Dot, now married, had sent him off to Georgia Military Academy, where he followed his duffel bag out his dormitory window and hitchhiked to Little Rock in search of sanctuary in our mother's home. He arrived in the middle of a blizzard, his navy pea coat with the gold buttons undone, an olive knit cap pulled down over his ears. Alan had Tom Cruise's chiseled jaw but not the actor's good looks otherwise. And he was short, with a perfectly combed pompadour and eyelashes as long as a girl's. But he was very strong, and there was something proper, almost military, about how he carried himself— offset by genuine warmth.

He'd hardly put down his suitcase before he was lying on the living room floor with his knees bent, hoisting Linda up and over them for a playful somersault through the air. Eager to follow suit, I took my place beside him, looking up to my brother even while I was lying down. But when Linda came running at me, I squirmed sideways at the last moment, laughing as she hit the floor. I will never forget how Alan looked at me: in a way that bespoke certain violence if I ever pulled a stunt like that again.

That night, with Linda in bed, Mom and Alan and I sat around the kitchen table under a bare bulb that gave the room a feel of capture and interrogation. Mom poured coffee into purple Melmac cups

("Cowboy Coffee" for me: one-fourth Folgers and three-fourths milk) and, under a swirling plume of cigarette smoke, she and Alan plotted my brother's future.

Now, if you were in the business of starting over, and Alan owned the franchise, Mom was the perfect backer. "You can do whatever you want, Alan Berg, once you put your mind to it." Now he was getting the Greek gods treatment, too. No one could do better than Millie Berg's children and certainly not the children of those *"goddamned rich Jews."*

For years I had been hearing from Mom about how she should never have let her baby live with "that momser father" of mine and "the whore he married" because Alan was frequently in trouble, which she blamed on Dad. Alan ran away a lot, did badly in school, and had a habit of antagonizing the fathers of neighborhood girls. (One man, whose wife found my fifteen-year-old brother in bed with his daughter, chased Alan down, put a gun to his head, and pulled the trigger, only to have it jam. And that's all I know about that story except this: that wasn't the last time someone tried to kill my brother before someone finally did.)

But talk about Greek gods: as far as I was concerned, Alan's arrival in Little Rock was like being introduced to fire by Prometheus himself. He took Linda riding on the handlebars of our Schwinn and then, in a single afternoon, taught her to ride it all on her own. He showed her how to jitterbug. He even brushed her hair. He was rather less delicate with me—like when he'd pin me to the floor with his knees and let a string of spit drip down while I turned my head violently from side to side until he slurped it back up. Or like when I sat on the toilet, the only one in our house, and he'd barge in, spread my legs apart, and pee between them, often hitting the bowl. And, of course, he treated me to many a dreaded Dutch Oven, trapping me under the covers with one of his rancid farts.

But his arrival made me feel safe in a way I never had. There was a man in the house! My friends loved having him around, too, and regarded him as something foreign and exotic that had invaded the neighborhood, even more exciting than when Mr. Gardner drove his brand-new Chrysler DeSoto up his driveway and we gawked at it like someone had just rolled the Hope Diamond into our midst. And all of us knew: if my brother was around, something big was about to happen—and he didn't disappoint. He organized us into a sandlot baseball team, elevating me from my prior status as last kid chosen ("You take David—we'll take a girl") to starting shortstop. He also showed me how to extend my arms and roll my wrists when I swung, and—dear God!—I could actually pull a ball way down the third-base line. When it came to doing his homework, Alan was about as disciplined as an adolescent lemur. But when it came to baseball practice, he was like General Patton, marching us to Lamar Porter Field even in the middle of frigid, wind-whipped days and sending us chasing after pop-ups and slow rollers—a subzero taste of the big leagues, Georgia Military–style. And we couldn't wait to start again the next day.

Baseball didn't stop for us once we left the field. We would gather in the stands at Lamar Porter to play a board game called Ethan Allen's All-Star Baseball. Major league players were represented by circular cards that fit over a silver arrow that you flicked hard with your forefinger: where it stopped determined your player's outcome at bat. Then you'd move your team's tiny pegs around the "infield," adjust the "scoreboard," and fit the next "batter" into place. My friends always wanted to bat Babe Ruth cleanup, but not me. I wanted Larry Doby, the Cleveland Indians' star center fielder and first Negro to play in the American League. One day, in the middle of a game, Piggy Waldrip grabbed my Doby card as he walked by—and tore it in half. When I told Alan what happened, he began grinding his jaws. "What time you get out of school?"

The next afternoon, as we rounded Valmar and 4th, there was Piggy, pacing the intersection, snarling, as usual, daring me to cross. I tugged Alan's sleeve and pointed to the builder's lot that my friends and I called "The Woods." Covered by a canopy of leaves and branches that left the ground mysterious and damp, it had plenty of places to hide, which is what I suggested we do. But my brother kept walking.

When Alan got to him, Piggy did not attack. He had something else on his mind, something monumental that he had learned about the Chosen People. Sneering down at us, he said:

"Daddy says Jooos cut off their kids' dicks with a rusty knife when they turn thirteen."

Alan reached up and poked his fingers into Piggy's chest.

"Your daddy is an idiot."

"Are you calling my daddy a liar?"

"No. I said he's an idiot."

For a moment, Piggy looked amused. Then Alan hit him with a hard right hook that landed flush against his cheek. He followed up with a dropkick to the scrotal sac, and Piggy sank to his knees. That's when Alan climbed aboard him like he was the 3:19 and began pounding the back of Piggy's head while my 175-pound nemesis cried for his mommy and condemned my brother as a "dirty fighter."

Our side's lone casualty was Alan's Speidel watchband, made of metal and guaranteed never to lose its shape. You could twist it and pull it this way and that and it would always snap back to its original form. From his supine position, however, Piggy managed to grab it and stretch it beyond its tensile strength. When he let go, it swayed back and forth before slipping off Alan's arm and onto the field of battle.

As we feared, Piggy's mom had called our mother, who left work early and, just inside our front door, without removing her winter coat (the one she called her "Russian mink" but felt like horsehide), screamed, "*MARCH YOURSELF IN HERE RIGHT NOW, ALAN BERG!*"

Uh-oh. Another whipping from Mom. And wait till she hears about the watchband. By now, Alan and I had become accustomed to an open hand to the face, or an array of rights and lefts to our shoulders, or her fingernails dug into our forearms, deep enough to leave horseshoe imprints that filled with blood once our hemoglobin came out of hiding. When the bloodletting was over, she would turn her palms skyward and cry, "You made my veins stick out!" Sure enough, there they'd be: blue and bulging, throbbing in censure of our bad behavior.

But this time Mom waited for Alan's side of the story. He hurried to get it out, with me standing behind him like a one-man Greek chorus, interjecting, "That's the truth, Momma!" Mom must have figured that no one could have made up the rusty-knife story, because when Alan was finished, instead of smacking him, she smiled broadly, wrapped her Russian mink around him, and began rocking him back and forth. "You did exactly what you should have done, *ketsila.*" *Ketsila,* the Yiddish term of endearment meaning "little kitten," meant to our ears, "For once, you're not in trouble." "That goyisha momser," she would mutter, and this we took to mean that she was glad Alan had kicked Piggy's fat, bigoted ass.

And from that day on, like a plant seeking sunlight, I inclined in my brother's direction.

Alan got a part-time job selling women's shoes and soon was earning commissions that rivaled those of the full-time salesmen. The best part, he told me, wasn't the money but looking up the customers' dresses, which they sometimes spread wide for the smooth-talking teenager, letting him slide his hand up so long as no one noticed but the satisfied customer. Every two weeks, on payday, he gave most of his earnings to Mom. For the first time, she was able to buy T-bones twice and even three times a month, and not worry about how she'd pay for it. Sometimes after school Alan would take me to Winkler's Drive-In, where he'd buy me a hamburger for a quarter and a Coke for a dime. If my friends were there, he'd buy them a burger, too. Once, I even found a dollar bill stuffed into the pocket of my pants. A dollar! That was sixty years ago, but I can still remember that burst of freedom and gratitude I felt finding a whole dollar in my pocket.

At Little Rock Central High, Alan joined the Drama Club and was cast as Nepommuck, the Hungarian linguist in *Pygmalion*. The night of the performance, Mom and I sat dead center, no more than ten rows back. When Alan came onstage, she gasped and clutched my arm. "Uh-huh, uh-huh, uh-huh," she whispered, which translates roughly into "You see? You see? When he lives with me he does great, but not when he lives with that momser father of yours and the longa-lecha nofke [long-legged whore] he married!" A month before the end of the term, however, Mom learned that Alan was not going to graduate, the victim of rules prohibiting crap games on campus. He also made five Ds out of fourteen grades and got into fistfights with boys whose racial views offended him. As the vice principal put it, "Your son spends too much time taking up for niggers and not enough time studying."

The next thing I knew, Alan was packing for Beaumont, Texas, where our father had opened his second upholstery plant (the first was in Houston, where he and Dot had settled) and wanted my brother's help after school launching the business. *If* Alan worked hard and *if* he graduated from the local high school, Dad would pay his way at Texas A&M. The deal was nonnegotiable—which to Alan always meant a starting point for negotiations. He convinced Dad to throw in a used car and, within the week, our father had bought him a green '49 Lincoln convertible the size of a small fishing vessel.

When Alan had arrived in Little Rock, it felt as though a limb I hadn't realized was missing had been sewn back on. When he left, I felt pain as profound as if it had been ripped off again. My own behavior at school—never perfect—spiraled out of control. In class I became a nonstop talker given to tantrums that could surprise even me. And when my fifth-grade teacher ordered me to Principal Hendrix's office, I shoved her into her desk and ran down the hallway, crying and screaming, "I miss my father!" Mrs. Hendrix was not moved.

My mother was summoned. Talking to both of us but looking directly at me, Mrs. Hendrix came straight to the point: "I am transferring David to a special school this fall. He'll either behave there or they will *pound* some discipline into him." When she described it in more detail, the school didn't sound so special; it sounded like a training camp for Hitler Youth.

Mom was in tears.

"I'm sorry, Millie, but your son needs a man's discipline."

"I know that, Mrs. Hendrix, but what can I do? His father lives in Houston."

"Then maybe you should send him there."

Mom quit crying.

"You have no idea what it's like in Houston, Mrs. Hendrix. My older boy lives there with his father and stepmother. That woman is a harridan."

*Harridan?* Mrs. Hendrix furrowed her brow—and offered her only concession. *If* I went to Houston and my conduct improved, *then* I could return to Woodruff for the last half of sixth grade. So, once again, Mom had to swallow her pride and call her ex-husband with word of a son in trouble. In her one-sided competition for Best Parent, she was now tied for last.

I was not thrilled by this prospect. I had heard terrible stories about the harridan. After our parents split up in Kalamazoo, Alan lived alone with our father for almost four years, moving from city to city as Dad sought better-paying jobs (ultimately, my brother would attend thirteen secondary schools in twelve years). With no time to develop friendships, Dad and Alan had only each other. When he came home at night, no matter how late, Dad would teach Alan card games that he thought men should play, like blackjack and poker, or he'd read him books that he thought a boy should know, like *Tom Sawyer* and *The Swiss Family Robinson*. But when Dot visited, Dad ignored Alan, who lay awake each night, unable to sleep, humiliated by the sexual sounds in the next bedroom.

In 1950, Dad and Alan moved to Atlanta, their fourth city in as many years, where my brother entered ninth grade at Grady High School and my father managed a national sales crew for a sewing machine company. That was also the year Dad married Dot, with Alan their only guest and best man. After the nuptials, Alan tossed a glass of water on Dot's new dress and she reacted, hitting him across the head with a Coke bottle she was holding. He crumpled to the floor—and that was the end of the celebration.

One year later to the day, on their first wedding anniversary, Dad withdrew all of their savings and announced that they were moving to Houston, where he was going into the upholstery business with $10,000 invested by the Rogers brothers, a wealthy Beaumont family he'd met when he worked there briefly. So Dad loaded Dot, Alan, and all their belongings in his black sedan, the driver-side door held shut by wire that he had to wind and unwind every time he got in or out, and headed for Texas.

No one knew why Dad chose upholstery or Houston, and, typical of most men of his generation, he wasn't much for explaining himself, but it didn't matter: for the first time in his life, our father's dreams of fortune panned out. Houston was a relatively new city, made possible by air-conditioning and wealthy from oil. A culture had evolved there akin to wildcatting itself, where risk-taking was the norm and understatement was not a virtue—witness the wildly popular "Diamond Jim" West, who tossed handfuls of shiny silver dollars from his Cadillac convertible, or the anonymous shit kicker rumored to have ridden a longhorn into a River Oaks party. Jobs there gushed like the wells that paid their wages, creating a monster postwar boom for the roughnecks, riggers, and pipe layers who worked the fields—and fanned out from them to the carpenters, electricians, and plumbers who built their houses, the department store clerks who clothed their families, and the gas station attendants who serviced their Chevys—each and every one of whom, our father believed, desperately needed his furniture reupholstered.

So Dad rented an office on what was then the western outskirts of downtown—a bleak area that would one day boast a score of graceful skyscrapers that leaped from Philip Johnson's sketch pad—but for now housed honky-tonks and the weathered men and women who frequented them, wearing faded jeans and handmade boots, listening to "Orange Blossom Special," and downing tequila shots. But Dad was oblivious to the depressing surroundings: he was obsessed with his new business, ran ads in the *Post* and *Chronicle,* put in long hours, sold jobs all over town and farmed them out to pieceworkers, the seamstresses and upholsterers who worked out of their homes. Soon he was able to rent an abandoned lumberyard that covered an entire city block and hire those workers full-time. And quickly after that, he and Dot bought out their backers for $30,000—triple their original investment. Now the business was all theirs and they could keep the profits in-house.

But, beyond the opportunities and welcoming environment, Houston, a flat, aesthetic nightmare, had little else to commend it—and in ways that could have sent our father packing. The heat and the Baptists could be oppressive. Besides the Alley Theatre, there was no cultural life of much merit. Houston's once breathtaking water attraction, Buffalo Bayou—banks covered with vegetation and studded with oak trees—was now a breathtaking blight, cut into deep *V*s and covered with concrete that funneled filth into the water below in a futile attempt to avoid flooding. Even River Oaks, with its slightly less-welcoming deed restrictions barring Jews and Negroes, was pockmarked with tasteless mansions next to stately ones. And all across town, the hodgepodge of U-tote-Ms and bars near or next to homes stood in tribute to a lack of zoning and the power of Hugh Roy Cullen, the richest oilman of them all, whose letter to the editor of the *Houston Chronicle* warning that a local zoning ordinance was a plot of "New York Jews" resulted in its repeal. And while Houston appeared to be an open city, it was run covertly by a tiny group of wealthy bankers, oilmen, and builders who met in room 8F of the Ben Milam Hotel, where they made wise if self-interested decisions about the city's direction. But with the town booming, nobody cared, much less knew, who was running the show, so long as the show didn't fold. And certainly not our father, who'd chosen well when he decided on Houston as his home.

But while Dad's business was booming his home life was not—not with his son around. Alan hated Dot and Dot hated him. She commanded their rented duplex at 1935½ Richmond Avenue with an implacable tone of voice and ludicrous rules. When Alan, who was fifteen, violated his twenty-two-year-old stepmother's *eight o'clock* curfew, she locked him out of the house, leaving him more than once to sleep all night in the yard. It did not help that Mom primed Alan to stir up shit whenever they talked on the phone. Alan knew what Mom wanted to hear, too. He'd call with reports from the battlefront: intelligence that each time convinced our mother anew that her ex-husband's marriage would soon be finished. "She's spending every penny he makes," she'd tell me, gleefully, after hanging up. Or: "She's got a new set of pearl earrings he can't afford!" If she was feeling generous, she'd lower her voice and say, quietly, "You know, that poor man, he's got a hellion on his hands," this time referring to Dot. It was from those calls that Mom developed the notion that she and Dad would soon be back together. Which might have happened had Dad and Dot not remained married for the next forty-eight years.

With no mother to counsel otherwise, and Dot urging him to get Alan out of the house, Dad first shipped him off to Allen Military Academy in Bryan, ninety miles away, isolated on land as foreboding as its harsh discipline, a fundamentalist institution that required even bellicose Jewish boys to attend Christian chapel service. Yet, to everyone's surprise, Alan prospered there. He made As and Bs, won the Daughters of the American Revolution Declamation Contest, and, generally speaking, stayed out of trouble. Which is why it was so puzzling that Dad moved him again, just after thirteen months, this time to Georgia Military Academy, seven hundred miles from Houston, where Alan promptly ran away to us in Little Rock and Mom pried these and other horror stories out of him.

Still, no matter how awful living with Dot might be, at least it would mean seeing Alan whenever he came home from Beaumont. I could handle a bottle upside the head if it meant spending more time with my brother.

That August, Dad drove thirteen hours to collect me for the fall term. When he came up the stairs into our living room, I saw that he was exactly as Mom had described him: a handsome dog. He lifted Linda and me up, one child per arm, and it didn't matter that I hardly knew him; I liked the way he smelled when he pulled us in and kissed us both at once. As he sank into the couch, he reached into his back pocket and ran his comb through his thick auburn hair, which in the manner of the day was slicked back with Vaseline that made a tiny squishing sound in the teeth of the comb.

Contrary to what I'd expected, my father did not gloat and my mother did not yell. They were worried. Both their boys were way off the playground, and nothing they had done had fixed things. After a while, Dad slapped his knees and said we ought to hit the road. He led the way with my suitcase, while Mom trailed a step behind. At the bottom of the front steps, Dad suddenly dropped my luggage, turned around, and grabbed Mom by the arms. Because she was still on the steps, they stood at eye level, looking at each other intently. Then they began to shake their heads and cry. My mother sank into my father and they kissed for what seemed a very long time.

I had thought that Millie and Nathan Berg hated each other. But for a moment the ragged edges of my family were seamed into something I couldn't name and only later identified as normal.

~

I arrived in Houston at a time of great controversy in the world of upholstery: Dad had advertised his plant there as the nation's largest, and a competitor had challenged that claim. The *Houston Post* set about resolving the issue by measuring the two plants and arrived at the conclusion that Dad was correct. They ran a picture of him holding the tape measure and looking triumphant and natty in a sharkskin suit that shimmered as if woven from Reynolds Wrap. Of course, one might question whether measuring two plants in Houston actually decides the issue, but it was good enough for me: my father was right, his competitor was wrong, the canard about size was resolved, and there in the newspaper was our name, *Berg*, and I loved the way it looked.

I wandered around Southwestern Upholsterers like Puck in the forest: my father *owned* this place. Dad called the upholsterers *artisans*, and my favorite was Mr. Spivey, whose name and long, spindly limbs made me think of a spider. Even when he squatted to say hello, I had to look up at him. Grabbing a handful of brass head tacks, he'd shove them deep into a bloated cheek, flip the tack hammer to his mouth, spit one onto the magnetized head, and snap his wrist hard, driving the tack right through the fabric and into the wood. Sometimes Dad would stop by to drape an arm around my shoulders and watch, too. "Beautiful job, Mr. Spivey," he'd say before moving on to make sure everyone was working.

Once a week, over the nonstop din of the plant, my father would yell, "Come on, son, lezz go," and off we went to Guardian Finance. There, one of several frosted glass windows would slide open and a disembodied hand would reach out and snatch a stack of contracts out of Dad's hand. Then the window slid shut and, five minutes later, reopened; the hand reemerged with an envelope containing a check that, this time, Dad snatched and stuffed into his inside coat pocket. Afterward he'd treat us to two giant, perfectly round hamburgers at the Cock & Bull Restaurant across the street. Between bites he'd open the envelope to savor the contents. "Three thousand dollars," he muttered once. In that moment, I believed my father the richest man in the world.

I was loath to admit it, but Dot was nothing like what Alan had described. She was . . . nice. And she and Dad took me everywhere—to movies and plays, and once we heard Mahalia Jackson sing "He's Got the Whole World in His Hands" at the old Music Hall, where ours were the only white faces in the auditorium and Dad made an irrefutable pronouncement: "If Jews had written that song, it would have been a dirge." Every Thursday we ate chicken cacciatore at Luigi's on Montrose, where the stocky little owner mounted a small platform to serenade us. It didn't matter if it was "Nessun dorma" or "Funiculì Funiculà," Dad's eyes would start welling up while Luigi was on the first few bars. When he did, I would squirm and hope no one noticed. It made me think of Mom's delight in telling us how Dad fell once and "screamed like a girl."

Once school started, my only chore was to do well. I began each day in the kitchen alone with Dad, who wore a linen apron over his silk tie and shirt and made the best poached eggs ever mounted on toast. Then he'd drop me off at school, frequently getting me there on time. Doing homework in the evening, if I asked him the meaning of a word, he'd scowl at me and say, "Look it up!" But in exchange for each A I made I was given new clothes, or extra spending money, and Dad bragged so much you'd have thought he made the grade himself. "What's the matter with you?" he loved to ask, even in front of strangers. "My son can't make a B?"

That December we bought a Christmas tree so tall it touched the ceiling and we doused it with so much tinsel you could scarcely see the branches. Dot modeled her new full-length mink coat, a large diamond ring, and a double strand of pearls—but that wasn't all. Dad had also bought her a pale-blue-and-white Oldsmobile Eighty-Eight about a half mile long. They were not yet in the Cadillac class (those irrepressible southerners labeled them "Jew canoes"), but they were getting close. For me, Dad had bought a collection of *Pogo* cartoons, which we read together on the couch, collapsing in laughter each time Pogo asked a question in congressional doublespeak. "What wox boggeth?" Dad would read in a funny voice and then we would just pound each other. For Dad, there was a trunkload of traditional gifts like shirts and ties that Dot let me help pick out. Just a few years before, in Kalamazoo, Alan, Dad, and I had sat on box crates watching in awe the flickering screens of TV sets through the store's window, never dreaming we'd own one. But there, in the middle of the pile, sat a brand-new twenty-one-inch Magnavox.

Unfortunately, I fell victim to my own good grades and glowing reports about my behavior. I had to go back to Little Rock, and Mrs. Hendrix had to let me back in school, a deal we both regretted very quickly. Exposed to the riches of Houston, the temptation of "Mr.

Prince Jesus" (as Mom was now wont to call me) had begun, and back at Woodruff I behaved worse than ever. I argued with my teachers and interrupted everyone constantly, singularly pleased with the sound of my own voice, an enthusiasm I apparently shared with no one else.

It was clear that Mom resented that I'd had a good time with Dad and Dot. She could not compete with their newfound wealth, and every time Mom lost her temper with me, I rubbed her nose in it. Even Momma Hattie said that I had a "*fisk* on my *punim*" (a mouth on my face), and my mother started calling me "Nat Berg Junior," as in, "Do you understand me? You are just like that son-of-a-bitch father of yours, Mr. Nat Berg Junior!" When I played with other children, she could hear my "obnoxious Nat Berg voice above all the others." When I talked back, I didn't just sass her; I sassed her with that "Nat Berg mouth" of mine. When I got good and mad, I gave her that "Nat Berg look." And just when I thought I'd heard the last of the Nat Bergisms, she'd warn me, "You better not speak to me in that Nat Berg tone of voice!" which was always a curtain-raiser on a whipping.

The more she compared me to Dad, the more I took comfort in the comparison. One day our battle culminated with the worst thing I could have said to my mother.

"At least she doesn't hit me!" I said of Dot.

Mom yanked me close by my hair and hissed fair warning in my ear: "*You better wipe that Nat Berg look off your face or I will wipe it off for you!*"

I didn't and she did.

She clamped my jaw between her fingers and thumb and, with her other hand, began slapping me across the face, one whack after another, popping and stinging and drawing blood with her nails. It saddens me to remember that my grandmother was there, too, holding my arms and calling me "Hellion." When Mom finished slapping me, she grabbed my shoulders, shook them so that my head toggled

23

violently back and forth, and screamed, in time with the shaking: "Do ... you ... understand ... me ... Mr. ... Nat ... Berg ... Junior?!"

She let go of my shoulders on a count that sent me backward into the front door, shattering three small panes. On the floor, I began to scream and pull glass out of my hands. Horrified, Mom pulled me to my feet and tried to brush me off. She began crying and put her arms around me, saying over and over: "I'm so sorry, *ketsila*, I am so, so sorry." Stunned, I looked around—at my sister, my grandmother, and my mother—and at that moment I knew that I was going to Houston and never coming back.

When school let out for the summer, Momma Hattie drove me to the bus station for another visit to Houston. Dot and Dad picked me up and, on the way to their house in my stepmother's new car, I leaned over the backseat and asked if I could live with them. Dot says that I told her Mom had hit me with wire coat hangers, the *Mommie Dearest* weapon of choice back then. I don't remember that, but whatever I said worked. Two weeks later, I returned to Little Rock, but only to pack. It was not hard to say good-bye to my mother. It was my grandmother I would miss.

This time I didn't take a bus: Dad bought his all-A student a ticket on the Texas Eagle. As I boarded, I said, "I'll write you from Houston, Momma Hattie."

"I'll Houston you," she replied.

A full moon rode alongside me as I lay in the pull-down bed. Until leaving to live with my father, I had never so much as held a five-dollar bill in my hand, much less slept in my own private room on a train.

# 2

Two months after I moved to Houston, Dad's upholstery plant burned to the ground.

Alan was in town and heard about the fire on his car radio. He careened into the driveway, honking and yelling for me to get in. On the way, we listened for updates, but the top was down and we couldn't hear very well. It didn't matter. It was a clear fall day, and, from miles away, the only cloud visible in the sky was the huge black one above our father's plant.

When we got there, Alan and I pushed through the crowd. He slipped his arm around Dad's waist. My brother was crying.

"I'm so sorry, Pop," Alan said.

"Me too, kid. Me too."

Then Dad pulled both of us close and for a while we stood together like that, just staring. Colors flashed in every direction: cherry red fire trucks parked at odd angles along Erath Street, yellow trench coats on firemen struggling with gray hoses to contain the blinding orange flames. But it was too late. Everything was tinder: the wooden building that surrounded the lumberyard like a horseshoe; aging furniture, with its dry, brittle frames; the polyfoam cut in squares to fill the cushions; the bolts of fabric; the wooden sawhorses; the glue and varnish, all ignited by sparks from the cotton gin where the fire had started—and now, all of it gone. Ashes and embers fluttered up and down on the wind and the air broiled over an ocean of filthy water where Southwestern Upholsterers had stood just hours before.

The next I remember, I was sitting on the floor of our living room. Two men in ties sat at the coffee table across from my father, whose face was reddened and singed from fire. Over the papers scattered between them, Dad peppered the men with questions about insurance policies and lawsuits. Their answers caused him to swear and shake his head. Remembering that I had a Boy Scout meeting, I ran upstairs and changed into my uniform, including the cap with the Troop 1190 badge sewn on. My hair was slicked down with Vaseline, just like Dad's.

"Dad, are you taking me to my Boy Scout meeting?" I asked, hurrying downstairs again.

"Goddamn it, David! I don't know if I even have a business. Get out of here!"

I don't fault my father for getting mad. Anyone would have been hard-pressed to give a shit about a Boy Scout meeting when he'd just lost his entire livelihood. But the greater significance of the fire is that my father never fully recovered, neither financially nor emotionally. The father I'd known—the father of shared hamburgers and funny Pogo impersonations and easy pride—was gone for good.

It was not simply about losing the plant. It also had to do with a terrible family secret, no less incendiary, and which I'd known about for as long as I could remember. My father's real dream had been to become a doctor, and he had come very close. He'd been admitted to the University of Arkansas Medical School when he was only nineteen *and* at a time of strict anti-Jewish quotas. Most likely Dad got in because he was considered by the school that rarest of men: the Honest Hebe. "Mr. Berg is to be preferred to many of the Jewish students that we have had," his college chemistry professor wrote to the Admissions Committee. "He seemed to be honest and upright in his work."

It would prove to be an ironic reference.

Three years later, in April 1935, Dad met Millie Besser. Mom had graduated as salutatorian of North Little Rock High and wanted to go to college, but her father refused to pay tuition for a girl, leaving her only one quick way out of his house: marriage. And Nathan Berg not only had smarts and a sense of humor, he also was Jewish *and* almost a doctor—for her, a real find.

By November Millie was pregnant. About the only legitimate detail on their marriage certificate is the rabbi's signature. Her age is listed as twenty instead of seventeen, to avoid asking her parents' consent, and their date of marriage is backdated to November 3, 1935, nine months and two weeks before their baby was due. In fact, Nat had insisted that Millie get an abortion, and it was months later before she talked him out of it and they married instead.

Nat dreaded telling his mother about his new wife. A Russian immigrant who reeked of boiled onions and a foul disposition, Mary Berg harangued her son to become a doctor while simultaneously undermining his efforts to become one. She frequently threatened to cut off Nat's rent and tuition, and in one instance she did—because he'd put his shoes on her burgundy velvet sofa. When she learned that he had not only married without her permission but also badgered him into admitting that his new wife was *pregnant,* she spit through her fingers three times and screeched at Millie, "I pray to God that child brings you as much heartache and pain as you've caused me!"

In Mary Berg's defense: in 1935, "having to get married" was news as rare and devastating as divorce or drug addiction. On the other hand, this was the same Mary Berg whom six-year-old Nathan had discovered fucking the landlord to pay the rent, and thus she was an odd source of moral indignation. Little more need be said about Mary Berg but this: her curse came true.

Nat and Millie borrowed $125 from Millie's parents to pay tuition for Nat's final year of medical school and moved into the Bessers' tiny home in North Little Rock. That made five of them in the house: Nat, Millie, Millie's parents, Daddy Joe and Momma Hattie, and Millie's younger brother, Maurice. Millie was soon so big, and the hallway so narrow, that it made it difficult for her and anyone else to navigate it at the same time.

Often, home late from rounds, Nat would wake Millie to exult about how he had spent the day treating patients, and, with her head tucked into his arm, she would listen until he fell asleep. No one, and especially not his wife, doubted that the confident and committed Nat Berg would make a fine doctor.

Six weeks before graduation, however, Nat walked out of his second trimester surgery final all but convinced he'd failed. After comparing answers with other students and consulting his textbook, he was certain. With his graduation and an internship in a Kansas army hospital jeopardized, to say nothing of what his mother would do, Nat panicked. That night he sat at the kitchen table, writing furiously. The next morning, dressed in his only suit, he hurried out into a miserable, overcast April day.

When he returned that afternoon, Nat was crying hard. He tried to tell his wife and in-laws what had happened but couldn't get a word out. He grabbed Millie and pulled her into the bathroom, where they sobbed loudly. Millie said over and over, "I'm sorry, Nat, I'm so sorry."

Daddy Joe, Momma Hattie, and Maurice sat on the couch in the living room, waiting and worrying that Millie, now five months pregnant, would lose her baby. The wailing grew so loud and so desperate that even Daddy Joe got concerned, wondering aloud if they might commit suicide. He and Maurice knocked on the bathroom door and Mom screamed, "Leave us alone!" So they sat back down and waited some more.

Finally, Nat and Millie emerged. Nat dragged two chairs across from the couch and clutched at his wife. He looked for all the world like a schoolboy caught cheating, which was exactly what had happened. He had offered a nurse $50 to substitute the paper he'd written the night before for his surgery exam. The nurse agreed—and then took the money and the paper straight to Dean Vinsonhaler, who came out of his office and told Nat to leave and not to come back. "It is my duty to inform you," read the eventual letter, "that the Committee on Discipline and Promotion has considered your case and recommends that you be dropped from the rolls of the institution."

So instead of becoming a doctor, Dad walked the streets of Little Rock's ghettos, knocking on doors and peddling life insurance that cost a quarter a month. Instead of awakening to another day at the hospital, he awakened each morning humiliated and consumed by his final hours in medical school.

He reapplied four times over the next six years, quitting for good when he received a letter from the dean in July 1942, the year I was born: "The senior class is comparatively large this year, and we feel that no additions should be made except under very exceptional circumstances. We felt that your case is not sufficient reason for that." If it wasn't clear before, it was now: he was never getting back in, neither there nor at any of the other schools he had tried.

Dad never, not once in his life, confessed his expulsion to anyone as far as I know, and certainly not to Dot, who learned about it from Linda ten years after he died. But we knew. Mom made certain of that, telling the story to Alan and me over and over, as proof of the failed character of the man whom she had "stuck by, hocked my rings for, worshipped—and how does he repay me? By marrying that whore!"

It had taken almost two decades, but Dad had clawed his way out of the hole he'd dug for himself in medical school. Now he had done himself in again. Out of cash when he bought out his investors, he had dropped his fire insurance. After the plant burned down, every piece of shit furniture in it suddenly became an expensive "family heirloom." With no money in the bank and no collateral for a loan, he had few means to fight the lawsuits that would dog him for years.

I was twelve years old at the time, still innocent enough to believe that my father would once again own the nation's largest upholstery plant. Very soon, however, I was disabused of my optimism by my potbellied eighth-grade civics teacher, Mr. Berman. A perfervid anti-Communist who referred to the USSR as the "Union of Skunks, Snakes, and Rattlesnakes" (often said while slapping his pointer against a map of the enemy nation), Berman had an ancient, 8-millimeter projector with monster reel capacity that he would wheel out of its closet at least once a week. Then he'd dim the lights and fire up "The Scourge of Communism," which laid bare "Brother Joe's" plan to seize control of an unsuspecting America. Mr. Berman's ranting about "Reds in the State Department" would end only as the film's voice-over, somber as a mortician's, began morphing from way too slow to way too fast, from slow-motion whale sounds to Alvin and the Chipmunks. My classmates and I used to mumble along as the narrator began:

"T-H-E S-C-O-U-R-G-E OF COM—M—UNISMMMMMMM-MMM!"

As far as I could tell, Berman loved all of the people and things that Dad had taught me to hate, namely Richard Nixon, Joseph McCarthy, Whittaker Chambers, and the House Un-American Activities Committee. When Berman called Senator Adlai Stevenson, the Democratic presidential nominee, a "traitor" and "known Commie," I laughed out loud. "And what is so funny, David Berg?" Berman asked. "You," I replied. That bought me a trip to the assistant principal's office and three swats with a specially designed paddle that had a large, donut-shaped ring cut out of it, to leave a lasting impression. It wasn't the first time I'd been sent to Mr. Viebig's office for a little corporal punishment. Just a few days earlier, I had gotten caught cutting class to watch the St. Louis Cardinals play their farm club, the old Houston Buffs (Stan Musial knocked a woman's front teeth out with a line drive!). Mr. Viebig swatted me then, too, prompting Dad to barge into his office waving Polaroids of my burnt umber ass and hollering, "*This* better never happen again!" Mr. Viebig, about six three and a former football player, chased Dad out and refused to see him.

This time Dad made an appointment. He insisted that Mr. Berman be present and brought Dot along, too. I sat between my father and stepmother and watched Dot cross her long legs so that no one in that room could have missed them or the black hair pressed into precise rows of tally marks by her nylon hose. From where I sat, for lack of a razor, we had already lost the argument.

I lowered my head and barely paid attention until Dad raised his voice.

"Number one, I don't want my son getting swatted all the time! Number two, if he acts up in class, goddamn it, call me! That will be the last time he does."

Before Dad could get to number three, Viebig was out of his chair.

"Mr. Berg, there is no call to take the Lord's name in vain."

Dad ignored him, instead looking at Berman.

"Number three, David is dead right. Calling Adlai Stevenson a traitor is pretty goddamn stupid."

At that, Berman leapt from his seat in the throes of an epiphany:

"I see where your son gets it! Don't you know when the Commies come your people will be the first to go?"

Dad stared at Berman, contemplating what he'd just heard. Then he shouted, "Are you nuts? Number one, what's my religion got to do with this? Number three, Viebig, if you ever swat my boy again, I will goddamn hire Percy Foreman to sue you!"

Dad had lost his count but not his punch: even I knew who Percy Foreman was. In a city without any other national celebrities, Mr. Foreman was it, our hometown hero. With his unrivaled track record—it was said he tried more murder cases in a single year than Clarence Darrow in his lifetime—daunting height (six five), and matchless skills, he had become one of the most famous and feared criminal lawyers in America. I had even seen him in person once, during lunch with Dad at the Cock & Bull, but we were too daunted to say hello, and besides, Mr. Foreman, sitting alone, didn't look too excited about company. Of course, it did not occur to Dad that Percy Foreman didn't handle civil suits and wouldn't sue the school, but then again, it probably didn't occur to Mr. Viebig, either, because he never swatted me again. Still, even if he had, I doubt Dad would have come to my defense. On the way out, he wheeled on me, tilted his head back, and located my face in the crescent-shaped bottom half of his bifocals. "You're on your own, Junior," he announced. "I've got a business to run."

And while Mr. Viebig might have been neutralized, Mr. Berman clearly was not. One day, rising at his desk, he announced to my class, "Everyone will be going on the field trip to Louisiana except David Berg. His father's check bounced." He wadded it up and threw it in my direction. "It's only fourteen dollars and fifty cents. I'm just a teacher and I've got fourteen dollars and fifty cents."

I picked the bad check up off the floor, put it in my shirt pocket, and waited with my head down for the bell to ring.

That night, I didn't tell Dad what Berman said. I just handed him the check. "Goddamn it," Dad whispered, fishing out the cash. So I ended up visiting Louisiana plantations after all, wondering all the while who had said what to their parents and what they'd said about mine.

At home, collection agencies started to call. So did the manager of a hotel in New York. "You should tell your father to pay his bills. He snuck out of here in the middle of the night like a *sneak thief.*" This time I told Dad exactly what I'd heard about him, hoping to be reassured that it was a lie. But Dad didn't say anything. The worst was when gentle Mr. Spivey called to ask why Dad hadn't paid him for an upholstery job. "I just don't know what happened to your father," he said.

I didn't either. I was fourteen, unaware of what self-loathing can do to you; I just knew Dad seemed ready to explode at everyone all the time. And when he wasn't angry he was silly, telling Jewish jokes that fell flat and did not improve with repetition. He punned nonstop and at restaurants became one of those "Did the hen lay the eggs yet?" and "Did you have to kill the cow?" customers. He developed a tremor in his right hand, which shook so violently that he couldn't bring a spoon to his mouth without spilling whatever was in it. When he yawned, which was often, his hand shook even more, and he was up to four or five packs of Camels a day, lighting one off another.

It was also then that my father embarked on a relentless campaign to drive my brother and me into medicine, to live out his life in his stead. And when Alan flunked organic chemistry at Texas A&M, Dad jerked him out of school, told him he was going to enlist, and personally drove him to the armed forces induction center in downtown Houston, where he lingered just long enough to see Alan walk in the front door but not long enough to see him march straight out the back. Alan reemerged three months later at Saint Louis University. God knows how he ended up at a Catholic school in a city he'd never even visited before, unless the respective answers are a girl and craps. That fall, Alan called Dad to ask for some help with tuition. Dad refused but made him an offer redolent of others: *if* he enlisted in the military, *if* he served his full tour of duty, and *if* he went back to A&M premed, Dad would pay his way. In moments like this, traces of the old Nat Berg would reappear: dropping his voice in a warmhearted, confidential way, whispering his most ardent goals for us with such rare concern and calling each of us "son" that it became difficult to do anything but what he wanted.

So in December 1956, Alan enlisted in the navy.

With Alan off on the high seas, I became the repository into which Dad poured his failed ambition and a captive audience for his irreducible maxims. "Doctors make twenty-five thousand dollars a year." "A depression can take your job but it can't take your medical license." "Everyone looks up to doctors." When he got wound up like that, I nodded like a bobblehead doll, knowing there wasn't a rat's-ass chance I would ever step foot in medical school, except maybe as a cadaver. I hated science. I hated studying. These are not early signs of a dedicated vet, much less a doctor. I knew what I wanted to be—according to Mom I told her when I was eight that I wanted to become a lawyer—but Dad did not agree with my priorities. "First," he said, "you become a doctor. Then you become a lawyer."

Once I hit adolescence, things really degenerated between Dad and me. Part of the problem was Dot, and while I am certain Dad would have wanted her to be a mother to his boys, if he thought that Dorothy Heinrich, whose name alone summoned up the Third Reich, was the mothering type, he had another think coming. Raised on a farm in northern Michigan by parents as icy as the winds off the nearby lakes, Dot was disinclined to bridge the differences that arose between Dad and his sons and ill-equipped to join in the political discussions that dominated Dad's table. (Also, raised in the anti-Semitic tradition of Martin Luther and the Missouri Synod, she is the reason, God forgive me, that I have never put a Lutheran on a jury.)

Because Dot wouldn't let Alan in the house very often, I fell prey to my father and stepmother's antipathy and one particularly unsettling problem. Dad rarely got home before eleven or twelve at night. I did my homework at the dining room table and waited for *The Huntley-Brinkley Report* on NBC like I was having company for dinner. Dot ran the office and came home late, too, but always before Dad, which was unfortunate, because I was uncomfortable being alone with her. She was my father's wife, but she was pretty and I had sexual thoughts about her. Fortunately, because God is great, my Oedipal thoughts quickly gave way to homicidal ones.

Then there were the Bs that had begun to dot my report card and the increasing amount of time I was spending with the Bellaire High School speech and debate team, both of which my father saw as alarming stumbling blocks to my medical career. Once, in Muskogee, Oklahoma, at a speech tournament attended by high schools from around the country, I placed first in extemporaneous speaking, oratory, and, with my partner, debate, ensuring a sweepstakes trophy for my school and for me. When I got home, I poured my medals and trophy on the coffee table and told Dad the results.

"What do you want?" he asked. "A pat on the head?"

It took me two decades and lots of therapy to admit that the answer to his question was yes, but even had I known back then, I would never have given my father the satisfaction. Instead, I started selling what I had done. I told him that my debate coach said she didn't think anyone had won that many events at Muskogee before.

"I don't care what that goddamn bitch said! I want you *out* of debate! It's ruining your grades!"

If Dad had taken debate, he would have been familiar with the advantages of a flow sheet: a piece of legal paper divided into halves by a line drawn down the middle. On the left side, the debater jots down the essence of an opponent's arguments and, on the right, bullet-point rebuttals to each. From those two entries, the contest is joined: point flows into counterpoint, and out of the competing views a rough truth emerges. Because the exercise is performed under the pressure of a live debate, it forces the young mind to think incisively. Over time, the debater develops a love of logic, intolerance for lies, and reluctance to be drawn into asinine conversations.

So I said nothing.

And Dad raged on, attributing my "shitty grades" and every other difficulty between us to "that bitch"—my debate coach. "You'll never get into medical school making grades like that. I'm calling that woman tomorrow. You are off that team! You are out of debate *as of now!*" Of course, I wasn't about to quit debate, which I loved—not when there were teams to beat, judges to persuade, and my name announced as a winner. Here's how debate made me feel: I wasn't *just another Berg*.

After that argument, Dad stopped speaking to me for three weeks. When my friends came over to pick me up, he went out of his way to say hello to them while pointedly ignoring me. I longed to hear my father say my name, but he didn't respond even when I apologized. I became nervous, an insomniac, unable to fall asleep until an hour or so before I had to get up for school. Compounding all the adolescent angst, I contracted impetigo, an infection that left my face covered with gray-black sores, which I picked at, making things worse and leaving scars. Our worst moment came in a darkened hallway in our home when I screamed at Dad that he had no right to criticize me when he was the failure—a mistake that I exacerbated by taking a swing at him, which he deflected by hitting *me*, for the first and only time ever, sending me into an antique lamp and breaking it. My sister was there, visiting from Little Rock, and says that I yelled at Dad, "You motherfucker, don't you know I love you?" Dot was there, too, complaining about the pieces of the lamp scattered on the floor. She still does.

It was into this delightful milieu that Alan came home on leave, thin but resplendent in his navy blues, wide collar over his back, bell bottom trousers, and a white sailor's cap crumpled in his hands. But he didn't come alone; he brought his girlfriend with him. Sandy was a sweet, well-educated Jewish girl from Boston. She was also pregnant.

Alan and Sandy sat together on the couch. Peering through a crack in the kitchen door, I could see only the backs of their heads and Dad standing in front of them, yelling.

"Goddamn it, Alan! You can't keep your pecker in your pants!"

"Dad, we're going to get married."

"The hell you are! You're too young to get married!"

"I'm twenty-one!"

"I don't give a good goddamn how old you are! You can't become a doctor with a wife and child around your neck! You haven't even graduated college!"

"Why are you screaming?"

"I'm not screaming! That's the way I talk!"

"Dad, quit yelling at us, please. Just listen to me."

"No, you listen to me. Number one, Sandy, I'm sure you are a very nice girl, but you are going to go home and get an abortion. Number two, you are not to see each other again. Alan becomes a doctor, you can see each other all you want."

Alan and his girlfriend began to cry. I opened the door the rest of the way and shouted at Dad to leave them alone. Alan turned around on the sofa and looked back at me, his eyes grown round. "David, don't get involved in this," he said, but it was too late. Now Dad was standing next to me, tilting his head, struggling to find me in his bifocals again, and so angry I thought that he was going to slug me. Instead, he unsheathed the deadliest weapon known to anyone who lives in a city of six hundred square miles and inadequate public transportation.

"Give me your car keys, right now! Goddamn it, give me the keys!"

"You took the car away three weeks ago, asshole," I said.

"Dad, please," Alan cut in, "don't be mad at him. He was just trying to help."

With Alan messing in my business, and me messing in his, Dad didn't know who to tell to stay the hell out of what. And then Alan and I made our worst mistake: we looked at each other and started laughing.

Dad exploded.

"Get out of this house, Alan, get out of here now, goddamnit! And take your goddamn girlfriend with you!" To me, he screamed, "And you get into your room and stay there! I don't want to see your face in here again! Go! Now! Get out of here!"

Alan and Sandy went back to their hotel, and Dad and Dot went to dinner. Alone in the house, I felt trapped and desperate. I wanted to set things straight with my father. I wanted things to be as they'd been during my first months in Houston. I wanted us to speak kindly to each other, as we'd done before. But I didn't know how to achieve any of this. I went into Dad and Dot's bathroom and looked in the mirror. My face was a horror, with all those sores. I opened the medicine cabinet and stared at a bottle of barbiturates—Dad's sleeping pills. I opened the bottle, emptied its contents into my hand, and slammed a fistful into my mouth, swallowing most of them. Then I lay down on my bed and grew dizzy and nauseous. I also became terrified that I might actually die. I lurched down the hallway and into the kitchen, where I picked up the phone to call Alan—but I didn't know where he was staying. Still, in my panic, I spoke into the dead receiver, blubbering to my brother about the stupid fucking thing I had done, and . . . was I imagining things? There he was, in the flesh, answering me, standing at the kitchen door, screaming, "What did you do?! What did you do?!" He had dropped his girlfriend off at the hotel and come back to have it out with Dad. Instead, he shoved me into his rental car and sped us to Methodist Hospital's emergency room, where I was soon splayed shirtless on a cold metal table under a blinding light.

The doctor said he'd keep an eye on me and that I should be fine after a while, a diagnosis that Alan evidently found wanting. He tapped the doctor on the shoulder and the two of them disappeared into the hall, returning with what looked like a length of garden hose that was inserted down my throat. Alan and I left the hospital a couple of hours later, and my brother asked if I wanted something to eat. Soon, with an esophagus that felt as though it had been scraped with a wire brush, I was wincing over pizza and spaghetti at Valian's, our favorite restaurant. For all his toughness, my brother was crying when he grabbed my hand from across the table and said, "Why are you so unhappy, kid?" I began to sob. For an hour or more, I unburdened myself to the one person I knew would understand. I kept talking until our waiter dimmed the lights and began hovering over us, grumbling that they were trying to close. But still Alan didn't get up. Instead, he leaned across the table and said, inches from my face, "Let me tell you something, kid. I love you with all my heart. But the next time you try to kill yourself, you better be successful. Because if you're not, I'll kill you myself."

The next time Alan came home the girl he brought was neither Jewish nor pregnant. She was, however, six feet tall and black. Before that moment, I had never been in a room with a black person who wasn't cleaning it. And this woman was stunning. She spoke confidently with no trace of the South and had obviously dressed for the occasion. Her sleeveless dress left her smooth arms shining under the lights in the den. Her hair, straightened, was parted in the middle and fell to just above her shoulders, like the movie star Hedy Lamarr's.

But even my father—a passionate integrationist who shouted down anyone who disagreed on the subject—was nervous and unwelcoming. This was no "Guess Who's Coming to Dinner" evening, where liberal old San Francisco Daddy reaches inward, confronts his own hypocrisy, and welcomes his black future in-law into the family. This was Houston in the fifties, where interracial dating could get you killed, especially if the Klan found out—and the Klan, which boasted many members in the Houston Police Department, was never far away.

Every so often, I would leave Dad and Dot to the glacial conversation with Alan and his girlfriend in the den, walk into the living room, and peek through a crack in the drapes, searching for any sign of trouble, quite literally fearful of seeing men in sheets on horseback. When I sat back down, Alan would glare at me—and I would turn away.

My brother didn't need to be asked to leave. Within a half hour he grabbed his date by the hand and stormed out of the house.

"That boy's going to get himself killed," Dad said as soon as they were out the door. Dot saw no such limitation. "He's going to get us all killed, Nat. You tell him not to do that again! Do you understand? I don't want that happening in my house again."

I didn't disagree.

Alan came home the next day, picked up his duffel bag, and headed back to his naval station at Quonset Point, Rhode Island. He told me he was never coming back to Houston—and I believed him. He was pissed and disappointed, and not just with Dad and Dot.

# 3

A lan didn't call much after that evening, and when we did speak I was afraid to ask if he was coming home for fear of the answer. Then, one hot December day in 1958, I returned from school and there he was, standing in our den, bathed in winter sunlight, shielded from the glare by sunglasses with frames as thick as Buddy Holly's, his duffel bag at his feet. He wore a starched white shirt, blue jeans, and the half smile that concealed his eyeteeth and easily could be mistaken for a smirk. And more shocking than that he'd come home: I was suddenly taller than my brother. I didn't know whether to hug his neck or shake his hand. "Hi, kid," he said, declaring the balance of power between us unchanged. Then he grabbed me and pulled me close.

Alan left the navy at virtually the same rank he went in, but two pay grades higher. He would have been discharged at an even higher rate had he not been caught running a (literally) floating crap game aboard his ship, the USS *Leyte*. He was snitched off by a swabie who'd lost all his pay and come running at Alan's bunk with a knife, screaming about how he was going to "kill the fucking Jew" who stole his money. Two other seamen, who, unlike Alan, were awake at the time, stopped him. Still, he had an honorable discharge in hand and cash in his pocket, leading me to conclude that his was not the first onboard crap game the navy ever uncovered.

There was no mention of Sandy or the black woman.

"I didn't think you'd come back," I said.

"I've been talking to Dad. I'm going to go back to school. I'm going to try to get into medical school."

"You don't really want to be a doctor, do you?"

"I don't know. I'd just like Dad to be less disappointed in me than usual."

"Are you kidding? He's disappointed when we do well."

Alan laughed.

"I'm not kidding. He wants us to fail. He hates when I do well at anything. Anyway, I thought you wanted to be an actor."

"Dad says I should be a doctor first, then an actor."

"What a coincidence. He says I can be anything I want provided I become a doctor first. 'Be a doctor. Then be a lawyer.' "

"You know why he wants us to be doctors, don't you?"

I knew, of course, from Mom, same as Alan, but I'd never discussed it with anyone other than her. Dad's secret weighed on me, made me feel somehow implicated in the bribery, forever wishing I could find a way to atone on his behalf. Now, at least between the two of us, it would be in the open and I felt enormous relief.

"Yeah," I said. "I know. He got kicked out of medical school."

"Have you ever said anything to him about it?"

"Shit, no. I've always wanted to, but—"

"It would kill him if he thought we knew. It wrecked his life, kid."

"*He* wrecked his life, Alan."

"Jesus, you sound like you hate him."

"I don't know how you don't. He treats you like shit."

"I made a lot of trouble for Dad."

"That's bullshit. You didn't do anything other kids didn't do except for being a bookie. I can't stand to be around him, Alan. He makes those stupid puns all the time. I haven't had a serious personal conversation with him since I asked him if my dick was ever going to grow."

"Don't worry, kid. Someday it will. Maybe not today, maybe not tomorrow, but soon."

We were seated at opposite ends of the couch in the den. Alan had yet to take off his sunglasses, despite being indoors the whole time, but at that moment he did and looked right at me.

"You have to understand, kid. Dad loves us. And he wants a family. But he only wants the façade of a family. He just doesn't know what to do to make it work."

And then he snapped the sunglasses back on.

We didn't spend the entire day indicting our father. Alan told me about attending the Newport Jazz Festival, just a few miles down the road from Quonset Point. He retrieved several albums from his duffel bag, including his favorites, the clarinetist Bix Beiderbecke and trumpeter Miles Davis, the latter of whom he'd actually heard in person for one dollar in a Newport nightclub ("He turned his back to the audience when he played!"). This was Alan's "schwee-bop" period, the slightly embarrassing sound he'd make scatting along with singers like Ella Fitzgerald and Louis Armstrong. And he'd snap his fingers to applaud riffs he liked and look to me to join him, which I did, snapping away and avoiding any question of how much I loved jazz, because I didn't—something I wasn't about to tell Alan, who obviously did. (This also helped explain the horn-rimmed sunglasses that he'd removed only that one time and which, he explained, were not at all like Buddy Holly's, but Dizzy Gillespie's.)

Alan also had books in his duffel bag—equal almost to the amount of clothing—and out came Jack Kerouac's *On the Road,* clarifying my brother's newfound hostility to the "bougie"—the bourgeois life. There was also some Dylan Thomas, whose poetry I, too, had escaped into of late. I told Alan that I didn't understand "Fern Hill."

"He's lying," Alan said. "If Dylan Thomas's childhood was so bucolic he wouldn't have died a drunk so young. Also, he peed on somebody's carpet at a party in New York."

Alan was going to stay with us until he found an apartment. In my bedroom, looking for a place to unpack his clothes, he opened one of my drawers, pulled out some worn underwear, and waved them around like a semaphore signaling the enemy's approach. "When's the last time Dad took you shopping?" he asked—and off we went to Sakowitz Brothers, where Alan bought me enough new clothes to outfit a small orphanage. In the fitting room, under the fluorescent lights, he looked closely at my face and winced. I explained about the impetigo. "I hold them responsible for this," he said, referring to Dad and Dot. The next day, he took me to a dermatologist.

And, just as he'd said he would do, he enrolled at the University of Houston, a few credit hours short of being a junior. For the next eighteen months, before I graduated from high school and left for Tulane on a debate scholarship, we spent long afternoons and evenings studying together at the kitchen table in his apartment on Binz Street, near the Museum of Fine Arts. Dad had forbidden me moving in with Alan, but I fell asleep so often on his pull-out couch that it was a moot point. I took comfort in those long, studious afternoons: just sitting there, drinking coffee and smoking, silent for a while and then talking about what we'd learned. Alan worked hard to compensate for the two years he'd lost in the navy. He even made a somewhat redemptive B in organic chemistry this time, leaving Dad encouraged. Maybe, just maybe, there was a medical school out there with a place for a Berg after all.

When Alan ran out of his navy money, he took a job at a used-car lot, its name long forgotten but not the dark blue '57 Buick sedan his boss lent him to drive back and forth to work. One day, the two of us drove to Galveston. Speeding down the Gulf Freeway, he patted the Buick's padded dashboard and said to me, "Someday we'll have a car like this, kid. A new one. I promise." Alan was skipping work that day and needed to call in "sick," so he pulled into one of the small towns on the way to try to borrow a phone. He knocked on several doors before a housewife allowed him inside. I waited in the Buick a lot longer than a phone call, leading me to suspect that he'd been welcomed into more than just the front door. When he finally emerged and got back into the driver's seat, he said, as though he'd never left, "But ours'll be a Cadillac."

We spent that day sitting fully dressed on the beach—it was not soaked in gummy particulates from the Mississippi Delta in those days—arms folded on our knees, watching the waves break, and plotting a future that would lead the Berg Boys to great success. We would share everything, we said.

When I left for Tulane in the fall of 1960, Alan continued to study hard. If he was being honest, he didn't go on a date for several months: he was that serious about getting into medical school, and his solid B+ average showed it. When the time came, Alan applied to twelve schools, including the University of Texas Medical Branch in Galveston, where my friend Jamie Gerson's older brother, Paul, had an interview on the same day. There were still restrictive Jewish quotas back then, making Alan and Paul competitors for the same few spots, and Paul recalls that they were so nervous that when Alan farted "incredibly loudly" in the UT men's room—an event that at any other time would have elicited at least an expression of admiration—the two of them merely washed their hands and wished each other good luck.

Dad found out from our family doctor that Alan's interview had gone well: the professor who interviewed him had been in the navy, and that's mostly what they had talked about, leaving him impressed with Alan's maturity and convinced that he was sincere about becoming a physician. Even with that feedback, the wait for a decision was excruciating, and not just for Alan. In fact, Dad and I probably sweated it even more than he, given that Alan had given up on getting in, having already been rejected by several other schools.

Still, that spring, mirabile dictu, just fucking wonderful to relate, Alan called me at Tulane and stammered into the receiver, "I made it! I got in! Can you believe it? I got in!" What a rutted road he had followed to this moment! He was crying, and then I started, too. Dad pulled the phone away. "That brother of yours is really something," he said, sounding more excited than I'd ever heard him. They had already called Mom, and when I asked how she'd taken it, Dad said she was probably still "kvelling," Yiddish for strutting while sitting down.

From then on, Dad called Alan "Junior" and steered all conversation around to his golden boy bound for medical school. This turn of events forced me to revise my view of my father. Maybe there was something commendable about his severity after all. Dad was hard on Alan, on both of us, but now my brother was going to be a doctor, and who could criticize that? Paul Gerson had been accepted, too, and in phone calls our fathers chortled over their sons' triumphs, all the greater for having beaten some pretty serious anti-Semitic odds. Becoming a doctor in the Jewish community was akin to knighthood, and my friends and their families were thrilled for Alan, too. "He's like a little senator," my friend Larry said. Somehow I knew exactly what he meant.

～

There is nothing so muted as a summer day in Texas, when you hear nothing but the cicadas murmuring under the relentless heat. On one such day that August, just before I was to return to Tulane for my sophomore year, I lay reading in my bedroom in Dad's house. Alan was getting ready to drive to Galveston for his first year of medical school. On his way, he stopped by to pick up an old black-and-white Zenith TV that had been sitting in a closet. But this was not acceptable to Dad. His hollering shattered the cicadas' drone and startled me clear across the house.

*"You are not taking a TV to medical school, goddamn it! Take it back into the house! Maybe someone else could watch TV and make it, but you can't! Now! Goddamn it! Now!"*

One might have expected our father, his hour come round at last, to pull Alan close, stuff an extra fifty bucks in his pocket, and (here I am dreaming) with eyes glistening tell him how proud he was of his boy. Or he could have said, "Son, I fucked up miserably in medical school and I've regretted it ever since. Do me a favor. Leave the TV set here. If you do well, once the semester is over, I'll drive to Galveston and buy you a new one myself. Deal?" But once our father got started, he was a wrecking ball. He began to scream about how Alan had barely gotten in as it was; with a TV to distract him, he'd flunk out for sure. Here's what I heard: *I'm afraid. I'm afraid that if you take the TV you might watch it and still become a doctor, like I never did. I've thought it over and I don't want you to accomplish more than I have after all. If you do, I'll resent it—and I will make certain that you suffer, too.*

I ran out the kitchen door into the driveway, swinging my fists, screaming at Dad to shut the fuck up and leave my brother alone. Dad whirled around toward me, beet-faced and ranting, oblivious to the neighbor peeping through her blinds and to Alan holding the TV above his head. My brother looked right at me. Then he closed his eyes. He wasn't angry. He was empty.

The TV fell at Dad's feet. I wish there had been an explosion— shattered glass and cathode tubes splintered across the pavement— but amazingly there wasn't. The TV bounced off the driveway into the garden and still wasn't broken.

Then Alan got into the car, slammed it into reverse, and peeled out of the driveway, even as Dad tried to reach through the driver's side window for the keys. But Alan escaped, driving so fast that we could hear him squeal around the corner half a block away.

I ran in front of Dad, who had picked up the TV, and blocked his way into the house.

"Are you happy, you motherfucker?! You don't want to pay for medical school, do you? Is that what this is about?"

"You can walk back to New Orleans. I'm not giving you another dime, you son of a bitch."

"It's always the money, isn't it. You and your cheap fucking wife don't do anything for us without putting a price tag on it, do you."

Dad stopped shouting and glowered at me, frozen, weighing what to do next. No one, especially not his sons, was allowed to criticize Dot, and I had done it often enough lately that I was afraid. Dad hesitated, then moved toward me, but instead of hitting me, juggled the TV set in his arms, shoved me aside, and stormed into the house.

And for the next three days we didn't speak a word, not until the next Monday, when we had no other choice. The dean of the University of Texas Medical Branch called, looking for Alan.

He hadn't enrolled.

Frantically, Dad and I called everyone we knew who knew Alan, but no one had any information. I looked all over town and went several times to Cougar Den, the student lounge at UH, and to a bar nearby where Alan and I used to hang out. Dad's efforts were no more successful. At the end of the second day, he called the Houston Police Department to report Alan as a missing person but they said it was a Galveston matter and Dad let it drop: he knew as well as I that Alan wasn't "missing." My twenty-five-year-old brother had run away.

The following Friday, the deadline for class registration, the school gave his spot to a grateful woman on the waiting list, and two lives were changed.

Dad never said another word about what happened in the driveway, remaining as silent about it as he'd been about that day back in Little Rock when Dean Vinsonhaler told him to clear out of medical school for good. Maybe it was the way of men of his era, but it was frustrating: my father never once accepted responsibility for a mistake, at least not out loud. I was stunned that he would sabotage his own son, no different from what his mother had done to him for an equally senseless reason, refusing to pay for medical school because he'd put his feet on her burgundy sofa. By now, failure to fulfill one's promise was beginning to look like a birthright of the Bergs. Dad's brother Uncle Harry was a licensed attorney who spent his life selling paint supplies out of his car, munching peanuts from a can. Their eldest brother, Uncle Phil, took post-baccalaureate courses in everything from Latin to economics, was a member of MENSA, and spent his career sorting letters at the post office. Now Alan was one of them, his failure to enroll a perverse triumph of loyalty. I'd convinced myself that he actually wanted to go to medical school—which is what made it even more difficult to understand how he had let this enormous opportunity slip by without even *trying*. How could he have put all that work into getting in and then simply walk away? And—shame on me—what would I say to my friends?

A week later, Alan called me from Las Vegas, up $2,500 from shooting craps. He told me he'd left school because he'd been blackballed by the Gentile medical fraternity he wanted to join.

"That's bullshit."

"Yeah." He laughed. "I don't think I ever wanted to be a doctor."

That was all that was said about that. Alan was eager to tell me all about how he was going to live in Las Vegas and become a professional gambler. He also said he'd wired me $250 through Western Union.

"I'm getting you out of there, kid. We're not going back." I was disappointed in my brother, but he was still my closest friend and cheerleader. And I believed, profoundly, that failure permeated my father's house like some deadly, undetectable gas that could poison my future, too. I told Dad I was leaving and why. He told me that I was a grown man and that I could make my own decision, "but if you step one foot out that door you cannot come back." The very idea kept me up, deliriously happy, the entire night. I calculated and recalculated the cost of attending Tulane. With my scholarship, Alan and I could pull it off easily; I could get a part-time job and spend summers and holidays with my brother in Vegas. The only thing that could keep me from leaving Houston the very next morning was my brother, and he did.

Alan called at 5:00 a.m., drunk. He'd lost all his money and told me to wire back the $250.

I told my father that morning that I had changed my mind, that I wasn't going to Las Vegas after all. He said that was a good decision and that I should stay away from that bastard brother of mine.

# 4

Sometimes I wonder whether my brother would still be alive today if only Dad had followed his own advice.

But that's not entirely fair. I was complicit, too.

Alan hitchhiked almost dead broke from Las Vegas to Dallas, where he borrowed some samples from a fabric wholesaler and peddled upholstery door-to-door. Within weeks he had bought a used Jaguar and moved into a two-story town house. But equally as quickly, he fell into our father's ruinous pattern, stiffing creditors and writing more than $3,500 in hot checks. Yet, knowing this, I never once refused the cash that he shoved in my hand each time I saw him. Still locked into the little brother role, I watched without saying a word as Alan orchestrated his own undoing.

In December, Alan sent me a plane ticket to Dallas and from there we were going to drive to Little Rock to see our family. On the way out of town, Alan stopped at Neiman's, saying he was going to buy Daddy Joe "something I've wanted to get him for a long time." Inside, he asked the salesman to show us the "twelve ugliest ties you have in stock," and when several of those did not meet that test, ordered him to bring even more repellent ones. Alan and I meticulously picked our way through the pile, eliminating anything that could be worn without having people laugh at you. Alan bought them all. When Daddy Joe, mumbling about the "goddamn waste of money," opened the boxes, he stopped at one containing a bright orange tie whose widest point featured a family of ducks floating in a brackish pond. He removed it like he was handling the Shroud of Turin and put it on. From what Momma Hattie told us, he seldom wore a different one after that.

Alan lasted fourteen months before he abandoned Dallas for Houston, pursued by the Dallas County DA for the bad checks. He set up shop in a dingy apartment on Old Spanish Trail and began selling upholstery door-to-door.

Not long after returning, Alan ran into Dad in a delicatessen. They hadn't spoken since the fight over the TV, but soon they were eating breakfast together, laughing and making up. Then Dad made Alan a proposition, something he said he'd been thinking about for a while: Why not become fifty-fifty partners in a new business, selling upholstery and carpet? "I'm not doing very well, son," Dad told him in his most persuasive, between-you-and-me tone. "I need you. You're a crackerjack salesman. And I miss my boy."

That was all Alan had to hear. Dad and that bastard brother of mine were in business.

To his credit, Dad had recently gone out of his way to make amends with me as well. During my junior year at Tulane, the year before my medical school applications were due, I managed to make a D in organic chemistry, an F in physics, and, for good measure, an asshole fraternity brother shoved a Q-tip I'd been using through my right eardrum. When I'd gotten back from the school clinic and was lying on the bed in my dorm room, half deaf and groggy from the painkillers they'd given me, it was my father who shook my shoulder and told me to wake up. "It's time to go home, son," he said. With the grades I was making, I knew I wasn't long for Tulane, but I would never have believed that Dad and Dot would come all the way to New Orleans to retrieve me—or that they would be so kind.

"Dot tells me I'm doing to you what Momma did to me," my father said. "You want to be a lawyer, go be a lawyer."

I was stunned.

So I transferred to the University of Houston, which I hated. Yet, in all other respects, my return to Texas marked the start of one of the happiest periods of my life. It was also a fairly happy time for my brother. By then, Alan had been married twice—three times if you believe the Mexico rumor, which I do. He and I never discussed it in detail, but Dad was pretty certain that Alan had been married to a Mexican woman for approximately twenty-four hours, a union annulled once the tequila wore off. He'd had a similarly drunken courtship and marriage in Houston, also ending in annulment. And there was even a third nonstarter: to a Jewish girl I'll call Sarah, whom Alan would divorce within a year after finding out that she had had an abortion without telling him. But during Christmas break of 1962, I had introduced Alan to Harriet Laviage, an old school friend of mine whom I'd taken out once myself. Harriet had thick black hair, tawny Andalusian skin, and, although she was only eighteen, the patience and understanding of Momma Hattie. Five months later, when Alan called to tell me that he and Harriet had eloped, I was thrilled, and immediately moved all of my belongings into their town house. The night they returned from their honeymoon in Galveston, I had dinner waiting for them: Mom's T-bones smothered under a pile of "red hot" spaghetti, a concoction of watered-down Hunt's tomato sauce and a spoonful of chili powder—Alan's favorite.

We sat up the entire night talking in their living room, alit with candles and our ambitions. Alan would build a business empire.

I would become a famous lawyer. Harriet would have babies, a houseful.

Soon I was driving to classes in Alan's red '63 MG with the top down, downshifting around the curves in Hermann Park while answering aloud the questions Johnny Carson surely would ask me one day about the monster case I'd won so quickly after being sworn into the bar. But it was Harriet who first made headway in the ambition department. By that summer, she was pregnant.

Some evenings, to pay for tuition and the occasional toddy, I waded into Houston's ghettos to try to sell the overpriced merchandise of Imperial Carpet & Upholsterers, the business Alan and Dad had started. They operated out of a large office space and plant near downtown, where two dozen women sat in tiny cubicles, cold-calling into the telephone exchanges of Houston's poorest neighborhoods, pitching whoever answered to let a salesman come to their home. This arrangement was called a boiler room, in 1963 still a relatively new means of attracting customers—a hustle that originated with the aluminum siding business that generated huge profits gouging its vulnerable clientele. Alan managed the sales crew, and Dad handled the finances, a deliberate division of responsibility that played to their respective strengths and, in theory, minimized arguments between them. With Alan closing almost every lead he took, business had taken off quickly.

Alan would "prequalify" his leads—call prospective customers beforehand to try to lock them into buying carpet or having their furniture reupholstered before he even left the office. Fresh out of one of my college lectures on Titian or Homer, I would settle into a chair across from my brother's desk and watch a true master at work. By then, and although he couldn't really afford it, my brother had begun wearing custom-made Italian suits and soft leather shoes that zipped up the sides. He had also abandoned his old pompadour for a hairstyle that drooped across his forehead like the Kennedys'; he'd even affected Bobby's habit of gentling it back into place when it fell too close to his eyes, a gesture he made often as he delivered his sales pitch—which was like something out of *Glengarry Glen Ross*:

> Mr. Beasley, while I have really enjoyed this conversation, I need to move on, I need to get some work done, because, like you, I work very hard, and talking to you, Vernon—may I call you Vernon? Great! Please call me Alan or I won't answer. As I was saying, Vern, talking to you is not work, it is a pleasure, a rare pleasure because I talk to so many people in my line of work and so few of them are so much [*pause for emphasis*] plain old-fashioned fun. So let me ask you this. I am considering coming to your house personally, to come myself instead of sending one of my salesmen. So before I saddle up and come riding out there, would you make me two promises? First, would you make me a cup of coffee so that I can sit down at your kitchen table with you and your wife and get to know you both? You would? Terrific. And second, would you promise me now, so I don't waste your valuable time or my own, that if you find a carpet you like at a price that's right and I could arrange some easy monthly payments, could I count on you to buy that carpet? And could I count on you to become a friend, Vern? Because I have a feeling you're not just going to be a customer. . . .

If Vernon Beasley said or did anything short of telling my brother to go fuck himself, Alan would set up an appointment and toss the lead, written on an index card, onto the stack in the middle of his desk. Occasionally Alan would miss a sale, and some that he closed fell through because of bad credit. But he rarely left a customer's home without a signed contract and new "friends," husbands and wives now deep in debt for carpet they could have bought at a third of the price at Suniland or any number of other stores like it in town.

Sometimes Alan and I would go together to a prospective customer's house. He would pull up his pant legs, sit cross-legged on the floor, and, upon spotting a small hole in the homeowner's upholstery, put a finger in and rip it wide open to demonstrate its fragility. Then, to redress the damage, he'd pull out an enticing array of fabrics "guaranteed to last," and the customers—while I sat astonished—almost inevitably agreed that it was high time to get it redone.

There was a reason Alan rarely lost a sale. He *listened*. Unafraid of a customer's objections, he would acknowledge their concerns, and by doing so, allay them. "I know what you're saying about the payments, Mr. Beasley—they *are* high—but on the other hand, you must spend thirty dollars a month on those cigarettes, and wouldn't you give 'em up to help pay for a nice carpet for your family?" Nor would he ever rush—or ever for one moment leave a couple alone while he used the bathroom—for fear they'd find the courage to tell him no. He could sit there like Buddha under the bodhi tree for hours if necessary, throwing in free drapes, a fresh paint job, and his final concession, always delivered sotto voce: "Vern, I am not supposed to do this, and I have to have your absolute promise never to tell another living soul—especially other customers should you meet them—but I am going to give you a twenty-five percent discount. Now say yes before I regain my senses."

And once they'd said yes, he'd "spike the deal"—take a cash down payment or stuff a chair into his trunk, ostensibly to "get the plant working on your job right away," but really to make it even more difficult for the customer to "kick out"—cancel the next day.

By contrast, high-pressure salesmen like our father did just the opposite: They talked like Faulkner wrote, which is to say without periods at the ends of their sentences, and so rapidly that they never gave the customer a chance to object: "Mr. Washington, I know you and your wife love this carpet and you want it and we're going to get it financed for five years so those payments will be very low and now just let me get you to sign this contract and we'll have it installed tomorrow afternoon at five and I assume that time is good for you but if not just let me know and let me tell you my friend you have just stolen this carpet . . ."

Often, pressured into signing and gripped by buyer's remorse, some of Dad's customers did kick out. But virtually all of Alan's stayed sold.

I learned many things about selling from Alan, but nothing more valuable than how to close a tough customer. "You know what, Mr. and Mrs. Tucker?" I'd say, when I was out on my own and the Tuckers hesitated, "I just realized that we might not even have enough of this carpet that you like in stock. I'm so sorry. Just let me call my manager, to check."

No matter where the phone was, I'd talk loudly enough for them to hear.

"Mr. Schmendrick, how are you, sir? This is David calling."

"Hey, kid. Can you close it?"

"Do you know how much of lot number ten fifty-eight we have left? It's that level-loop pile in dark brown."

"Did your penis ever actually grow?"

"That's right. Forty-eight yards in dark brown. Please check the warehouse. We're going to lose some very nice customers if you don't have it."

"We're going to Lee's Den for dinner, so close it and get home."

"That's right: forty-eight yards. I'll wait."

While "Mr. Schmendrick" checked, tensions escalated. Mr. and Mrs. Tucker would lean forward nervously, asking, "What'd he say? Do you have the carpet?" As luck would have it, "Mr. Schmendrick" always located precisely enough square yardage in dark-brown level-loop pile to cover the Tuckers' entire house—and then, feeling magnanimous, would be moved to give the Tuckers an unprecedented 25 percent discount just to move it out of the warehouse. Twenty-five percent! With savings like that, the Tuckers could hardly wait to sign the contract—and soon I would be sitting with Alan and Harriet at Lee's Den, exultant over egg rolls and ribs and my latest commission.

Life went on like that for a while. We had a lot of fun, my brother and Harriet and I, but looking back I have to acknowledge the troubling undercurrents that were gathering as well. I had learned to be careful with money from Daddy Joe and Mom—but Alan had not, not from any source. He loaned friends thousands of dollars and (until his credit went south) cosigned their notes. He failed to pay his bills and some months paid as much as $500 in bad-check charges at Industrial State Bank—a fortune back then. And then there was the boiler room. It was a seedy operation, staffed largely by former used-car salesmen, some of whom had criminal records. Of course, I can't say that I had the integrity to walk away from it; I didn't, and I made and spent money from the deals I closed. But I knew it was just temporary, not a career but a means to a better end—and I suppose I wanted to believe that it would be that for Alan, too.

Late one humid evening in March 1964, I finished my leads and returned to the office, where my brother and Harriet were waiting to take me to dinner. With my very pregnant sister-in-law in the passenger seat and me in the back, Alan began backing his car out of the company lot. As we passed the loading dock, a stocky man with dirty-gray stubble came running toward us with a paper bag over his hand. When he reached the car, he jammed his hand through the open window and the bag against Alan's temple. Alan braked, hard.

"You goddamn son-of-a-bitch, pay me the money you owe me before I blow your brains out!"

I was sitting right behind my brother, and I could see the butt of the gun.

Alan, who always drove with his left leg crossed over his right, swiveled slightly in his seat and calmly asked the man how much he was owed.

"You know goddamn good and well how much! A hundred twenty-five dollars, you fucking Jew bastard!"

"*No*, I really didn't know the amount. Now that I do, I will be glad to pay it."

"Pay it or your brains will be all over this car!"

"I'm going to reach into the back and get my checkbook. Take the gun away and I will write the check."

"*FUCK YOU!* Give me my money!"

Back then, checks were kept, four to a page, in a three-ring binder on perforated paper attached to a stub where all the details were recorded. Terrified, I handed the binder to Alan, who rested it on the steering column and opened it up. His legs were still crossed, and the gun was still at his head. Alan gentled back his hair, then began filling in the pertinent information. "Tell me again," he murmured to the gunman, "how you spell your name?" When all the information had been filled out, Alan tore out the check and handed it to the gunman, who backed away with his pistol still trained on my brother, screaming that he ought to kill him anyway.

Finally, he turned and ran away.

Alan backed the car out of the lot, drove a block away, and pulled over. Harriet was crying.

"I have got to get out of this business," he said. "And you"—he turned to me—"are never going into it."

"Jesus, Alan. Why'd he do that?" I asked.

"We owed him money for an upholstery job."

"Why didn't you pay it?"

"We didn't have it."

"Is that check any good?"

"I'll get the cash from Dad and take it to the night deposit."

"Alan, please do it. Don't screw around. That guy was serious."

"I know, kid. I know."

Then he started up the engine and we drove off. I leaned forward and put my hand on his shoulder. Harriet settled back into her seat. They were both crying now.

I wanted to believe what Alan said about getting out. But somehow I knew that my brother was going to be trapped in that shit business until the day he died.

# 5

T here was one way in which the University of Houston was superior to Tulane: at UH I could actually get dates. One of those girls was Mary Beth, whom I met in comparative religion class. She was of that species of Texas women classified as "rode hard and put up wet," with big blondish hair piled on top, tight-fitting blouses, and a cigarette cough. Sitting directly across from me in the semicircle we formed around our professor, Mary Beth began slowly crossing and uncrossing her legs, revealing a little more thigh each time until it became apparent that she had, in modern parlance, gone commando. She licked her lips and smiled a wicked smile in my direction. I was not stupid. She was flirting.

Mary Beth and I went out, double-dating with my buddy Jamie Gerson and a girl whose name I'm not sure I ever knew. Jamie was at the wheel as we rounded the billowing Mecom Fountains on South Main, their water spraying high into the air. Mary Beth pointed at the Museum of Fine Arts, which is nearby.

"I just luuv that place. I go there and just get ingrahssed en rahdin."

"You what?"

"I get ingrahssed en rahdin."

"Ingrahssed en rahdin?"

"Yes. I love his statutes."

Solicitous to a fault, Jamie asked, "What the fuck are you talking about?"

"I just *tole* you! I get *ingrahssed en rahdin!*"

Frequently, I had been ingrahssed en rahdin my own self. The museum had a piece of his called *The Walking Man.* But even more important than our common interest in Rodin was our common interest in matters of the flesh, with special emphasis on the word "common." On the way to Galveston, in the dark of the backseat, she slid her hand up my thigh, her fingers coming to rest on top of my zipper. "I'm all horned up," she whispered in my ear. Suffice to say, so was I. In Galveston, Jamie and his date disappeared to one end of the beach and Mary Beth and I to the other. By sunrise we were picking sand out of our respective crevices and reconvening to head home.

I went out with Mary Beth once more, in a manner of speaking, following a class when she reprised her leg-crossing performance, revealing slowly once more the sainted area where I had lingered days before. We ran to her apartment and repeated the beachfront exercise indoors. That was our last encounter. Separated by language—I couldn't understand half of what she said, with the exception of the oddly crisp way she referred to "Jewing" someone down—our relationship foundered. And when she started wearing jeans instead of miniskirts to class, it was clear that we were done.

I graduated from UH in '64 and joined the Peace Corps, inspired in equal parts by President Kennedy and the desire to get away from my father and Houston. I left for Hilo, Hawaii, to train to teach English in the Philippines. Dad was not happy. "Get your law license first. Then go into the Peace Corps." This time he was right.

In Hilo, my fellow volunteers and I took immersion classes in Tagalog, the Filipino dialect: *"Magandang umaga po!"* the teacher would exclaim. *"Magandang umaga po!"* we repeated until we had mastered this arcane greeting for old Filipino men. The training begged the question: Why were we teaching English to our little brown brothers when they had a perfectly good language of their own? Within days I knew I'd made a mistake. I was miserable. I wanted to go home. I wanted to go to law school.

One afternoon, an instructor pulled me out of class. He said that my brother was holding on the line for me and that it was important. I ran as fast as I could to the training center's pay phone, closed the booth, and picked up the receiver, assuming bad news. I wasn't disappointed.

"Hi, kid," Alan said. "Listen, Mary Beth got pregnant."

"You're kidding."

"No, I'm not. She called me a week ago and told me."

"I bet I'm not the father."

"Didn't you fuck her?"

"Yes, but just twice. . . . Well, that's stupid, isn't it?"

"She says it was you."

"She can't be certain. She probably fucked half the guys in our class."

"Well, it's over now. I took her to get an abortion."

The booth was stifling. I was sweating and shaking.

"The guy turned out to be a butcher," Alan continued. "I thought she was going to bleed to death. I couldn't take her to a hospital or we'd have both been arrested, so I brought her home and got a doctor to come over and help her. Harriet and I let her stay until she got better and then her father came and took her home."

"Well, I'm coming home, anyway. I hate it here. Wait a minute. Did you say her *father* picked her up?"

"I begged her not to tell him, but she did anyway."

Then Alan paused.

"Are you serious about coming home? Are you really dropping out?"

"Dad was right. This is a huge mistake. I want to go to law school."

"*Jesus H. Christ*, David. You can't come home. Her father says he's going to kill you."

"Oh shit, Alan. He'll do it. That guy's brutal."

A few days later, I received a thick envelope from my brother. Inside were a round-trip ticket to London, a Eurail pass, and some spending money. I called him at work.

"I can't believe this. Jesus, I thought you were really mad."

"Well, we know how much you want to see Europe, and you really can't come home."

"We? You told Dad?"

"I'm on the phone too, son. Alan told me about the girl. It's probably better that you don't come home now."

"Who is this? What have you done with my father? Put my father on the phone."

"I couldn't have afforded this without Dad, kid."

"I don't know what to say. I'm stunned. You have no idea what this means to me."

Now Alan mimicked Dad's voice. "I have one suggestion before you go."

"What?"

"Keep your pecker in your pants."

"I do *not* sound like that!" Dad said, and we all started laughing.

The next day, on money that my family didn't have, I left Hawaii for Europe.

After going to Florence, where I spent three days visiting every church, statue, and painting I'd studied in art history, I took a train to Paris, where I was scheduled to take the Law School Aptitude Test at the American University. But the night before, at Harry's Bar, I met a New Yorker named Steven Winter, who was studying at the Sorbonne and wanted to be a writer. I had never given even passing thought to being anything other than a lawyer, but there I was, an English major enamored of the American novelists and poets of the twenties and thirties, in the city that nurtured them, and in the bar Hemingway made famous; by 3:00 a.m., I wanted to be a writer, too—and worked myself into such an expat frenzy that I went lurching for a payphone to call my father. Dad greeted me the same way he always did when I called collect from Tulane: "Make it snappy, son. This is costing money." I explained that I wanted to stay in Paris and write. Dad himself made it snappy: "Are you nuts?" he asked, none too cheerily, and the conversation was pretty much over.

The next morning, while I sat for the LSAT, drunk and struggling to stay awake, my brother was in the Admissions Office at the University of Houston Law Center, persuading them to accept me even before the results were in. (Dad was right: Alan really was a crackerjack salesman.) But for all my resolve to become a lawyer, I nearly flunked out my first year of law school. I found no poetry in the cases we studied, just stultifying facts illustrating arcane legal theories. I hated every minute of classes and rarely studied. Prior to my criminal law final, I stayed awake for three days and nights cramming on some green pills with white dots that my friend Larry had brought back from Mexico. About halfway through the exam, I started braying like a donkey and had to leave the room. And, of course, I failed.

At the end of my first year, A. A. White, my contracts professor, sent word for me to come to his office. Dean White was the school's most respected faculty member, beloved by his students and elegantly tall and spare in both appearance and speech. He did not rise or offer his hand when I walked in. Instead, he motioned toward a chair, waited until I had sat down, and said, "Your exam reads like a Gilbert's outline." He was right. I don't think I'd read a single case. What I *had* read was Gilbert's, the equivalent of Cliff's Notes for law students. "Your answers are superficial," Dean White went on. "You didn't discuss issues; you just listed them." Then, still seated, he leaned across his desk, folded his hands in that Protestant way that supplants screaming, and said, "Mr. Berg, you are a corner cutter." In the past, I had always found "underachiever" lectures perversely flattering, but this was something else. When Dean White said, "You are a corner cutter," what I heard was, *You are just another Berg.*

Faced with evidence that he might be right, I could not dismiss his comment. It ate away at me. During the next two years, I worked much harder and raised my average considerably. (I did fail Admiralty, having taken the course on the theory that it would be all Moby Dickish, only to discover it wasn't.) In July '67, I sat for the bar exam in Austin. I don't know where Larry was getting his pills, but this time he gave me a giant red one that allowed me to fall asleep. It did not, however, allow me to wake up, at least not on time, so on the final morning of the exam, I arrived an hour late and still finished thirty minutes early, drawing scattered applause and several "attaboys" as I walked out.

Dad's close friend Sol Rogers, a member of the powerful Beaumont family that backed him in the upholstery business, arranged a job for me in Washington as a clerk to a member of the National Labor Relations Board. Two months after arriving, in September '67, I received word that I'd passed the bar (by a single point). I called the chambers of a US Supreme Court justice, Abe Fortas, and talked his secretary into getting him to agree to swear me into the Texas bar, along with a Houston buddy of mine, Stu Nelkin, also working in DC. The next morning, with my hand in the air, repeating words after a *Supreme Court justice,* I realized with sudden force the power of that license. And when he was through reciting, I was a lawyer!

Three months later, anesthetized by government work, I returned to Houston and the local NLRB office, plotting to open my own practice as quickly as possible.

By then, Alan and Harriet had two children, Lisa and Jonathan. My brother's favorite word was *yes*, and he used it all the time with his growing family. You could see that he was the kind of father he wanted Dad to be. Each evening, he would rush home, clamp an affectionate hammerlock on his kids, and wrestle them into bed. Once they were under the covers he'd sing "Down by the Station" and "chug-chug, toot-toot," off they'd go. Given his history, it hardly seems plausible that Alan would have been a good husband, but with Harriet he tried very hard. Each evening, before he left on his leads, he'd tell her, "Don't make me any dinner, I'm going to be late," but Harriet always did anyway. They'd eat together no matter when he returned, make love, talk through the night, and fall asleep just before dawn. When the kids woke up, it was Harriet who got up with them, letting Alan sleep until noon. On their fourth anniversary, May 4, 1967, Harriet found this letter on her pillow:

My dearest Harriet,

I know that I could never express on paper how much I really love and appreciate you—besides, you know how much I love you. Why else would I give you a fishing glove for Mother's Day? So, I'll make this real short.

You're the nicest person I've ever known, the best friend I've ever had and the greatest, loveliest, most understanding wife in the world. If that sounds like an awful lot of adjectives and adverbs thrown together, I can't help it, because it's the way I feel.

Thank you for the four happiest years of my life, my Dear.
I love you,
Alan

So after three failed marriages and God only knows how many abortions, my brother had finally gotten this part of his life right. I envied him this. While I was in law school, I had met and married a girl named Dayle Black, a bright, remarkable woman, but we did not make a good match. I did love her, and she provided invaluable emotional support over the harrowing years to come, but the most compelling reason for me to get married was that my father was against it. By contrast, Alan's marriage seemed to me about as idyllic as marriage can be. Certainly I could not have imagined the extent to which he would risk throwing it away.

~

In late 1967, Sol Rogers offered my brother a way out of the carpet business. *And* it was almost 100 percent legal, a fraction my brother could always work with. A Spanish count named Ibarra had outfitted his yacht, the *Cabo Izarro,* with gambling equipment and advertised seven-day cruises from the Port of Galveston to the Yucatán Peninsula. Twice, however, the boat had set sail nearly empty, and now the count wanted out. Given that gambling was both illegal and widespread in Texas, Sol decided that the cruises hadn't been promoted well and decided to charter the vessel. But he needed Alan to front for him because Sol and his brothers owned an interest in Caesar's Palace and he was precluded under Nevada law from owning any other gambling interests. In return for promoting and managing the ship, Alan would receive 10 percent of the gross revenues.

Then Sol brought in Ted Lewin, a Las Vegas bookie and gangster, to run the ship's casino. Among the first to hear were FBI agents, who invited Alan into their offices for questioning. Alan went with his close friend, a nonpracticing attorney named Fergis Ginther, who did well at the meeting, ferreting out a lot of information by remaining quiet and allowing Alan to speak only sparingly. At any rate, the agents weren't interested in the boat, or my brother, or Sol Rogers. They were building an interstate gambling case against Lewin and wanted Alan to testify against him. But what little Alan said was dangerous: he denied gambling with Lewin—and lying to federal agents is a crime. When the agents interviewed Sol Rogers, Sol lied, too, denying there was a deal for the boat and Lewin's involvement in it. Then, not thirty minutes after the agents left his office, Sol called Alan and killed the deal.

Unfortunately, Alan had already begun gambling with Lewin. In January 1968, he placed a $500 bet on the "Game of the Century": UCLA versus UH at the Astrodome. Both basketball teams were undefeated, with UCLA ranked number one and UH number two nationally. Lew Alcindor, who would later be known as Kareem Abdul-Jabbar, played for UCLA, while UH had Elvin Hayes, a six-nine All-American shot-blocker. UH won, 71–69, and even I began to tell people where I'd gone to college. But this first win was an anomaly for Alan: he had booked basketball games but he had never bet them; he knew next to nothing about that sport. Besides, Alcindor played the game with an eye injury and had the worst game of his college career. Still, UH *barely* won.

Soon Alan was hooked. He told me that he was betting on basketball games, but I had no idea how often or how big. At first his winnings and losses offset one another—as much as $25,000 in a week—so he hadn't ever been out of pocket, at least not yet. Then he and a friend bet $7,500 on UH when they played against UCLA in the Final Four. Alan was so certain he'd win that when the friend backed out, Alan covered the entire amount himself. Even Lewin, his own bookie, tried to talk him out of it, telling him that the smart money was on UCLA, but to no avail.

Dayle and I watched the game on TV with Alan and Harriet at their house. Just after it started, Alan told me about the bet. I felt sick.

My brother didn't have that kind of money to lose; in fact, as far as I knew, he didn't have it at all. As UCLA began to pull away, Alan fell apart, muttering, "Oh, God" and "Oh, shit."

UH lost, 101–64.

When the game was over, Lewin called. Alan told him he'd need some time to make the payment, and I could hear screaming through the receiver. Alan knew by now that Lewin was dangerous—the FBI agents had told him that he'd had people killed—but, still, he didn't seem worried. First he tried to borrow $10,000 from Dad and then his brother, our uncle Harry. Both turned him down. Finally, he enlisted Sol Rogers to negotiate with Lewin, who ultimately agreed to a payout of $1,000 a week.

Alan insisted that he was going to quit gambling. I'm sure he meant it when he said it, but I wasn't convinced. My brother loved the possibility of quick money.

He wasn't the only one.

By then, Dad and Alan had expanded their business into San Antonio, forcing my brother to make the three-and-a-half-hour drive a couple times a week. Alan liked the idea of expansion but he hated being away from Harriet and the children, so he placed an ad in the San Antonio papers for a locally based manager to run the branch office. The first person to respond was a man named Frank DiMaria, who had experience in the aluminum siding business in Kansas City. Eager to put commuting behind him, Alan interviewed DiMaria, liked the five-foot-two Sicilian well enough, and hired him on the spot.

Dad was upset that Alan hadn't called any of DiMaria's references, but soon the hire looked like an act of genius. DiMaria could really sell. Within three months he had trained a sales crew of seven or eight men, had the boiler room churning out leads, and reported sales of as much as $15,000 in a single day. Despite significant start-up costs, the office recorded a paper profit of $17,000 the first three months DiMaria was there. The operation exceeded Dad and Alan's expectations so much that, before DiMaria asked for a raise, they gave him one, along with check-writing privileges and the promise of a 10 percent commission on all San Antonio sales.

It wasn't long, however, before Dad told us he'd received worried phone calls from San Antonio employees reporting that customers were demanding their money back. They had put down a deposit but weeks later their carpet remained uninstalled and their furniture still hadn't been delivered—and Frank the Wonder Boy wasn't returning their calls. Panicked, Dad and Dot drove to San Antonio and went through the books and bank records, which showed that there had never been a $17,000 profit, or any profit at all. They were outraged, convinced that DiMaria was stealing from the business—pocketing down payments, cashing in contracts, and keeping the proceeds for himself.

That night Dad called DiMaria and ordered him to come to the office. He also called the police, but DiMaria never showed—and he was never charged with a crime, at least not over this. Maybe DiMaria had his side of the story, although Dad never thought so, or maybe it was because of his check-writing privileges. Whatever the reason, the San Antonio debacle threatened the entire business—and Dad set about to get even. Through their San Antonio salesmen, still in touch with DiMaria, Dad made certain that word got to him that he was trying to get him indicted. Soon, incredibly, to Dad and Alan, DiMaria moved to Houston and was trying to borrow money to open up a carpet business of his own. When our father found out, he called every lending officer he knew and cold-called the ones he didn't, warning them off of "the thief who stole us blind." For a while, it worked. DiMaria couldn't get his financing and Dad got to tell his story repeatedly, depicting himself as both victim and hero—while simultaneously ingratiating himself with the very bankers he might need to borrow from, and soon.

For several months, Dad and Alan tried to scrape themselves out of their latest hole. They could barely make payroll, much less lay the carpet and reupholster the furniture on jobs DiMaria and his crew had sold. The pressure led to vicious screaming matches between Alan and Dad. They would disappear into their offices and lock the doors, but employees could hear them throughout the building and speculated about whether there was going to be a business at all the next day. Then, virtually every night, Harriet got on the phone and mediated Dad and Alan's differences and they would reconcile, laughing and pledging that things would change. But the next day it would start all over again until finally, in the spring of '67, my brother walked out and opened his own operation. As usual, their separation didn't last long. The following October, Dad resuscitated his business with a $50,000 small-business loan, gave up the upholstery line, and talked Alan into coming back and helping him expand Imperial Carpet statewide.

One night, Linda, visiting from Little Rock, was alone at Dad and Dot's when she heard a noise in the hedges outside. She looked out the window and saw a man staring at her. When she screamed, he took off. When Dad and Dot got home, Linda described the man and his height, or lack of it. They both said that it had to have been DiMaria.

Another evening, I picked up the phone at Dad and Dot's. The caller asked who I was. I told him and asked who was calling.

"Frank DiMaria."

"Do you want to talk to my father?"

"You're the one who's a lawyer?"

"What do you want?"

"I want you to tell me what you think that painting in the living room is worth."

"What are you talking about?"

"I'm going to sue and take every penny from that fucking father of yours."

Dad snatched the receiver from my hand.

"Goddamn you, you son of a bitch, stay away from my family!"

Dad's response to DiMaria's harassment was to escalate his own. He upped his attacks at the banks and repeatedly told the DiMaria story to his captive sales crew, boasting that he was going to run the dwarfish Sicilian out of town. True to the cutthroat nature of the boiler room business, some of his salesmen went to work for DiMaria and told him what Dad was saying. The same thing happened in reverse: when salesmen returned to Imperial they all said that DiMaria was outraged by Dad's accusations—that it was Dad and Alan who cheated *him* out of thousands of dollars in San Antonio.

One night, my brother was headed home on South Braeswood when a driver ran him off the road, pushing Alan's car down a wet embankment and nearly into the waters of the bayou below. Afterward, unharmed but for once really scared, Alan told me that the car looked like DiMaria's.

Now I was terrified, and Alan and I agreed that we should sit down with our father and try to convince him to quit bad-mouthing DiMaria. We found Dad in the employees' kitchen and asked everyone else to leave. Then we locked the door behind us and sat down at the table: Dad on one side, Alan and me on the other. The sun was behind Dad, causing me to squint. Alan wore his sunglasses. We began with the obvious.

"David and I have been talking, Dad. We think DiMaria is dangerous, crazy. You've got to lay off him."

"So? He stole from us. I have to do something. You don't just overlook something like that."

"It's been more than a year, Dad. David and I think it's best if we figure out a way to put this thing with Frank behind us."

"David is a kid."

"I'm not a kid, goddamn it! Listen to me, please! I'm scared he's going to hurt somebody."

That did it. When my father heard "scared," he was on his feet, yelling and heading for the door.

"Dad!" Alan said. "*Please* sit down. Let's talk."

"Goddamn it, Alan, *you* got us into this! You didn't even check him out! Now drop it! I'll handle this my own way."

"Dad, *please* quit screaming. Everyone can hear you. I don't want Frank to find out about this."

"I don't give a good goddamn what he knows!"

"Dad," I said, "Alan and I are just trying to stop this before something bad happens!"

"Nothing bad is going to happen! I'll shut him down and that will be that!"

Alan jumped up.

"Dad. Please. Stay here and talk to us. He's not the first employee to get caught with his hand in the till!"

"I'll do whatever the goddamn hell I please!"

Like father, like sons: now we were all yelling, even though there was nothing more to say. It no longer mattered if Dad and Alan had ripped off DiMaria or the opposite was true. What mattered was that Alan and I were right about the potential for violence and our father was wrong and there was no triumph in that for any of us.

~

In May 1968, I opened up my own law office downtown in a tiny space I sublet from another lawyer, with walnut wainscoting and a desk of slick, indeterminate material that left little room to turn around. Alan was my first visitor. Skinny as he was, he still had to squeeze between the wall and my desk to get a better look at the picture of Justice Fortas swearing me in.

"You made it, kid. No more selling carpet."

"I may have to come back. I don't want to starve."

"Do me a favor. Starve."

"What if I die?"

"I'll give you a great funeral. I'll carpet your coffin."

"Sure, in some lime-green shit you can't move."

That picture of Justice Fortas still hangs on my office wall, although now with a touch of irony: in 1969, Fortas got caught taking a bribe to lobby the SEC and LBJ on behalf of a stock swindler and was forced to resign. But back then the picture was still an image of pure honor, and my eternally supportive brother saw it as a harbinger: his kid brother would do great things.

"I'm getting you bigger offices as soon as I can swing it."

"Alan, I'm off the dole. You don't need to worry about me anymore."

"Of course I do. You're an idiot."

Alan leaned closer to Fortas.

"How can he do that? Swear you into the Texas bar?"

"He can do anything he wants. He can intern your ass if you piss him off."

"Actually, I've been thinking about going to law school, too. I've got seventy-five hundred dollars saved up. I wouldn't have to work, at least for a while. I could concentrate on school."

"That's great."

In truth, I thought it was anything but great. If not for Alan sweet-talking my way into UH law school, to say nothing of the roof over my head, the encouragement and the cash he'd been stuffing into my hands since I was ten, I might not have been in that office. But that didn't mean I wanted *him* to become a lawyer. If he did, he'd want to practice with me, and with his get-rich-quick schemes, he'd probably get us both disbarred. Besides, if he had $7,500 saved, why didn't he pay off the bookie?

He read my mind. "I've already paid back most of the bet. I only owe twenty-five hundred dollars now."

"It sounded like he was going to kill you that night. I could hear him yelling across the room."

"Ted and I are friends."

"He didn't sound like a friend."

"He's okay with the payout. I have to keep as much money on hand as I can. I can't work with Dad anymore. I told him I'm quitting. And I'll need it to live on."

"What did Dad say?"

"He went nuts. He said I'm leaving him with all the debt. He's not talking to me."

"I thought you and Dad were doing better."

"It never lasts. We still have screaming matches every day, and every night he gets Harriet on the phone to patch things up. Then the same thing happens the next day. I hate it. I don't know how to stop it other than to leave. It's killing me, kid."

"You don't think he can make it without you, do you?"

"He said that himself."

"And you always go back. You seem chained to that place. Please don't go back this time."

Alan stayed most of the day, sunk into the chair on the other side of my desk. This was a strange reversal of position. Always before, it had been Alan behind the desk and me sitting across it, usually with outstretched hands. If it hadn't been the other way around for so long, and if I hadn't been so broke and unsure of my own future, I might have told him to quit the carpet business once and for all and offered to help put him through law school, despite my misgivings.

Alan picked up a box he'd brought with him and began ceremoniously unpacking his start-up gifts. There were reams of typing paper, carbon sheets, a Big Chief tablet, an eraser shaped like a duck, and a Roy Rogers and Dale Evans lunch kit with a picture of the King of the Cowboys and Trigger on the side. "Let me ask you something, kid," Alan said, holding the lunch kit aloft. "Do you find anything disturbing about the way Roy's looking at his horse?"

My brother didn't seem to want to leave. After a quiet moment he said, "Hey, you hear about that Schacht kid?"

He was talking about Danny Schacht, a young Houstonian who'd been sentenced to a federal prison for his part in an antiwar protest. Not long after, someone had shot up Schacht's car and firebombed his family's home.

"That had to be the Klan," my brother said. "And the cops will never investigate. There's too many in the police department." Alan paused. "I wish you could get a case like that."

"They'd never hire me. But I'd kill to represent him."

"You have to admire that kid. At least he *does* something. All we do is talk. Talk—and cheat black people."

Dr. King had been assassinated the month before. We were all horrified, but Alan was absolutely inconsolable. He'd read the "I Have a Dream" speech so many times that he knew long passages by heart. The highest compliment Alan could pay something was to call it "logical," and he'd once told me that speech was the most logical thing he'd ever read. That was why the next thing he said surprised and worried me:

"The Black Panthers are right: Dr. King was naive. Nothing much has changed since that speech, even with the Civil Rights Act. Maybe black people should take to the streets. I've even thought about doing something to help the Panthers. I don't know what. But something."

"But things are different for you now," I cautioned him. "You have a family." Harriet was expecting their third child.

Alan's only reply was to lift his hand to the hair that had fallen across his forehead and gentle it back in place, which that day seemed to me a melancholy gesture.

At about six, he left to go out on a lead. I rode down in the elevator with him and we walked through the lobby: black marble walls that contrasted with a white floor, an elegant touch that masked the sad little offices upstairs. Alan's driver was waiting for him at the curb, a tribute not to his prosperity but to his haste: with thousands of dollars in parking and speeding tickets, he'd lost his license. Before he got in, my brother leaned against the open door of his car. He was bathed in sunlight, just like when I found him in our den the day he came home from the navy. He put on his sunglasses.

"I could never have done this if it weren't for you, Alan."

"That's not true, kid. You would have done this with or without me."

Then he hugged me and said, "I love you, kid. I'm really proud of you." I hugged him back, told him that I loved him, too, and watched him drive away.

# 6

A month later, Alan disappeared.

Harriet called me at four in the morning.

"David, Alan's not home yet. Do you know where he is?"

"Oh, shit, Harriet. I don't have any idea. I haven't heard from him. Have you?"

"He said he'd made a sale and was meeting Fergis for a drink at the Brass Jug. I was hoping you'd know where he was."

"I don't."

"Oh, God, David, he has never done anything like this. I'm really worried."

"Have you called the police?"

"Do you think I should?"

"I don't know. He'll probably come rolling in the minute you do."

"He better. Maybe your father knows where he is. And Fergis. I'll call them both."

Then Harriet hesitated. "Can you come over? I'm scared."

Dayle was awake now, too. She said to wait and she'd come with me. I walked onto the balcony of our apartment and lit a cigarette.

My T-shirt stuck to my skin; the air was oppressive. My stomach jerked.

"Oh, fuck, Alan," I said, "don't do this, don't do this."

The phone rang again. It was my father.

"Alan hasn't come home yet," he said. "Do you know where he is?"

"I don't. I told Harriet that. I haven't heard from him."

"She called you already? I'll be damn. She and I are pretty darn close."

"He told Harriet he'd made a sale. Do you know who to?"

"No. He takes the leads with him."

"Do you know if Harriet's called the police?"

"No. I'm going to call them as soon as we hang up."

"He'll show up soon. He's probably still with Fergis somewhere."

"That bastard better not be with another woman."

That, of course, was exactly where I wanted Alan to be: asleep with another woman, in calamitous trouble with Harriet—as long as he was okay.

Dad and I drove to the Brass Jug, in the heart of Houston's Sin Alley, an area notorious for bars, drugs, and obliging young women that had sprung up so quickly, and in such close proximity to River Oaks and its Church of St. John the Divine—just five minutes away— that it shocked the entire town. And it was there, just across from the entrance to the Brass Jug, that we found Alan's Cadillac, parked and locked. We knocked on the club's door, but no one answered. As we walked back to Dad's car, he said:

"This looks bad, doesn't it, son?"

"He'll show up, Dad. He's probably asleep somewhere. You know how late he can sleep. Give him a couple hours and he'll show up."

"What do you think? Do you think he's okay?"

"I don't know, Dad. I just don't know. This isn't like him."

"Should we tell your mother?"

We agreed we shouldn't, not yet. If Alan reappeared of his own accord, she would have suffered for nothing, and if he didn't, well . . . she would call us every five minutes looking for an update, and what good would that do?

After agreeing to come back to the Brass Jug when it opened that evening, I went to Harriet's, and Dad went home. Meanwhile, Harriet had called Fergis, who, assuming Alan had gone off with a woman, tried to cover for him, telling Harriet that he and Alan had had a drink and that he'd left Alan at the table by himself and gone home. But when Dad and I returned to the Brass Jug that evening, no one remembered seeing Alan come or go and we learned nothing. From the club, Dad called the Houston Police Department and was referred to the Homicide Division, where the detective declined to come to the scene, even with Alan's car undisturbed. "Lots of husbands take off without saying good-bye," the detective said. No matter how vehemently Dad insisted that Alan loved his family and would never do that to his wife and kids, the cop dismissed Alan as a runaway husband and refused to open a file.

Three days later, we still had no word from Alan, and *still* the police refused to act—so my father did. He posted a $5,000 reward, a good chunk of the cash that Dot had been squirreling away over the years since the fire.

The first tip came from a lawyer Dad knew from our synagogue, who said that Alan had been spotted in Chicago and that all he needed to bring him home was $500 and airplane tickets for himself and his private investigator. Ecstatic, Dad gave him what he asked for and told us all that Alan would be back soon. But for seven days and nights there was no word from the attorney, until, finally, he returned, "just heartsick" about what had proven to be "a case of mistaken identity." Sometime later, Dad found out the lawyer had gone to Chicago with his girlfriend.

81

Then the homicide detective Dad had spoken to on the very first day of Alan's disappearance called to say that he had been thinking about the situation and was concerned about security at Dad's house. Given how little interest the detective had shown in Alan previously, my father interpreted the call as a change of heart and gratefully agreed that the detective and his deputy could come by and check things out. When they arrived—neither man was wearing an officer's uniform, and in fact one of them was not a cop, but a private detective—they sat down with Dad and Dot in the den. When the detective suggested that they move into the kitchen so that his "partner" could check the den and the remainder of the house without distraction, Dot was suspicious and refused to budge, but Dad insisted. Soon after moving into the kitchen, they heard a loud crash. Dot ran into their bedroom and, seeing that a painting had fallen, told the investigator that she didn't have a wall safe, so he could quit looking. Then she kicked them out. Within the month, their house was broken into and all of Dot's jewelry was stolen, including the 2.5-carat diamond ring Dad had given her for our prosperous Christmas fifteen years earlier.

Luckily, Dot recently had parked their remaining savings, about $12,000, in a certificate of deposit with a California savings and loan, where she got a higher interest rate than she could get in Texas. They also had Dad's income from Imperial Carpet, but as he became more and more obsessed with finding Alan, the business fell apart. Sometimes, even in the middle of a carpet pitch, he would bolt to his car, possessed by a need to "look for Alan" around town.

When Alan had failed to call her for a week, Mom knew something was wrong—and Linda told her the truth. After that, hysterical and rambling, Mom called Linda several times a day, and sometimes Dad and me as well, asking whether we were ever going to find her baby. Once or twice she could not resist blaming Alan's disappearance on Dad's "rotten" business, and they'd scream at each other, but, mostly, she and Dad just cried together, leaving me yearning for the days when they fought because Alan had turned up somewhere he wasn't supposed to be.

Late in June, a man named Dan Hughes called me at my office. He said that he knew where Alan was and that he was safe. I had never heard of Hughes before, but the Houston Police Department had: someone on the homicide squad told me that he was the head of the black rackets and that I shouldn't worry; he wouldn't do anything to a white man. That night, I walked into his club on Southmore Street, in the ghetto. The music was loud. The jukebox had little dancing figures whirling around on a colorful neon screen. Looking for Hughes, I cut across the dance floor, through customers obviously puzzled by my sober white presence.

Hughes, a huge man wearing two gold watches with front teeth to match, told me to take a seat at the bar and then left me there for an hour, which I spent doing tequila shots. Finally, he returned and motioned for me to come into his office, a dank place with dim lighting and walnut walls.

"You can stop worrying," he said. "I got your brother sat down in Mexico."

"You're kidding. How do you know it's him?"

"Because he tole me so, baby. He tole me so."

"You've seen him?"

"Course I seen him. Why would I say I seen him if I hadn't?" Hughes leaned across his desk. "He run off with his chippy. He don't want to come back. But don't worry. Ole Dan'll bring him home. He won't have no choice."

Ole Dan told me to go back out to the bar and we'd talk business when his customers had left. I agreed, even though what he'd said was bullshit. I could believe that my brother might cheat on his wife but there wasn't any "chippy" and he wasn't in Mexico. But even propping up the bar at Dan's Club was better than sitting impotently back at my desk or in my apartment or in Harriet's house, longing for an unlabored breath. I was glad to be doing something, no matter how absurd, to find Alan. I was also a little drunk.

Before the last customers had left, I pushed open the door to Dan's office and walked in.

"What will it take to get my brother home?"

"Twenty-five thousand dollars. That reward ain't shit for what I'm doin'."

"I want proof you actually have my brother."

"It don't work that way, baby. You put up the money. I bring him home."

"It don't work that way, Dan. You bring Alan home. Then you'll get your money."

I walked out and never heard from him again.

Then a former Imperial Carpet salesman told Dad that a nightclub singer he'd "been banging" knew something about Alan. Her name was Jenna Coy Huddleston, and my father persuaded him to phone her while Dad taped the call and listened in. Huddleston said that she'd heard a club owner say that Alan Berg had "gone off on a trip and wasn't coming back" because he'd told a gambler that the UH–UCLA game was fixed and the gambler lost $109,000. When Dad told the police, they said that Huddleston was a con artist who'd say anything for the reward. Sure enough, she called later the same day, demanding the $5,000 from Dad in exchange for information about Alan— unaware that he'd heard and taped what she had to say already. Dad slammed down the receiver.

So my father's reward had launched both of us into a world of hustlers and cons. Dad, especially, was defenseless, like a cancer victim running to Mexico to be cured with melon rinds, vulnerable to anyone who offered even the slightest clue, no matter how implausible, no matter the cost. An agonizing month passed before we finally got our first solid tip from a credible source. At the end of June, Dad hired Claude Harrelson, a private investigator and former Houston policeman with an excellent reputation among law enforcement agencies. Harrelson's uncle had been warden of the Lovelady unit of the Texas Department of Corrections, and his father was a guard there. Another uncle was a former FBI agent.

Not three days after being retained, Harrelson called Dad and asked to speak to him in private, away from both of their offices. They met at the Avalon Drug Store, where lots of oil deals were done. Dad found Harrelson sitting at a corner table. He seemed scared, my father told me, and warned Dad not to repeat what he was about to tell him to anyone, especially the authorities, because if word got out, Harrelson would be killed. Dad agreed.

Then Harrelson told my father that Alan had been murdered.

Dad felt at that moment that he might die. Everything was spinning: the walls and windows and Harrelson, too; he clutched the table to keep from falling to the floor. Dad finally asked him to repeat everything he'd said so he could decide what to do next, and when he still couldn't concentrate, told Harrelson that he was going to call his personal lawyer to come help him discuss the next steps. Harrelson said he'd walk out but Dad convinced him that the lawyer, Jim Cowan, had to keep the matter confidential—and the investigator agreed to stay. Then, with the three of them seated around the table, Harrelson said that for $3,000 his sources could turn up Alan's body. Dad said that made no sense; the reward he posted was already $5,000. Harrelson said he didn't understand it either but that was his sources' demand. Dad and Cowan left the Avalon and drove straight to Fannin Bank, where his loan officer listened to the story and advanced him $3,000 on Dad's promise to pay him back immediately out of the California CD. Then Dad wrote a check to Cowan, who was to endorse it over to Harrelson once Alan's body was found.

Dad drove home to wait for Harrelson's call. Harriet, Dayle, and I waited with him and Dot in their den, but hours went by and the phone didn't ring. Around midnight, my father covered his head with his hands and said, over and over, "I want my boy back. What have they done to my boy?" Then he left the room, sobbing and apologizing.

I followed him into his bedroom and sat down next to him on the bed.

"What more can I do?" he said. "I put out thousands of dollars. I've hired half a dozen investigators and nothing happens. The cops don't do anything."

I reassured my father that he had done all he could and that if we kept looking, we might still find Alan alive.

"You don't really believe that, do you, kid?" He put his arm around my shoulder and said, "You know, I do love you."

"Do you think it's too late for me to go to medical school?"

"Never."

At three in the morning, long after Harriet and Dayle and I had left, Dad's phone rang. The caller's voice was muffled. He said that the price was now $6,000. But it was a Saturday; the banks wouldn't be open, so Dad said he'd get the additional money first thing Monday morning. The phone went dead.

On Monday, at 6:00 a.m., he got another call, and the same muffled voice told him that the price was now $10,000. Dad assured whoever was on the phone that the money would be there. But in fact he'd had enough. That morning, with me listening in, Dad called Harrelson and told him that he was going to pick him up and that the two of them were going to the police. Harrelson refused. Dad pleaded with him but Harrelson insisted that going to the authorities would get him killed. Dad lobbed a volley of "goddamns" at him that did us both proud.

Then Dad and I went to the police, who listened politely as my father described what Harrelson had told him. The officers agreed that Harrelson was a believable source and that his tip probably did bear some truth, but if they ever questioned him, we never knew about it, and I don't believe they ever did.

So we were back to zero. Every day was excruciating. With each tip there followed interminable parsing of the informant's every word and inflection—but nothing ever turned up except more bribes and torment. One day at work, Dad got a call from another former sales-man, telling him that Alan had been put through a meat grinder in a packing plant. Afterward, my sister sat by helplessly as he cried and vomited. Dad often phoned Alan's friends to pick their brains for something new, and no matter how seemingly insignificant the detail, he would follow up and obsess over it for days.

As tight-fisted as she was, Dot never said a word objecting to the money my father was spending on his search. But Dad looked else-where for warmth. For the first time in Linda's life, Dad leaned on her, calling her, hugging her, recalling funny stories about Alan and, many nights, stopping by her house to play with Linda's two-year-old daughter, who distracted Dad and calmed him down—for a few hours, anyway.

While it is said that everyone's suffering is unique, no one's could have exceeded Harriet's. With Alan gone, money was tight, and Harriet took a secretarial job at the county hospital. Sympathetic cowork-ers would show her unidentified corpses when they came in so she could see for herself whether it was her husband. "They bring in bod-ies that were found in the mud, facedown, filthy," she told me. "It's awful. It's never Alan." Nonetheless, she refused to burden her children, Lisa and Jonathan, now four and two, with her anguish. She told them repeatedly that their father loved them all very much—even the baby in her tummy—but he could not come home right now because he was off on a trip and she hoped he'd be back soon. While the adults around her dissected tips from Houston's underbelly, Lisa sat in the front yard and blew dandelions in the air. She said the "floaty" parts were her daddy and let them fall over her.

~

Dad fired Harrelson and hired another private investigator, this one recommended by one of Houston's most respected law firms. The investigator's name was Bob Leonard, and he always dressed like an FBI agent right out of the movies, in a gray suit and pretzel-thin tie. Almost immediately, Leonard discovered something valuable: he'd homed in on a possible murder site in Fort Bend County, just thirty minutes south of Houston. No one had found a body, but after talking to one of the officers who'd stumbled on the scene, and then visiting it himself, Leonard felt certain that a murder had been committed there.

Leonard convinced Dad that the only way to flush out what had happened in Fort Bend was to go to the papers.

The following Sunday, August 4, 1968, the *Houston Post* ran the first media report about Alan's disappearance, a front-page story with the headline:

## Bloody Trail in Weeds: Was It Alan H. Berg's?

The article described how, on May 29, the morning after Alan disappeared, Fort Bend County deputy sheriff Roy Schmidt had pulled onto Levee Road at exactly 4:00 a.m. while listening to a weather report. He was performing a routine sweep for "car strippers," thieves who sold parts off cars they had stolen.

He saw car tracks on the freshly graded dirt road. He thought he saw a small white light blink. He drove a few yards down the road to an old dump, keeping his eyes on the tracks.

"The tracks were dug out," he said. "It looked like a car had got away in a hurry." The next morning, a ranch hand contacted the sheriff's office. He said he thought someone had slaughtered a calf on Levee Road. Schmidt drove back to the same spot, this time asking Deputy Ed Chesshire, his on-duty replacement, to meet him there.

There were signs of a fight beside the road, a pool of blood, and a bloody trail leading across the dump to a freshly dug hole near some trees. In a cow track near the dump were two or three cups of blood.

"I knew it wasn't a calf that was killed," said Schmidt. "No reason to bury a calf."

He searched the trail of blood—"enough blood for a man to bleed to death. Everybody laughed when I got down on my hands and knees and crawled down the trail. But I told them I was going to pick up something."

He did: a human hair, a Schaeffer pen like one Mom had given Alan, a broken hatchet handle, and a tuft of red carpet of a variety that Dad and Alan sold. The blood in the dirt was type A, which matched the "carpet executive" Alan Berg's, but there was no record of Alan's Rh factor—not even in the navy's files—that could prove definitively that the blood was his.

Dad and I were both interviewed for the article and I'm still appalled by what we said. I was quoted as saying that my brother was "a wild gambler, who gambles infrequently and badly." My father told the reporter that he thought Alan had been called into the FBI for questioning "about interstate gambling." From that point on, in the media, "carpet executive Alan Berg" became "gambler Alan Berg."

The article concluded almost like a eulogy:

> Friends say his marriage is "the most successful thing about him." Perhaps, they add, he might even be considered over-protective. He had bought his children a swing set, but was afraid for them to play on it. He was afraid for his wife to drive at night.
>
> He loaned money to everyone. The family has paid one $1,000 note he cosigned before he disappeared.
>
> They have posted a $5,000 reward, which they hope will tempt someone who knows where he is. "Somebody here in Houston knows where that boy is—alive or dead," Nathan Berg says.

*Alive.* Even confronted with the *Post* article, my father tortured out scenarios that led to the possibility that "that boy" was alive.

Leonard was right about using the media: the *Post* article forced the HPD into opening a missing-person file (seventy days after his disappearance) and even persuaded the fabled Texas Rangers to lend their statewide authority to the investigation. Encouraged, Dad raised the reward to $10,000. And then, in the most unlikely development so far, a freshman congressman ramped up the search for my brother: George H. W. Bush.

Sol Rogers had arranged for Dad to meet with his local congressman, Beaumont's Jack Brooks, one of the most powerful men in Washington. But when Dad met with him in his DC offices, to try to convince the congressman to trigger an FBI investigation, Brooks discouraged him, saying it sounded like an essentially local matter, despite kidnapping being a federal offense. When Dad emerged from Brooks's office, disappointed and angry, he spotted Bush walking down the hall and pursued him. Bush welcomed Dad into his office, where my father once again laid out his reasons for getting the FBI involved. Bush listened carefully, then, making no promises, advised Dad to go home and reiterate what he'd said in a letter, which Dad wrote as soon as he got back.

My father had no right to expect Bush to do anything for him. Dad was a Yellow Dog Democrat who believed Republicans a species born without opposable thumbs. He didn't live in Bush's River Oaks district; in fact, he couldn't have lived there even if he could have afforded it, because Jews were excluded in the deed restrictions. Nonetheless, the same day he received Dad's letter, Bush forwarded it to J. Edgar Hoover along with a note of his own: "I would greatly appreciate your looking into this matter and advising me of your findings." One week later, on October 2, the FBI opened a file on Alan, citing as its jurisdiction the gambling case it was seeking to bring against Ted Lewin, with Alan as a potential witness—but mostly because Bush had insisted. The congressman then assigned his administrative aide to keep pressure on the FBI and to field Dad's calls when the congressman was unavailable. I don't know what Mr. Bush and my father said to each other, but their conversations comforted Dad like nothing else. I remember thinking that maybe the most compelling reason for George Herbert Walker Bush to spend so much time on the phone with Nathan Berg was, very simply, that— no matter how different the circumstances—Bush knew what it was like to lose a child. His first daughter, Robin, died of leukemia when she was only four years old.

With the FBI involved, field reports began flooding in. One of the earliest listed Alan's life insurance policies, each with double indemnity provisions that would pay Harriet a total of $80,000 if it turned out that Alan had been murdered. In addition, there was a $50,000 "key man" policy on both Alan and my father, a condition for obtaining Dad's small-business loan of the same amount—with the lender as the beneficiary to pay off the balance. Another report stated that my brother ran "a 'boiler shop operation' where high pressure telephone sales pitches were made by about 30 of his employees soliciting carpet business. Most of the customers are Negroes." The same report also stated something even we hadn't heard before: that Alan was a suspect in a bank robbery that had taken place a few days after his disappearance. In yet another report, an agent quoted a confidential informant as saying that Alan "dressed like a queer" (which might account for Mr. Hoover's personal interest in the case). But then the same informant had added, "Berg also did not run around on his wife and is quite a home-living [sic] individual who stayed home usually each day until about noon. The story that he was going to meet a girl at the time of his disappearance does not jibe with his pattern of normal behavior."

*Normal behavior.* For months we had lurched from one phony tip to another, rallying when one suggested that Alan was alive, plummeting when another said he was dead. And with each successive false lead we became even more anxious and uncoupled from any semblance of normal life.

~

By October 1968—five months after Alan's disappearance—we knew little more than what we had learned in the *Post* article that had run on August 4. I distracted myself with my law practice, working as hard as I could to keep it afloat, with little success. In the first six months, I brought in a total of $1,250 in fees, not even enough to cover my overhead. Our only dependable income was Dayle's $75 per week from the ad agency where she was now a secretary.

It was then, with so few clients, that I began spending time watching Racehorse Haynes try cases. I can't remember a single trial that he lost in those days—a track record that put him in competition with Percy Foreman, the famous Houston criminal lawyer my father had once invoked to scare off Assistant Principal Viebig. Foreman was an old-fashioned "fact lawyer" who prepared so doggedly that he normally knew more about the case than anyone else in the courtroom. But he was a hostile man and a loner, an ordained Baptist minister who learned to speak and preach on the old Chautauqua circuit, the circus-like revivals and lecture series where he'd pounded his Bible and moved audiences to rapture. It was said that Percy tried more murder cases in a year than Clarence Darrow did in his entire career. Even more remarkable was that out of almost one thousand cases tried by Foreman, just fifty-five of his defendants had gone to jail and only one got the death penalty. Still, Foreman himself had been charged with several crimes, from using foul language in the presence of a minor girl to subornation of perjury (knowingly putting on false testimony). Representing himself, he won them all, only burnishing his unbeatable image.

Haynes had worked for Foreman for six months following law school but quit out of concern for his reputation. Within just a few years, he had established a remarkable one of his own, which is what led me to spend entire days on the back benches of Harris County courtrooms, watching him in awe. It was good for me to be there, learning from Race; it felt productive and it distracted me from my brother's absence and the tidal wave of dishonest men who wanted Dad and Dot's money.

Soon I didn't have to stalk Race in the cafeteria; I was a regular at his table, thrilled and flattered to be included in the famous lawyer's inner circle and moved when he called me "Brother." And it didn't matter that he addressed others the same way.

In late October of that year, Dad received a call from a Dennis Weadock, who said he had worked briefly as a salesman for Imperial

Carpet, quitting just after Alan disappeared. Weadock sounded "terrified" and told my father to go to a phone booth and call him back. When Dad got him on the line, Weadock said that Alan had been murdered and that for an extra $5,000, in addition to $5,000 for leading authorities to the body, he would "name names." He also needed $200 plane fare to fly back to Houston from Los Angeles, where he now lived with his girlfriend, whose name was Sandra Sue Attaway.

By now even Dad was skeptical of these calls, especially from someone dumb enough to negotiate for a $10,000 reward that Dad had already posted publicly. "Why," he finally asked Weadock, "do you need $200 when you're going to get $10,000 if your information is good?" Dad told me that this was followed by a long pause ("You could hear the adding machine in his head") and then Weadock responded that he needed the plane fare because he was broke. He also said that if word of this leaked out, the man who'd murdered Alan would murder him, too. That sounded familiar to Dad—like the same runaround Claude Harrelson had given him. This time Dad said he'd think about it, and hung up. "He didn't make sense," Dad told me. "Number one, he said he worked for us selling carpet and I don't remember him at all. Number two, how stupid is this guy? The reward is already ten thousand dollars, without his blackmailing me. And number three, just before I hung up, he said, 'Mr. Berg, you could make a fortune.' What the hell is that supposed to mean?"

Dad turned to Bob Leonard, his investigator, who called Weadock and, after hanging up, told Dad to wire the $200. "I figured," Dad said, "I've been screwed out of so much money, what's another two hundred dollars?" Leonard also instructed Dad and Dot to cash in their remaining CD and withdraw $10,000 from their savings, in case they needed it right away for the reward.

Eight days after his initial phone call, Weadock, as promised, flew into Houston Hobby and was picked up by Leonard and Emmit Williams, an off-duty HPD officer who worked with Leonard part-time. Then they picked up Dad, who recognized Weadock after all, and the group went to a restaurant. Shortly after sitting down, Weadock said that Alan had been a "nice boss." And then he told a bizarre story about Lucky Pierre's, a seedy bar on Kirby Street where local characters played cards and drank. Weadock was a regular there, and one day, during a card game, a "midget" complained that "a prick" named Alan Berg had undercut him on a carpet sale and cost him "thousands of dollars."

"I'd like to murder the Jew bastard," the "midget" added.

And that was when "Chuck," a drinking buddy of Weadock's, tossed a business card on the table that read "Have Gun, Will Travel" and everyone laughed.

Dad had had enough. "Tell me," he begged Weadock, "is my baby alive?"

"We got business to do first," Weadock replied.

Dad agreed that if and when the information proved true, he would have the $10,000 reward delivered in cash to Weadock's brother-in-law, the president of Farmers State Bank in nearby Brookshire, Texas, who would then pass it on to Weadock. Then Weadock complained that everything "looked fuzzy" and refused to say anything more until he'd had a chance to rest. The next morning, when Leonard and Williams knocked on his motel door, Weadock opened it holding a revolver at his side. When he saw who it was, he put his weapon down and at last told the investigators where Alan's body would be found: wrapped in a blanket and lying in a ditch near a clump of cedar trees nine or ten miles east of Surfside, near Galveston. But Weadock refused to draw a diagram or accompany Leonard and Williams on their search; he was terrified, he said, that if he did, the killer would find out.

Leonard and Williams drove to the location Weadock described and spent hours searching in a driving rain, walking up and down two miles of cedar trees while thunder exploded and lightning flashed overhead. Finally, they turned to head back, certain that Weadock was trying to scam my father.

And then there it was: a piece of a blanket.

Leonard pulled it back but saw nothing underneath, so he walked deeper into the brushy area beyond—and there, under the largest tree in the cedar break, he saw my brother's skull, half buried in the shales of a narrow ditch.

His torso lay several yards away.

⁓

Dad called me to his house around dusk. When Dayle and I arrived, we found him sitting alone in the den: the same room where I had welcomed Alan home from the navy almost exactly ten years earlier. That day, my brother had been bathed in sunlight. This day was dark and rainy.

"My boy is dead," Dad said. "They found Alan. He's gone."

Dayle began to cry. I felt a strange sort of relief.

Then my father said, "That son of a bitch Claude Harrelson is the killer's brother. That's how he knew where Alan was. He's in this up to his neck."

Now I was reeling.

Leonard had told Dad that Frank DiMaria was behind Alan's death and that the motivation was spite: he wanted to destroy Dad. He had paid someone else to commit the murder: Charles Harrelson, a thirty-year-old contract killer whom the Texas Rangers suspected of having murdered a dozen men or more.

I wanted to be the one to tell Harriet. I didn't want her to hear it on the radio. I left with Dayle while Dad called Linda and her husband to come over to get the reward—$10,000 in a brown envelope—and to deliver it to Weadock's brother-in-law, who was waiting at the bank in

Brookshire. On the way, Linda heard the words "Alan Berg's skeletal remains" on the car radio and became hysterical.

Meanwhile, Dayle and I had sped to Alan and Harriet's house. Harriet saw our car through the front window and came outside as we walked up the sidewalk. She wore a dress that was green and big as a tent; she was exactly one week away from delivering their third child. The other two were playing at a cousin's house.

"Alan's dead, isn't he," Harriet said when she saw our faces. "He's dead."

"Yes, Harriet, he is gone. Alan is gone."

I somehow thought Harriet would be relieved that it was over, too, but of course she wasn't. She was devastated. She stood at the door, arms moving at someone else's command: flailing about, drifting to her mouth, wafting back to her sides. "Who killed Alan? Who killed my husband?" she asked again and again.

That's when I thought a terrible, unutterable thought:

*Dad did.*

As we helped her to her bedroom, Harriet's cries became wails, filling the hallways. Dayle and I laid her down in their bed and then climbed in beside her. We remained there for a long time, while Harriet sobbed and cried out my brother's name.

"I knew it," she said when I mentioned DiMaria. "I knew it." And then she began crying even harder. Sometime later, she abruptly sat up in the bed and laughed out loud.

"Remember when we got married, I lost all that weight? You know why? I had to. Alan wore smaller jeans than I did."

The next morning we woke up to Alan's story on the front page of the *Post*. Above the fold there was a picture of my brother's skull cradled in a deputy's palm.

# PART II

~

*What the detective story is about is not murder*
*but the restoration of order.*

—P. D. JAMES

# 7

Alan's suffering was done, but not that of those who loved him: we were collateral damage. In the months after we found Alan's remains, I was inconsolable, paranoid, and explosive. Then, as years passed, almost against my will, the pain eased and I moved on. But very early along that continuum, without realizing it, I stopped talking about my brother almost entirely. When his name came up, I went silent. Eventually people quit mentioning him to me.

It took a quarter century before I thought about writing this book. I was out on Long Island, taking a short break between settling a case in New York and trying one in Texas. I was changing into running clothes on the screened-in porch upstairs when a flock of Canada geese flew overhead in such huge numbers that dusk turned dark. On and on they came, wave after wave. I ran downstairs and watched them until the din of their honking faded and the last bird disappeared from the horizon. In the days that followed, I could not quit thinking of that astonishing sight and how they flew in almost perfect, undulating Vs along migratory paths charted over millions of years—and of how little choice they had in the matter. My mind drifted to our own lives and how difficult it is to change direction. Consciously or unconsciously, we tend to follow the path of those who've gone before.

Suddenly Alan's memory burst into my consciousness like an ancient shipwreck breaching the ocean's surface. I began to remember things about him that I had forgotten or repressed. I knew that our father had marched around in my brother's head, Dad's life dictating how Alan would live his own. But in those moments I had to admit that my brother, despite his struggles and rebellions, had not been able to change the many ways he was like our father after all. I also realized that, like Dad, I had kept a painful secret from my own two sons and that they, like Alan and me, let me keep my silence for fear of hurting their father. It was ironic: for someone who had spent half his professional life speaking about the heinous acts people commit, I could not bring myself to speak to my own sons about a crime that deeply affected their family—and them. And that's when I decided: if I couldn't say it, I would write it.

I began to research Alan's life and death and his murderer's trial as I would a case in my law office. I enlisted my sister's help and we began to accumulate all manner of records, from Alan's elementary school transcripts to redacted FBI files obtained under the Freedom of Information Act. That led us to Dad's transcripts, too, all the way back to Crane College of Chicago, and most important, to his file at the University of Arkansas.

Of course, there was much that I already knew about Alan's murder, but I wanted to understand even more deeply, if possible, how someone that close to me could meet such an end. I was confident I knew who killed him and who paid to have it done and how he was lured to his death by a pretty young woman's voice over a phone; I even felt certain about the motive, petty as it seemed. But there was still a lot that I did not know—for example, about the very last moments of his life. Ironically, it was the pretty young woman who would give me a fuller account of Alan's murder, and her role in it, not only during two lengthy phone calls years later but also, primarily, from the detailed statement she typed and signed in a jail cell six months after Alan was murdered.

～

Twice married and divorced by age twenty-three, Sandra Sue Attaway abandoned her young son to her mother's care in rural Texas and moved to Houston to become a waitress in a bar and "sample the club life." Shortly after arriving, she went to a party on a Thursday night and met a good-looking guy who introduced himself as "Chuck." By the following Monday they'd gone out on a date. By Wednesday they were living together.

About a month later, they left Houston for Las Vegas, where, within a day, Chuck got ahead $5,000 and then just as quickly lost it back. From Vegas they went to Des Moines, where Chuck, trained as a repairman for dental equipment, applied for a job with the Den-Tal-Ez Manufacturing Company. He'd fallen in love with Sandra Sue, he said, and wanted a "straight" job because he was ashamed of what he'd been doing for a living—although what he'd been doing he didn't say.

It wasn't just his real job that Chuck kept from Sandra Sue. He also failed to mention his current wife, and three sons from another, earlier marriage. Nor did Sandra Sue know about his rap sheet, which included everything from drunk driving to armed robbery. What she *did* know was that he was a pimp. When she asked him to stop, he did. But that was as straight as he got.

He declined the job in Des Moines and he and Sandra Sue lived in San Diego for a while. He knew people there and thought he could make a living gambling, but he did so badly that they had to leave town a step ahead of angry men he owed money for baseball bets he'd lost. Still, Sandra Sue was enthralled with Charles Harrelson, who exuded power but could also be gentle and romantic, in the beginning, at least. From California they drove through the Utah mountains, where Chuck sang love songs as they navigated the winding roads. Then they stopped in Vernal to buy a .25-caliber pistol before continuing on to Fort Worth for a Thanksgiving visit with Sandra Sue's mother and son. Sandra Sue did not ask why Chuck needed a pistol; she trusted that his reasons were good enough.

Everyone who knew him, even the police, said that Charles Harrelson was a smart man. His grammar was good, his vocabulary impressive, and he was an avid reader. Still, even smart guys make stupid mistakes. In a motel room in Fort Worth, Harrelson dry-fired his new pistol and discovered only too late that it wasn't dry. Sandra Sue ran in from the bathroom to find that he'd fired a single round into his leg. He was turning white, all the while insisting that he'd thought the gun was empty—the hallowed explanation of every Texan who accidentally shoots himself in one limb or another. Sandra Sue rushed Harrelson to the hospital, where the surgeon removed the bullet, gave it back, and sewed him up. Shaken, Harrelson tried to sell his pistol to the officer on duty in the emergency room, who declined because the slide did not move freely.

From Fort Worth, Harrelson and Sandra Sue drove back to Houston, where she took a job waitressing at the Cork Club—owned by a drunk named Glenn McCarthy, the notorious oil tycoon who inspired the character Jett Rink in Edna Ferber's book about Texas oilmen, *Giant*. When I was eighteen or nineteen, Alan had taken me there and attempted to introduce me to McCarthy, whom he knew, sort of. Surrounded by showgirls at his table, McCarthy looked up from his drink and barked, "Get that kid away from these broads."

McCarthy looked a bit like James Dean, who played Rink, but had a clownishly thin mustache and black hair as drenched in oil as his bank account. He hired only sexy women, and Sandra Sue met that qualification, but only until the second week of her job, when she showed up with a broken nose and two black eyes. She blamed it on the nerve in Chuck's leg; as it had begun to heal, he suffered tremendous pain and took it out on her. But instead of subsiding along with his symptoms, the beatings became worse. Black-and-blue and out of work, Sandra Sue decided to run away if she ever got the chance and by then understood that there was much more to Chuck than what he'd told her. When Sandra Sue finally dared to ask him if he "hurt people" for a living, he replied, "Of course."

Meanwhile, gambling debts continued to plague Harrelson, and in April 1968 he was offered a job that would make him $2,000 for less than a day's work. But he needed Sandra Sue's help—and it is at this point that her statement first mentions Alan, whose name is misspelled throughout.

> I asked about the job and little by little he told me that a boy named Allen Berg who sold carpet had cheated a man named Frank DiMaria out of $7,000 sometime in the past and he would get $2,000 for convincing the boy to pay it.

I have never learned for certain whether it is significant, or mere coincidence, that $7,000 was only $500 less than the amount of money Alan lost to Ted Lewin on his basketball bet.

> On a Tuesday night, Chuck came into the apt. and said he wanted me to make a phone call and he would tell me exactly what to say and that I was to repeat what Allen said so Chuck could tell what was being said.

Harrelson instructed Sandra Sue to tell Alan that she had seen him at a jazz club in Old Market Square and that she thought that he was cute. Jim Hathaway, a salesman we all liked, later said that through the office's "paper-thin walls," he and a few other employees heard Alan say, "What do you want with me? I'm not rich and I'm not good-looking."

Then: "Are you attractive?"

A moment later, Alan walked into the adjoining office and asked the guys gathered there, "What would you do if a woman called and said she had seen you on Market Square and just had to meet you? That she wanted to give you a blow job?"

"I'd be careful," said Jim.

Alan told Jim that he'd agreed to meet her outside the Brass Jug that night at about nine-thirty. Jim offered to go with him, but Alan declined. However, he did accept the same offer from his friend Fergis Ginther, whose opinion was that the phone call sounded like a joke or some sort of setup. "You ain't that cute, podner. Now, if it had been me she called cute or offered to suck my dick, it would make sense." Still, Alan and Fergis agreed to meet at the club around nine.

At eight-thirty, Alan called Harriet and told her that he'd had a rough day and would she mind if he met Fergis for a couple of drinks? It was true that things had gone badly at work. Three of Alan's salesmen had just "kicked him in the teeth," in Dad's words. The week before, Alan had cosigned a bank loan for one of them, only to learn that he and the other two had used the money to open their own carpet business. And then Alan could not help himself: he'd spent hours on the phone trying to kill their financing with the banks.

Alan dropped his driver off at his apartment and drove to the Brass Jug. But as soon as he sat down at their table, he told Fergis that he'd left his glasses in his car. He went outside to retrieve them, unaware that Harrelson and Sandra Sue were circling the block in Chuck's red Cadillac convertible, waiting for him. Sandra Sue was driving.

Chuck jumped out and forced Allen into our car by use of a gun and a shove. He also jumped into the back seat and told me to turn right on Westheimer. He told Allen this was a kidnapping and Allen said that his daddy would furnish whatever money was needed. Chuck kept telling me where to turn and we were in an area completely unfamiliar to me. I got the car stuck in some mud in front of a gate leading up a road to a house. Chuck became extremely angry at me and at first hit me and used profanity and told me to hold the gun on Allen. Then he told Allen to get out, that he was going to put him into the trunk in case anyone came from the house. He opened the trunk and Allen said he would be quiet so Chuck just tied his hands in front of him and said for him to be quiet and that if anyone came from the house he would kill all of them. He then got the car out of the rut and mud, made me drive again and once more directed me up and down unfamiliar roads. He said that he was looking for a certain spot but that it had been a long time since he had been out there and couldn't find it. Finally he was getting more and more nervous, I could tell, and he said to stop right where we were. He and Allen got out of the car and he closed the door and I could hear them walking to the back of the car. I assumed that he was going to beat on the boy and so I didn't look because I knew what it felt like to be hit and I was shaking inside because when he was nervous like I could tell he was, he was liable to do anything. Then I heard a shot.

The autopsy report was wrong. It took more than a gunshot wound to the head to kill my brother.

I jumped out of the car and looked behind the car. Allen was laying on the ground on his face. I couldn't see any blood but

Chuck later told me he had shot him in the temple. He looked at me as he put the gun on me and said to get back in the car or I would get the same thing if I did the wrong thing. I did this and sat there. I heard a noise and moved over the seat to the right and saw him dragging Allen by the arms and shoulders across the dumpy looking area. In a few minutes he came running back and I rolled down the window and said what is the matter. He said there was no water as he thought down there and he was going to have to bury the body. He opened the trunk and removed a shovel and went back out in the dump. He called me in a few minutes to come down where he was which I did. He took off his coat and tie as it was hot and told me to take them back to the car. I heard a gurgling noise coming from Allen and said what was that. Chuck said that evidently the boy was not dead and that he would have to choke him. I was shaking and sick and said please could I go back to the car. He said to go sit in the car and not to do anything but be quiet. I ran back to the car and sat there and then he called me once more to come down. I did and he handed me the shovel and said that the ground was too hard to dig and for me to take the shovel back to the car. I did this and looked back and he was dragging Allen by a rope around his neck. He pulled him to the car trunk area by walking backwards and opened the trunk and put the boy and the shovel into the trunk. He then got into the driver's seat and started driving. We drove for a long time and he said that he was looking for a spot to drop the body in water. He finally drove over the Intercoastal Canal Bridge near Surfside and turned left on a narrow road and drove for 9 or 10 miles. We were in an area where we could see lights in the distance but there seemed to be no people near. There was a vast area of brushy growth on our left and he stopped the car and told me to stay there and look for cars coming. He opened the trunk and yanked the boy out on the road and dragged him into the growth through a ditch with water in it and threw the quilt which was in the trunk which had blood on it over the ditch to the right of the body and then came back and got in the car. After a minute he told me to drive so he could change clothes as his were wet. Then he drove again. He told me to look in the back seat for anything there as he had not seen the boy's glasses. I looked and the glasses were there. Back at the place where he left the body he had given me a watch to hold which changed colors in the map light of the car. It was a very expensive watch with a very flexible band but was so small that I could not see the brand name. He said that he had left everything else on the body but had to have the watch to show that he fulfilled the contract and the man would recognize the watch. We drove over a toll bridge onto Galveston island and to the Galveston Causeway. As we drove over the bridge to the Gulf Freeway Chuck took the clip out of the gun and pitched the gun out and over the car to the right and into the water. He then changed lanes to the left and pitched the glasses over that side. We came back to Houston and to our apartment and he told me to wash the blood out of his clothes which I did and left them in the sink with cold water. The next morning he left, telling me he was going to wash the car and collect his money. In two or three hours he returned with $1500 in cash. He did not tell me where he had cleaned the car and I did not again see the shovel but he told me on the phone in October while I was working at the Le Bistro Club to have Jerry Watkins get a shovel from Crawford Booth and dispose of it. I told Jerry and I assume this was the shovel.

Alan must have thought he'd talk himself out of that car. After all, it wasn't his first time facing down a gun. Still, this time had to seem different, and not least because of Charles Harrelson's eyes: they looked like they'd been seared into his skull with a branding iron.

But even if talking wouldn't save him, my brother had other chances. Sandra Sue could have stopped Harrelson herself when he set about freeing his Cadillac from the mud and asked her to hold his gun. She could have shot him or held him captive while Alan ran to the nearby house and called the police. For that matter, Alan probably could have taken the gun from her, even with his hands tied. Or when Harrelson got him outside to put him in the trunk, Alan could have run deep into the woods. You can't hit shit at night with a .25-caliber pistol.

Of course, it's inevitable to ask oneself over and over: *What if?* But then again, when Charles Harrelson set about to murder someone, he never failed, as far as I know.

∾

Two days after killing Alan, Harrelson and Sandra Sue were staying in a motel near the Houston Astrodome when they were visited by his friend Pete Scamardo. Scamardo had brought some Mexican heroin in a condom and asked Harrelson if he could sell it. If so, they'd split the proceeds and Scamardo, with his clean record, would smuggle more across the border at Reynosa, Mexico. It sounded like a good deal to Harrelson—and necessary. He had already pissed away the money he earned by murdering Alan. After nearly a week of trying, however, Harrelson still hadn't managed to move the drugs—not even, as Sandra Sue put it, to "a big Negro with a gold front tooth who hung around Lucky Pierre's and was a driver or some sort of body guard for the little dwarf named Mousey." So Harrelson called Frank DiMaria, who was from Kansas City and put Harrelson in touch with some possible buyers there. But in Kansas City, Harrelson was stopped by the police, who had heard about the heroin from an informant and obtained a search warrant. Harrelson lucked out, sort of: while the police searched his car he kicked the smack into a sewer and they never found it. What they did find was a sawed-off shotgun in the trunk and a gun clip in the glove compartment—the one he'd neglected to toss in Galveston Bay—and that was enough for the US attorney to charge him with federal firearms violations.

Harrelson called Sandra Sue, who was back at their motel, and told her he was in jail. She then contacted DiMaria, who agreed to help; later that day a lawyer named Furry showed up and posted Harrelson's bond. That night, June 5, Harrelson was freed from jail—a few hours before Sirhan Sirhan assassinated Bobby Kennedy. Now all the men Alan and I loved were gone.

With the heroin lost, Harrelson owed Scamardo a favor. The two of them agreed that Chuck would kill Sam Degelia Jr., Scamardo's closest friend since the first grade, both of them part of the close-knit Sicilian community that blanketed the rich cotton farmland of the Brazos River Bottom. Scamardo's reason? Degelia and Scamardo were partners in the grain business, and if Degelia were to be murdered, the grain business would collect $100,000 in life insurance: $50,000 that went directly to a bank to pay off their business loan, and $50,000 Scamardo would pocket by stiffing their other creditors. For his part, Harrelson would receive $2,000. This time he left Sandra Sue at home in favor of another accessory: Jerry Watkins, whom Harrelson had met at Lucky Pierre's just two weeks before. According to Watkins's own statement, while he waited in a car outside a shack in McAllen, Texas, he heard pistol shots from inside, where Harrelson murdered Degelia.

Not too many days later, stoned and drinking in Watkins's den, Harrelson grew reflective: "Isn't it hell," he said, "when your best friend kills you to collect the insurance?" Then he took Watkins into his confidence, telling him about "different things" he'd done, like killing Alan Berg, and about how Sandra Sue had been along for the ride, just as Jerry had been down in McAllen. When Sandra Sue found out, she told Chuck he talked too much. In response, Harrelson hit her in the face. But then Sandra Sue did her fair share of talking, too—beginning with Claude Harrelson, Chuck's brother—days after Dad, by sheer coincidence, had hired Claude to investigate Alan's disappearance. According to Sandra Sue's statement:

> Chuck started talking about trying to get a reward for Allen's body and he and Jerry worked on this off and on but I was told little about it as they assumed that our phone was bugged and did all their calling outside the apartment. Claude Harrelson . . . had been contacted to try to find the boy as his father thought he had disappeared of his own volition. . . . About this time (first of July) Chuck called Claude and asked him to meet him at Lucky's for a drink. I had been drinking and was badly in need of food. Chuck asked Claude to take me to eat, which he did, and it is foggy but I believe that this was the time that Claude tried to pump me about Allen Berg. I probably did not deny strongly enough any knowledge now that I think about it. I cannot remember what I said, but later when Claude tried to pump me in Le Bistro he told me rather than asking me too many things, and at this time I told Claude nothing and just listened to what he said. I believe now that I had probably told Claude too much the day I had been drinking.

And that's when Claude joined the conspiracy and tried to extort the reward money from Dad, telling him at the Avalon that for $3,000 his "sources" could lead him to Alan's body. It was after the second muffled phone call (possibly from Charles himself), the one upping the price to $10,000, that my father demanded that Claude come with him to the Homicide Division and he refused. And that's when they abandoned the shakedown. According to Sandra Sue, "They gave up as they said that too many phones were bugged and it was too dangerous."

Toward the end of the summer of '68, Charles Harrelson reentered the chosen field of his youth: pimping, this time in Las Vegas. But he bounced so many checks at so many hotels he had to get out of town before they caught up with him. Once back in Houston, he learned from a friend of his father's in the Houston Police Department that the Texas Rangers had questioned Scamardo and were looking for him, so he and Sandra Sue hit the road again, but not without first stopping at DiMaria's new carpet store. There, DiMaria agreed to help him cash a $200 check from Scamardo. When they returned from Highland Village State Bank, Harrelson asked DiMaria if he would give him a good job recommendation if he needed one. DiMaria agreed. Why wouldn't he?

From Houston, Harrelson and Sandra Sue drove to Midland, where he won $100 hustling pool. From Midland they drifted through Denver, Vail, and then Vegas, where they met with Harrelson's confidant, Jerry Watkins, who warned him that the Rangers had questioned him, too. In Reno, Harrelson hit a lucky streak and went up $1,000. That was when Sandra Sue, encouraged by his good mood, asked him if she could have $200 to rent an apartment and send for some belongings still in storage back in Houston.

> This made him extremely angry and he knocked me down in the casino and grabbed me by the neck and yanked me to the car and beat me outside then threw me in the car and beat me around the head with his gun. I was very weak and bleeding from the nose and the head and he kept hitting me with his hand as he drove and telling me that he was going to kill me that night

and dump me out in the desert. Finally he stopped this and drove back to the motel and threw me in the bathtub and turned on the cold water.

The next day, when Harrelson went gambling again, Sandra Sue stole away in his car and drove to San Francisco. She contacted an old boyfriend to send her money so she could stay in California, but the money never came. So with a credit card and what little cash she had left, she drove seventeen hundred miles to Sherman, Texas, to see her mother and son. But when she got there they were gone, so she doubled-back the ninety miles to Fort Worth, found them there, and stayed for four days while her injuries healed. Then she drove back to Houston and got her job back waitressing at La Bistro.

Soon Sandra Sue was spending time with Harrelson's poker-playing buddy Dennis Weadock. Ever since he first met her with Chuck, Weadock had "wanted a piece of Sandra Sue," as he later told me, but was terrified to ask her out while she was still "Chuck's woman." But now she wasn't and in fact needed protection from Harrelson, who'd tracked her down at work and called to say he was on his way to Houston to kill her. First she told Jerry Watkins, who said he'd try to talk Harrelson down; then she turned to Weadock, who suggested that Sandra Sue hide out with him, and she agreed. A few days later, afraid that Harrelson was after them, the pair drove to Los Angeles, where they rented an apartment in Culver City. On the road, Weadock began asking Sandra Sue what she knew about my brother's death.

Eventually after Dennis kept talking about Allen I told him that Chuck had killed Allen and about where the body was— that it was near the big bridge near Surfside. I also told him

about Jerry and Chuck doing the job [on Degelia] in the Valley.
. . . Dennis then told me that Mr. Berg had offered a reward
for information leading to anything concerning his son. I told
Dennis that there was not any way to get the money because
the bullet would still be in his head and Chuck had told me that
if they had the bullet they could trace it to him as the gun clip
from the gun was in the custody of the FBI in KC and they would
eventually tie this together. Dennis agreed with me and said that
maybe after Chuck was caught doing something else as he was
likely to be, perhaps something could be done then. This was
the last time he said anything about this. The Wednesday night
before he left on Thursday he picked me up at the club where I
worked and was very excited and said that he had to go to Fort
Worth and Houston and someone was sending him the money
to go. He said that he was going to see a friend of his in Fort
Worth who was married to the daughter of Amon Carter and
had plenty of money and also to Houston to see Grady Hall and
Crawford Booth and that he thought that he could borrow $500
from each of them. I put him on an airplane Thursday afternoon
and was supposed to hear from him at the club but of course
never did.

She never did because Dennis Weadock was in Angleton, telling Sheriff Gladney everything Sandra Sue had told him about my
brother's murder. At 3:00 a.m. on the morning after Alan's remains
were found, two Texas Rangers knocked on Sandra Sue's apartment
door, cuffed her, flew her back to Houston, and deposited her in a cell
in the Brazoria County courthouse—where a typewriter was waiting.
"You got the keys to the jailhouse in your purse, Sandra Sue," Sheriff
Gladney told her. "All you gotta do is tell the truth."

Sandra Sue cried for a while and then finally began to type. She did not stop until she had completed twelve single-spaced pages.

And you would have thought that such a detailed confession alone would have been all it would take to convict Charles Harrelson, but you would have been wrong.

# 8

After Alan's remains were found, an administrator at Harriet's conservative synagogue sold me a grave site, sight unseen, on the outskirts of the cemetery. Only later did I learn that this is where Jews bury criminals, suicides, and other impious people.

If nothing else made Alan's death real, the deed for the grave did. It was on legal-size paper folded into four parts, and the pages were stapled to stiffer paper called a blueback. In the synagogue's parking lot, I paused to read the terms, set out in the commonplace language of any land transfer: "Beth Yeshurun Cemetery Association, for and in consideration of the sum of Three Hundred Fifty Dollars ($350.00), to it in hand paid by David H. Berg, does hereby grant unto the said David H. Berg, forever, the use of a certain burial plot of land, to wit: Single grave, in Lot No. 258, Section No. D, in Harris County, Texas."

I opened the car door of our Chevy, steadied the frame with my left hand, doubled my right, and threw my fist into the window.

My mother had come in from Little Rock and had scorched her chest while draining spaghetti at Linda's. When we all convened at my father's house on the morning of the burial, she was a tiny presence among Dad, Dot, Linda and her husband, Dayle, and me. She began to cry. "Oh, Nat, I don't want to go," she said, tugging her blouse away from her chest. "It hurts so badly." Remarkably, it was Dot who put an arm around Mom's shoulders and said, "Millie, you need to stay here." And she did, in Dad and Dot's living room, while the rest of us drove away.

When Dayle and I pulled up to the cemetery, the gravediggers weren't quite finished. It was drizzling and muddy. Dad was standing beside their truck, a good distance from Alan's coffin, staring at the workmen. I walked to him and we hugged, then held on to each other for a bit while he cried. "My boy is gone," he said again.

No more than twenty people huddled under the green canopy where Alan's coffin perched on the tracks that would lower him into the ground. Harriet's family's rabbi officiated, and, knowing next to nothing about my brother, spat out his vapid prayers like a jackhammer. The tracks moved and the coffin was lowered. We threw in clumps of wet dirt, ashes returned to ashes, and then everyone turned to leave. My good friend Larry was there, and he shook my hand and said what he'd said when Alan was accepted to medical school seven years earlier: "You know, he was like a little senator." I was glad for that.

As we walked back to our cars, my sister was still sobbing. I put an arm around her and promised to be there for her like Alan had always been. Then, for the second time in as many days, I doubled my fist and threw it, this time into the brick wall surrounding the cemetery.

❧

Immediately following Alan's funeral, my father ("well-groomed" and "immaculately dressed," according to the *Post*) drove to Brazoria County to appear before the grand jury. The most critical witness, of course, was Sandra Sue, whom Sheriff Gladney ushered in, her head covered by a piece of cloth. (If the media published pictures of her, the sheriff explained, "I might as well get ready to go to a funeral.") Later that day, another witness, Crawford "Big Man" Booth, told grand jurors that he had loaned his friend Harrelson a Sharpshooter shovel and that he had returned it on May 29, the day after Alan's disappearance. Prosecutors assumed that was the same shovel Harrelson had used when he tried to dig a grave in Fort Bend.

Another witness, Claude Harrelson, sat nervously in the hallway outside, waiting and talking to reporters. The next day the *Post* ran a story under this headline:

## Ironic Coincidence in Berg Case

When Nathan Berg hired Claude Harrelson to look for his missing son several months ago, neither man had any idea that Harrelson's younger brother would eventually be indicted for the murder of the son.

But that is what happened Wednesday afternoon after a grand jury session in Angleton.

Both the victim's father and his former private investigator testified before the grand jury. And when they faced each other Wednesday in the hallway outside the grand jury room, each knew what he had not months before.

"Facing Mr. Berg was the hardest thing I've ever had to do," said Harrelson, whose 30-year-old brother Charles was indicted for the murder.

"I know a lot of people are going to think there was something wrong," he said as he waited to testify. "But I worked on it (the Berg case) as hard as I knew how."

Harrelson bowed his head and rubbed his hands together.

"I never suspected anything," he said and added that when the father did not agree with some of his advice, he burned his notes and dropped out of the case.

Sandra Sue's statement told a different story. Claude had informed her "straight out that he knew Chuck had done this [murdered Alan]." The Brazoria County DA, Ogden Bass, could have indicted Claude for lying to the grand jury, but perjury cases are difficult to make, and besides, he had an even better option. Claude, his brother, and Jerry Watkins had committed a far more serious felony when they tried to shake down Dad for the reward money. And because there was no crime of "attempted" extortion under Texas Law, Bass could have waltzed his file over to the US attorney's office, where a federal grand jury would have returned an indictment against the trio for conspiracy and attempt to commit extortion, which carried a twenty-year prison term. And while Sandra Sue's testimony alone would have been insufficient to convict the three men—given that she had said in her statement that she knew little of the specifics of their scheme—that's where Dad and Jim Cowan would pick up the story, testifying in detail about their meeting at the Avalon with Claude, how he informed them that Alan had been murdered and demanded $3,000 for his "sources" to tell them where to find the body. Plus, there was the cold, hard evidence of Dad's check for that exact amount, made out to Cowan and to be endorsed over to Claude if his information panned out. Dad would conclude with the story of the weekend of harrowing calls demanding more and more money and—here I could confirm—Claude's refusal to go to the police department with us to tell them what he knew.

People have spent lifetimes in jail on a lot less evidence than this—and the egregious facts made their convictions all the more likely. Had Bass obtained such an indictment, he would have held the whip hand, a legal Damocles sword that would have forced the men to "flip" or face a lengthy prison term. And Charles Harrelson's only bargaining chip was to give up the man who hired him.

But the only Harrelson indicted that day was Charles, who fled immediately to Scamardo's hometown of Hearne, where he met with Scamardo on the outskirts of town and ditched his rented Ford in a gravel pit before driving off in Pete's '69 Oldsmobile—which Scamardo reported as stolen to cover his own ass. On November 19, the same day Harrelson was reported as seen in Mexico and Texas, he was positively identified in Atlanta by a resident of a boardinghouse where he was staying. Local fugitive detectives kept him under surveillance until just before dawn the following morning, when Texas Ranger Skippy Rundell, two Harris County police officers, and Jimmy Jones, chief investigator from the Brazoria County DA's office, arrived, knocked on Harrelson's door, and told him that he was under arrest— at which point, the accomplished hit man surrendered, sobbed, and begged to be allowed to keep a comb in his cell.

The next day, the *Post* said that Harrelson had registered at the boardinghouse under the name "Terry Southern." I was taken aback. Terry Southern? Alan had once recommended his books to me and, I think, gave me one. Before I could catch myself, I found myself impressed that Charles Harrelson knew of Terry Southern, one of America's greatest writers, perhaps even enjoyed his work. But what was I doing contemplating my brother's murderer's literary preferences? If I were the one in the ground, Alan would not have given my killer a single humanizing thought. I felt disloyal.

The officers flew Harrelson back to Houston on a Department of Public Safety twin-engine plane. The next day, the ever more attentive *Post* ran a picture of him being hustled toward a sheriff's car. Once in Angleton, accompanied by a single deputy, Sheriff Gladney sneaked Harrelson into his jail cell through the tax assessor-collector's office. "The boy don't want to see any news media and he don't want his picture took and I'm going to do my best to see that it ain't unless he changes his mind," Gladney said, as though he were talking about Elvis.

With Harrelson in jail and Sandra Sue free on $5,000 bond, there remained only the indictment of DiMaria. It had been hinted at in news stories coming out of Angleton, but months passed and it didn't happen, despite my father's increasingly angry questions of the DA. One day, returning from a doctor's appointment, Harriet found herself and her young son in an elevator with the man she was convinced had ordered her husband's murder, and he was grinning.

~

Even before Alan disappeared, my ties to Dad were frayed to breaking. Once we'd found his remains, I could hardly stand to be around my father at all. I felt he bore considerable responsibility for what had happened to Alan, especially because he refused to listen to us that day in the employees' kitchen, and yet it never seemed to occur to him that he wasn't the only one grieving. That said, I did not welcome condolences; I found them mawkish and embarrassing. The exception was a handwritten note from Congressman Bush, written as if he were speaking to a friend, when all that connected us was my father and a letter I'd written him thanking him for his help and commending him on his courageous vote for the Fair Housing Act of 1968 (which, among some of his River Oaks constituents, had earned him the epithet "nigger-lover"). On November 25, 1968, Bush wrote:

> Dear David,
>
> I was distressed to hear about your brother. I just got back to Texas from a trip to the Bahamas.
>
> You must be sad, and I just wanted you to know that you have my heartfelt condolences.
>
> Best,
>
> George B.

I could have done without the reference to the Bahamas, but still his letter touched me when little else did, not even my wife's constancy. I simply could not mourn my brother, or at least not in the way that I have come to understand mourning for others I have lost since. Instead of remembering the moments that had brought us so close together, I imagined Alan's final hours so often that *I* could have been the eyewitness to his murder. I heard him scream Harriet's name and mine. I watched as Harrelson trapped his neck beneath his boot and pulled the trigger. I thought about the last face Alan saw and wondered what he thought before everything went black, which I assume is the color of death. But I felt powerless to avenge all of this, despite the many violent scenarios that played out in my head. DiMaria bouncing off the hood of my car. Harrelson drowning in a pool of his own blood.

I also felt powerless to alleviate the longing that I felt for my brother. If I went to a movie—and I needed to see movies, for respite from the ones in my head—I would drift from the action onscreen and begin to feel his name claw its way out of my throat. *ALAN!* I'd scream. Then I'd sink down in my seat and wait to be thrown out. But I never was. My wife would shake the popcorn in my direction or I would hear the actors' voices again. I hadn't said a word.

One day, a man at a bus stop pointed a rifle right at me as I drove by. I swerved into oncoming traffic and pulled back just in time to avoid a collision. Clear of the threat, I looked back and saw that he was carrying a broom.

Driving a client to court in Dallas, I saw another man with a gun: this one walking along the sidewalk with a very real pistol in his back pocket, his shirttail hung up on the gun butt. Suddenly he whirled around, pulled the gun, and aimed it at me, point-blank. Again, I swerved my car, this time into the curb. The man took off running while I sat, terrified, no breath in my chest or blood in my face. My client—the man whose defense and protection were *my* job—had to calm me down.

"What's the matter?" he asked, laughing. "Ain't you never seen a nigger with a gun before?"

Apparently the man on the sidewalk had never even turned around, much less reached for his weapon.

Harriet's mom once told Alan and me that she'd never met brothers as close as we were—and that made me proud, because there was no relationship I cared about more than the one I had with Alan. But now there were daily reminders—like picking up the phone to call my brother or seeing Linda's husband behind Alan's desk a few days after we buried him—that the thing I valued most was gone.

By New Year's Eve at the end of 1968, my depression had become profound, and I felt certain that something bad was going to happen. I hate it when people say things like that. My mother, the Nostradamus of Valmar Street, did it all the time, claiming that she had predicted virtually every disaster of the twentieth century, including Al Jolson's death ("I knew it . . . I just knew it. I told you this was going to happen."). But then something did happen, and that very night: at only fifty-one, Dayle's wonderful mother, Gertie, died of a cerebral hemorrhage. So we had thought we were through with death, but death was not through with us. Overwhelmed with grief, my sweet, pregnant wife grew sullen and withdrew from everyone but her sister. Meanwhile, I was seething, seeing things, and hearing voices. What a fun couple we must have been.

I dreamed about Alan. His face was bloated, waxy, and yellow, as if he'd been in water a long time. He was leaning against the wooden pillar of a wharf, wearing his old navy pea coat and a brown beret, hands dug into his pockets. Wherever he was, it was cold. Behind him was a bright blue ocean and above him a yellowed newspaper headline that said something about "Alan Berg's Return." He seemed apologetic. I sprang up in my bed, my T-shirt drenched, and yelled, "MOMMA!"

That was the last time for forty years that I would remember having a dream about my brother, but it wasn't the last time I lurched upright in the middle of the night calling for my mother.

# 9

That winter, while Harrelson languished in jail awaiting trial, I did my best to immerse myself in my work, which wasn't easy. You can't immerse yourself in next to nothing. But then I got a phone call from a young man named Tim, and everything changed. Tim explained that he and his girlfriend had been hurt in a motorcycle accident. "Do you handle personal injury cases?" he asked. "Tim," I said, "are you kidding? Do I handle personal injury cases?" Sometimes the Talmudic response—answering a question with a question—beats the honest one.

It wasn't as if I knew *nothing* about accident cases. I'd clerked during law school for a personal injury lawyer, who disabused me of the notion that a crippling injury is necessarily a bad thing. I once overheard him on the phone with a client's doctor: "The pain goes all the way down her legs?" he said cheerfully. "Oh, those are *good* injuries."

Now, with Tim talking about retaining me, it wasn't Dean White or Racehorse Haynes whose voice I heard. It was Alan and Dad's, whispering: *Spike the deal!* Straightaway, I drove to Tim's apartment and spent an hour drinking coffee with him, his girlfriend, his mother,

and his grandmother. I commiserated about the young couple's griev-
ous injuries and swore that such unforgivable negligence would be
avenged in the courtroom. I pulled out a boilerplate contingency fee
agreement and Tim and his girlfriend signed up.

Then Tim's mother asked if I handled divorces.

"Oh, my God," I said. "Are you kidding?"

I signed her up.

Then his grandmother asked if I could draw up a will.

"Are you *kidding*???"

That might have been a mistake on her part. I have drafted a grand
total of three wills in my life and two of those clients, including Dayle's
mother, died an uncannily short time later. I have no idea how long
Tim's grandmother lived after executing hers, and I don't want to
know. In the public interest, I have not drawn up a will since.

Anyway, by the time I left Tim's house, I had done everything but
sell his mom forty-five yards of carpet, and I was thinking I was finished for the day. I was wrong. On the way out to my car, Tim asked
if I handled criminal cases. Now we were talking! I'd been shadow-
ing Racehorse Haynes around the Harris County courthouse for six
months! I *lusted* after a criminal case. "Criminal cases?" I asked, and
Tim needed no further assurance. Within thirty minutes I was in the
Reasoner Street jail, where Dad and I had gone several times to talk to
homicide detectives—but never before had I heard the chilling "clank"
of a cell door as it slammed behind me in the attorney waiting room.

Tim's friend was in on drug charges. While I waited for him to
come down from his cell, I stared through the thick plate glass that
separates lawyers from the lockup while roaches tap-danced around
my feet. An officer appeared with James, removed his handcuffs,
and sat him down opposite me. Even after three weeks in jail, James
still looked strung out, his hair matted and his face gaunt. Speaking
through a circular slot in the window, he described how the police had

spotted him on the street, jumped out of their car, and found heroin in his pocket. It was true: James was an addict and sold everything from marijuana to meth to support his habit. But the police had had no warrant or cause to arrest him other than his long hair, and that, obviously, was not enough.

Racehorse had told me that clients should always sign a fee agreement, even when there was no chance you'd get paid. That way, if the client referred anyone else, the prospective client would know going in that it was going to be expensive. "Plus," he said, "you never know when a rich relative will turn up." I told James that my fee was $2,500. He didn't flinch. Why would he? As far as I knew, he didn't have two buffalo nickels to rub together. The jailer passed the papers, and that was it: I had signed up my first criminal case.

As I stood to leave, James told me that he was going to call his father and get him to call me. "He's a brain surgeon in Denver," he said.

*Of course he is,* I thought. *And Daddy Joe founded the NAACP.*

That night I arrived home ecstatic—as would any rookie lawyer who'd started the day with almost no clients and finished with five new ones. As Dayle and I sat down to a celebratory dinner, the phone rang. It was James's father, thanking me for visiting his son in jail and apologizing for the late call, explaining that he had just gotten out of surgery. My hands started shaking and, in an attempt to sound older than my twenty-seven years, I lowered my voice. He'd already booked a flight into Houston for the following day and, when we met under Justice Fortas's approving smile, the first thing he did was to ask if I would mind receiving my fee in two installments. "Well," I said, "normally, I don't string out payments," which was literally true, given that I'd never had anything to string. "But in this case I'll be glad to make an exception." Then the neurosurgeon wrote out a check for $1,250.

I did not know, as it is said in Texas, whether to shit or go blind.

Being both a doctor's son and white went a long way in the Harris

County criminal courthouse. When I arrived for James's hearing—on the motion to suppress evidence, based on the illegal arrest—the prosecutors were talking to his father. They told him that if his son didn't take probation and then lost his motion, they'd send him away for ten years—an offer I'd already rejected, because I was certain I'd win and the case would be dismissed. They shouldn't have been talking to my client's father, and I was pissed. But he'd already agreed, and James walked free that afternoon—which, despite my opposition to his pleading guilty, was nevertheless excellent advertising for my fledgling practice.

I attracted even more cases like James's and won a steady succession of them—fighting the Klan-ridden Houston Police Department, whose officers stopped kids for no reason but their long hair and the vans they drove with peace stickers on the bumper—often planting "throw-down" drugs when they found none and stealing whatever money they found. (In several cases, including one of my own, a particularly twisted narc shoved his pistol into the vagina of women he'd arrested.) Hundreds of unshorn kids swarmed "Hippie Hill" in Hermann Park on Sundays and began to circulate my cards, whispering to one another that they should "call this guy" in the event they were arrested.

Soon, with some good press and word of mouth, cases began coming in from around the state—not a lot, but enough to send me speeding down long, empty highways once or twice a month toward distant Texas towns. It was in Laredo, on the border with Mexico, that I tried my first federal case, and it was also there that a skeptical Judge Reynaldo Garza called the lawyers to the bench and in a voice calculated for the jury to hear characterized the government's lead witness—a Mexican pharmacist who not only sold my clients barbiturates illegal in the United States but also snitched them off to US Customs—as the "nigger in the woodpile." And so it was, owing little to my courtroom skills, of which I had few, and much to the judge's bigotry, of which he had aplenty, that I won my first federal case.

Thoreau didn't just say that most men lead lives of quiet desperation; he also said, in the next breath, "From the desperate city you go into the desperate country. . . ." At first, those long drives were difficult for me; I was afraid to be alone with my thoughts. But I can romanticize carrying out a sack of garbage into carting a slain enemy over my shoulder, and that is what I did—I bought myself some boots and imagined myself an actual Texan on a mission for his clients, speeding down highways surrounded by dust and cactus and the occasional Esso station with its RC Cola signs and listening to eight-track tapes of Johnny Rodriquez ("Johnny Rod"), Waylon Jennings, and, somewhat out of character for my redneck period, Enrico Caruso. And, as out of place as the breathtaking mesas that popped out of the West Texas desert, I also stopped in honky-tonks, drank beer, and shot pool with cowboys over sawdust-covered floors.

It was during those trips that I discovered that among the hard-ass prosecutors and judges, there were many others, from the largest cities to the most rural towns, who shared not only the secret language of the law but also a devotion to justice—and for me, there was no more vivid example than in a drug case in Van Horn, near the New Mexico border. A college student—the nephew of my criminal law professor—was busted there, along with his cousin and thirty bricks of marijuana poorly hidden in his Volkswagen van. The professor, who'd flunked me, retained me. "I've been keeping up with your cases," he explained, which I found flattering, until he added, "But you better do a damn sight better for my nephew than you did for me." To represent the cousin, I brought in my friend Stu Nelkin, who'd recently returned from DC. When we got to Van Horn, we watched the circuit-riding judge from El Paso land his single-engine plane in the dirt and emerge with a single passenger: the prosecutor. If that wasn't worrisome enough, I peeked in at the jury panel and saw row after row of sunbaked heads with slicked-back hair and no sideburns, starched khaki shirts, and blue jeans, Anglo ranchers incapable of using "not" and "guilty" in the same sentence. The only thing separating our clients from the Texas Department of Corrections was our pending motion to suppress evidence, arguing that the traffic stop that resulted in our clients' arrest was illegal, a contention we based in part on my professor's scholarly *Missouri Law Review* article on that subject. I was surprised. The judge asked for the article, retired to chambers, and emerged half an hour later with a command of the material and a ruling in our favor—excluding the marijuana from the trial. Without any evidence, the prosecutor was forced to dismiss the case. As soon as he did, we bolted from that courthouse before the judge could change his mind and drove nonstop six hundred miles home.

With time, I was no longer afraid of those long drives, and, in fact, welcomed them—they meant fees, trial experience, and isolation. I did not realize it then, but those desolate highways had become a metaphor for freedom for me. I was on my way—and not just to distant Texas towns.

And then, in August of that very successful year, my phone quit ringing. I didn't sign up a single client. Each day was hard. I felt like someone who loses a hundred pounds and still thinks of himself as fat. Never mind the fees thus far, I still thought of myself as broke—and destined to go without signing up another new case ever.

Still, new cases or no, there was never a better time to become a lawyer—at least one with my political views. While ultraconservative Houston was not a hotbed of antiwar or civil rights protests, some measure of the ubiquitous social upheaval across America inevitably found its way there, creating great cases and great causes. For a long while, I was the Houston lawyer most willing to take them on, even from the subversives at the American Civil Liberties Union. My clients were reviled: flag burners and antiwar marchers and kids kicked out of school for long hair, and one young Hispanic student expelled from a local junior college for wearing a mustache, coincidentally, a day after his pro-Castro essay was published in the campus newspaper. In addition to ACLU cases, I also represented some black men arrested for being black, like the young epileptic accused in 1969 of assault on a police officer—the default criminal charge whenever a Negro sassed a cop. On the morning of the trial, I asked Judge Jimmy Duncan for additional recesses so that my client could take his anti-seizure medication, to which he responded by pulling a .45 out from under his robe and sliding it on top of the bench, nonchalantly spinning it as he responded, "We've had niggers throw fits in here before." I tried my case and four days later, when the jury returned with its verdict, I watched him read their decision to himself and knew from his curled lip what they had decided. I couldn't help flashing him a shit-eating grin as he spat out the words, "Not guilty." And how odd it was that he smiled back at me and winked.

Then, on the Friday before Labor Day, just as I was leaving the office, the phone finally rang. All the time, effort, and commitment I'd invested in those cases was about to pay me back exponentially. Marty Elfant, a political activist I'd met through the ACLU, was on the line, asking if I could help a friend's son with a serious problem. The friend's name was Ezra Schacht. The US marshals had an arrest warrant for his son, Danny.

This was the case Alan had said he wished I could get the last time I saw him. I was flabbergasted—and thrilled.

I knew the facts of Danny's case from TV and the papers: he and a friend had staged a skit in front of the armed forces induction center in downtown Houston to protest the killing of innocents by our troops in Vietnam. Danny wore parts of an army uniform (including an officer's insignia, but upside down) and pointed a squirt gun filled with red ink at his friend dressed as a coolie. "Be an able American!" Danny had shouted as he squeezed the trigger. Then he ran to the fallen "coolie," splattered with "blood," and shouted, "My God, this is a pregnant woman!" The two young men repeated the skit several times and then went home.

That night, armed FBI agents cornered Danny's car and arrested him as he left his father's electronics plant. One of them bragged to Danny that he had spent the entire day trying to identify a federal crime they could charge him with—and finally dug up "unauthorized wearing of a distinctive part of the military uniform."

Danny's case landed in the court of US district judge James Noel, a pro-prosecution reactionary who seemed to think that his job was to promote convictions. Danny went to trial with another defendant, the improbably named Jarrett Vander Smith III, whose only role had been to pass out antiwar leaflets. (Somehow the "coolie" had escaped prosecution.)

Here was Danny's defense: the statute he was charged with violating—designed to preclude civilians from impersonating members of the armed forces—had an exception: an actor in a theatrical or motion picture production could wear an armed forces uniform but (and this was the catch) only if the portrayal did not discredit that branch of the military. Put another way, it was okay to wear an army uniform while acting as long as you spoke lovingly of the army. On the stand, Danny agreed that he had worn unmistakable parts of an army uniform during his skit (which his lawyers argued constituted a theatrical production) and that his intent was to discredit the army. But as he also told the jury, he believed that the restriction on what he could say about the military violated his right of free speech.

Well, lots of luck with that defense in the Southern District of Texas in 1968. During closing argument, the assistant US attorney, "Moose" Hartman, pointed at Danny and yelled, "If Schacht comes to my house and expresses himself like this he won't be able to walk into this courtroom to stand trial." Then he moved toward both boys: "The only thing I gather from the argument of these defendants is that they are displeased with the government and the war. But I have a single answer to that. There is a plane and boat leaving two or three times a day for other parts of the world. I can probably name you gentlemen the place to go. . . . If you don't like it, get out!"

Noel refused to declare a mistrial and later, when Danny's lawyers pointed out that the prosecutor had slipped in the word "betrayal" for "portrayal" in the draft jury charge, Noel commented, "Some might view it as a betrayal." The offending word came out, but there was no doubt where Judge Noel stood: he read the charge to the jurors in a tone that practically mandated Danny's conviction. The jury was out only briefly before finding both men guilty.

At sentencing, Noel gave Jarrett probation. Then, while punching holes in a piece of paper with a pencil, Noel glared at Danny and said, "Schacht's express purpose was to discredit the United States, of this army in Vietnam, to leave the impression to all watching that the soldiers of the country were attacking innocent people who were being killed by shooting. . . . In my opinion, the defendant acted heedlessly and he has expressed not the slightest bit of remorse." Noel sentenced Danny to the maximum possible term under the statute: a $250 fine and six months in a federal penitentiary.

Sixteen days later, on March 16, 1968, US army lieutenant William Calley led his troops into the tiny village of My Lai, where they slaughtered at least 347 unarmed men, women, and children. And, as Danny had learned from stories and pictures in Quaker newspapers—and Judge Noel could not imagine—that wasn't the first time our troops had massacred innocents.

Out on bond during his appeal, Danny and his father met with the board of the ACLU, which agreed to finance costs through the US

Supreme Court and appointed Will Gray, an experienced appellate specialist, to handle the case. The first stop was the Fifth Circuit Court of Appeals, and the first step was to purchase the trial transcript—but the ACLU's check bounced. It was replaced with a cashier's check, but Gray remained rankled. Gray did argue the case, but that was all he did: the conviction was affirmed and Gray did not appeal the decision to the Supreme Court. To be precise, he failed to file Danny's petition for writ of certiorari, the document setting out all the reasons why the high court should hear the case and the only possible way to get his conviction overturned. When the deadline for filing passed, the conviction became final, a warrant was issued for Danny's arrest, and that's when I got the call to represent him.

That night, Danny and his father came to our apartment. Ezra Schacht also was an activist—and he, too, had been arrested once, for putting up yard signs in support of a black candidate for Houston City Council—but his black hair, graying at the temples, was combed neatly and he was dressed as though he'd just gotten back from Neiman Marcus. Danny, on the other hand, wore an untucked blue denim shirt and tattered jeans and had curly brown hair way out to here (a style labeled a "Jewfro" by the country-and-western singer Kinky Friedman and most definitely not calculated to win favor with a Southern District jury). But Danny seemed to me an extremely gentle and thoughtful person, truly baffled by his circumstances, and terrified of prison. When I explained that Gray never filed his petition in the Supreme Court and that it was unlikely that the justices would hear his case this late, Danny buried his head in his hands so that there was nothing to see but his curly hair. "I don't understand what's happened to humanity," he said, beginning to sob.

The Schachts didn't want the ACLU involved anymore. We agreed that I would take over the appeal and I set a $2,500 fee, although I couldn't have cared less whether I was paid. As soon as the Schachts left, I hightailed it to the tiny law library I shared with the lawyer I sublet space from. I could have argued the First Amendment issue from the years I spent living with Dad, but I could only find two cases where the Supreme Court had discussed the late-filing issue, and both times it was mentioned in footnotes, meaning to me the matter was unsettled. Worse, from what I could tell, no criminal case had ever been heard filed as late as Danny's, which was already seventy-five days past due—and I hadn't even begun work on the brief. So not only would I have to prove that Danny was in no way at fault for the failure to file—so-called excusable neglect—but I would also have to motivate the Court to overcome its predisposition against taking late-filed cases, no matter how meritorious they might be.

I awoke the next morning with my head on top of a law book and a Styrofoam cup of cold coffee nearby. The irony of my sleeping among the very cases I had avoided so scrupulously during law school was not lost on me.

Meanwhile, Ezra had gone to Gray's office to ask why he'd failed to file the petition. Gray's young associate, Bob Hunt, told Ezra that Gray wasn't coming in, but Ezra sat in their waiting room for two and a half hours, refusing to budge. Finally, Hunt emerged from his office and said that Danny had never paid for the filing fee and therefore Gray hadn't filed his petition. That astonished Ezra; after all, the ACLU had agreed to pay the expenses.

On the Tuesday after Labor Day 1969, Ezra and I surrendered Danny to a deputy US marshal in the federal courthouse. Then I made a huge yet providential mistake. I went to a pay phone in the courthouse and called Judge Noel's chambers. His secretary asked why I needed to talk to him. I told her that Danny's lawyers had failed to file the appeal and I wanted to know if the judge would continue his bond until the Supreme Court ruled one way or the other. I assumed that she would be moved—and she was: to anger. "I'm getting Judge on the line," she snapped. "Don't you dare hang up!" When Judge Noel got to the phone, he said that my call was the most unethical thing he'd heard of in all his years on the bench. At the time, I was unaware I'd done anything wrong, but he was right: I should not have called him without including the prosecutor on the line. Still, Noel didn't listen to a word I said and only got madder when I tried to apologize. (Dad? Is that you?) And then he unwittingly taught me something that proved crucial: he demanded to know if I was accusing Will Gray of negligence.

Negligence? No one sued lawyers back then. The concept of lawyer malpractice had been utterly foreign to me prior to that moment.

"That's exactly what I'm saying!" I blurted out. "Gray never filed the petition and that's about as negligent as you can get."

Noel exploded.

"Young man, I'll see you in my court at two o'clock! We are going on the record!"

That afternoon, the marshals escorted Danny—dressed in prison-issue khaki shirt and pants—down from the tenth-floor holding cell. Once in court, they removed his handcuffs and sat him next to me at the counsel table, where I had been waiting for an hour, alone, fidgeting, wondering if I was going to lose my license. Fittingly, Will Gray and his associate sat with the prosecutor. Then the courtroom door reverberated with the three jarring bangs of the knocker that herald the entry of all federal judges, and Noel flowed in, his black robe billowing about his tall frame.

He called the case, and both sides announced they were ready. Then there was a long silence. Finally, Noel looked down and said, "Well?"

Well, what?

I was twenty-seven, not even two years a licensed lawyer, had been in only one other federal court—*and* the judge-for-life already hated me. I was lucky not to wet myself. Finally, I rose at my chair and asked that Danny be allowed to remain on bond. Noel took the request under advisement, meaning that he would wait until after he heard the testimony to fuck us.

Danny took the stand and testified that the ACLU had agreed to pay the filing fee and that he'd had no idea that Gray hadn't filed until I told him the previous Friday. On cross-examination, the prosecutor asked Danny how often he'd been in contact with Gray, assuming, as he had every right to, that the answer would be "frequently." Instead, Danny testified that he hadn't met with Gray since their initial conference and that Gray never once returned his calls. Danny did say that Gray's associate had called him a couple of times but had never mentioned that there was an issue about getting the filing fee paid.

Then I called the chairman of the ACLU, who had sat uncomfortably in the courtroom listening to Danny's testimony. Once he took the stand, he unloaded on Gray, telling the judge that his board had "unequivocally" agreed to pay the expenses of the appeal and that he'd said that "personally" to Gray. I now had evidence of lawyer negligence, but I needed to prove that Danny was not responsible at all for the failure to file, or, as long as the odds were already, the Supreme Court would never take his case. The best opportunity to prove just that came in the person of Bob Hunt, who fairly ran to the stand to reclaim Gray's reputation. Under the prosecutor's questioning, he insisted that he'd told Danny that he had to pay "in the neighborhood of five hundred dollars"; he also said that he had told Danny the due date for filing.

The former dean of Northwestern Law School, John Henry Wigmore, famously said that the greatest engine ever invented for the discovery of truth is cross-examination. That holds true even for a very lucky rookie lawyer. Under my questioning, Hunt told a different story: he confessed that he did not remember telling Danny the due date and could not even tell me what that date was, not even the month.

Then I asked questions about the filing fees that elicited answers so hostile that they just might get the Supreme Court's attention:

Q. Did you ever ask the ACLU for the money for the filing fee?

A. Personally, I am not going to ask the ACLU for nothing.

Q. Just answer the question.

A. No.

Q. And although you knew Mr. Gray was a volunteer ACLU lawyer, you didn't make any attempt to get the money from them?

A. I have made attempts in the past on other cases.

Q. No, I mean on this case.

A. No.

No more questions, Your Honor.

Next, Gray took the stand. He testified about the ACLU's check bouncing and (although it had been replaced) added, "I didn't see why I should put down five hundred dollars for the transcript and filing fees. If nobody else cared, why should I knock myself out?" Then, with no question pending, Gray let out a deep breath, slid down in the chair, and cratered. "I feel pretty bad about this. I know that we would have won in the Supreme Court, but I didn't want to put up the money." Then he looked right at Danny and added, "I would like to get to the Supreme Court on this."

Too late, Mr. Gray. My case now. And just wait until I tattle on you to the Supremes.

Judge Noel, his bushy white eyebrows pumping up and down like overheated pistons, denied my motion to continue the bond and condemned Danny for his irresponsibility. I expected that. It was when he praised Gray for his excellent representation before the Fifth Circuit that I found myself on my feet, as angry as Dad at Assistant Principal Viebig. "I don't know if I'm out of order or not," I said, meaning: *Not only do I not know, but I don't give a shit.* "If Danny is a criminal, he is an ideological criminal and what he is being punished for is the crime of protest." Meaning: *I hate to bother the court, you heartless prick, but would you mind recommending a prison that is not filled with hardened criminals?* Judge Noel said that was not up to him, remanded Schacht to custody, and swept out of the courtroom. The marshals cuffed Danny and led him back upstairs. And while the Bureau of Prisons did assign him to a minimum-security prison, it was still a prison—and Danny Schacht did not deserve to be there.

Now I needed help, so I called in Stu Nelkin again. He pitched camp with me for the three weeks it took us to prepare both a motion asking permission to file Danny's petition late, with the transcript of the hearing in Noel's court attached, *and* the petition itself, seeking reversal of his conviction—a delay that felt sinful, given Danny's imprisonment. But we wanted the papers to be perfect, and when Alpha Legal Brief finally delivered them to my office, they almost were. (My secretary, an old-school stickler, discovered a typo and broke down crying.)

I don't know why it bothered me, but the first thing I noticed was how thin the documents were. After all that work, I had not expected the brief to be so, well, brief. Anyway, Ezra and I placed the justices' copies in two small boxes and took them down to my office building's lobby, where we sat down together on the white marble floor to wait out a terrible thunderstorm. While we were speaking I realized Ezra had begun to cry. He said that as Danny was taken off to jail, he'd seen his son as a tiny child crawling in his crib. "I thought, you know, you can never know what the world holds for a baby." And while he spoke quietly about Danny, I remained fastened on the image of a baby in the crib and his unpredictable future.

When the rain stopped, we took off our shoes and socks, rolled up our pant legs, and ran through ankle-deep water to Ezra's car, where we threw the boxes into the backseat, and then he headed for the airport. The next morning, September 22, 1969, Ezra arrived at the office of the clerk of the US Supreme Court, handed him the briefs, and paid the $100 filing fee. With that, case number 628 was filed, 101 days late.

Approximately one month later, the Fifth Circuit unexpectedly granted our motion to recall the mandate for Danny's arrest, giving Noel no choice but to reinstate Danny's bond. He let Danny sit in prison for another week and then summoned him to court, where he announced that he was readmitting Schacht to bail because of a letter Danny had written expressing "remorse" for his acts. My client rose in his chair and began to complain, "You're distorting the meaning . . ."—and I kicked his leg as hard as I could. That was quite enough principle for one day.

Eighty-four days after we filed in the Supreme Court, on December 15, 1969, I was driving to Austin, switching channels on my car radio, when I thought I heard something about Danny. I swerved into a gas station and called my office from a phone booth. My secretary said that a telegram from the clerk of the Supreme Court had just arrived: The justices had agreed to hear the case!

I put another quarter in the phone and called Stu.

"You are fucking kidding me," he said.

I flew home several feet above the surface of that highway. I was going to argue in the Supreme Court of the United States! *Time* magazine once said it perfectly about a case I no longer recall: that a practicing lawyer arguing before the Supreme Court was like an airline pilot flying to the moon. Not only that, but I was going to argue against Erwin Griswold, the solicitor general of the United States and former dean of Harvard Law School. "The Dean," as everyone still called him, was also a renowned civil rights advocate—among the first to condemn Senator Joseph McCarthy—and had argued more cases in the US Supreme Court than any other lawyer in history.

There was one sobering note: Three justices had voted against hearing the case because of the late filing. If just two more came around to thinking the same way, the petition would be dismissed as having been "improvidently granted." As we thought, the main battleground was going to be over the tardiness issue—and given that courts always look for procedural reasons to dismiss cases, two votes turning around was not out of the question.

Upon learning that Danny was bound for Washington, the local media squeezed into my office and spilled into the hallway. Dayle was there, beaming at me from over a cameraman crouching in the doorway. Danny and I answered questions while I did my best not to voice a nasty thought: *I hope Judge Noel is watching.*

Dad was watching, for sure, and reveling in the different kind of publicity the name Berg was getting—if not in my five-o'clock shadow. "If you're going to be on TV, junior, you better wear some makeup. You looked like Richard Nixon."

Stu and our wives and I arrived in Washington the day before the argument. The first thing Stu and I did was to run, like Muslims to Mecca, to the Supreme Court building, where we watched an argument, awestruck. It is one thing to see one famous person; it is quite another to see eight of them (Justice Fortas had resigned and had not yet been replaced), and several of those your heroes: Hugo Black, William O. Douglas, Thurgood Marshall, William Brennan, and Potter Stewart, the latter a pragmatic jurist famous for writing that he couldn't define pornography but knew it when he saw it. In that era of social and political upheaval, it was those justices in particular who acted as a pressure valve for a society about to explode—ruling most often in ways that expanded and protected civil liberties.

After watching the argument, Stu and I wandered up and down the rows of cream-colored law books and mahogany desks in the Court's library. We searched for any recent, relevant cases that we might have missed, but we found none. Then Stu suggested that we call Professor Charles Alan Wright at University of Texas Law School. Wright was one of America's greatest legal minds and a coauthor of the leading text on federal procedure. Stu dialed him from a pay phone, and while he laid out the late-filing issue to Professor Wright, who had picked up the phone himself, I waited anxiously outside the open glass door. After a few quiet moments listening, Stu hung up and smiled triumphantly. Then he repeated what Wright had said: "It's interesting you called, because Ernie [Griswold, the solicitor general] called me last week about this very issue. I told him I thought he was in trouble on this one. I read your brief. You're right. The Court made the rules. The Court can suspend the rules. Don't make it any more complicated than that."

I wish I could say that a great calm swept over me that night. On the contrary: my guts were churning and I was rapidly approaching tachycardia. Desperate for reassurance, I called Racehorse, waking him up. He offered me this optimistic view on our profession's anxieties:

"Look at it this way. A trial lawyer is never constipated."

"This is an appeal, not a trial."

"Okay, brother. Have it your way. An appellate lawyer is never constipated either. Good luck and good night."

I took a long shower and finally fell asleep around two. At five I awoke and lay there in that peaceful moment between sleep and consciousness. Then I grabbed my stomach and whispered, "My God, the Supreme Court of the United States." Dayle woke up, put her arm around me, and said, "You'll do great." Then she said something that

I am embarrassed to repeat and probably will never be forgiven for doing so: "You're my Hercules."

Danny and his girlfriend, Scout, a sexy hippie with long hair and canvas pants, were already at the courthouse when we got there. Even Danny, the consummate sixties radical, walked around in wonder, touching the marble.

I went to the clerk's office for my instructions. They were written on a crummy index card with the case number at the top. I was disappointed. If I was going to argue in the Supreme Court, I wanted my directions on scrolled-up parchment—in Latin.

The card read:

Do not interrupt the Chief Justice to ask how much time is left.
Do not interrupt the Justices while they are asking a question.
Stop talking when the red light is on.
The charge for lunch is $1.25.

Before heading for the area where participants gather preargument, I looked back at Dayle. She was radiant, just beautiful. I ran back and kissed her, of the variety that pleads, "Tell me I'm not going to make a fool of myself."

"You'll do great," she said again.

When Stu and I had sat down at the counsel table, Erwin Griswold, looking every bit "built like a block of granite," as the *New York Times* described him, walked over, introduced himself, and asked about our trip from Houston, while idly leafing through our brief as if he'd never read it before. At 9:00 a.m. the justices roared out from behind their burgundy curtains like lions freed from captivity. The marshal sang out the venerable call to order: "The honorable, the chief justice and the associate justices of the United States Supreme Court. Oyez! Oyez! Oyez! All persons having business before the honorable, the Supreme

Court of the United States are admonished to draw near and give their attention, for the Court is now in session. God save these United States and this honorable Court."

There was another argument before ours, a death penalty case out of Arizona that droned on for an hour while my mind somersaulted over the questions I knew were coming my way. Finally Chief Justice Warren Earl Burger called our case—"*Schacht versus the United States*"—but he mispronounced Danny's last name as "Shocked." I took this as a welcome sign that at least one of the justices was not made of granite. Otherwise, Burger was straight out of central casting, with flowing white hair and a relaxed, welcoming smile.

The white light on the lectern came on. At this point in the tape recording of the argument, a disconcerting forty seconds passes in silence. Finally Chief Justice Burger says, "Mr. Berg, you may proceed whenever you are ready."

After I'd summarized the charges and the outcome in the district court, Chief Justice Burger asked the first questions.

Burger: "Has he served his prison sentence?"

Berg: "No, sir, he has not."

Burger: "He hasn't served any part of it, he's . . ."

One question, one wrong answer. Of course Danny had served some time. Still, Chief Justice Burger's question had the same effect on me as getting hit for the first time has on a football player: I relaxed. And I immediately corrected myself.

Berg: "Well, inadvertently, he did. The petition was filed out of time. He was in prison for three weeks. We lodged a motion to submit out of time. It was granted. He was released from prison."

Burger: "I noticed, counsel, that you described this in your factual statement as a demonstration in front of the recruiting headquarters or some such thing. You do not make the claim that this is a theatrical production?"

*Jesus*. Had he read the brief? That was our main contention—that the demonstration was a theatrical production that entitled its participants to free speech protection. Why else would the Court have granted Danny's writ? Now the question became: Could I control what Momma Hattie labeled the fisk on my punim? To my credit, I did.

"Yes, Your Honor," I responded respectfully, "we do make that claim. . . ."

"Then your describing this as a demonstration was not intended to preclude your claim in your brief?"

"No, sir."

"I wondered if you were changing your position."

"This was, as it were, a play within a play—within a demonstration."

Dear God. Did I just say "as it were"?

A few minutes in, Associate Justice William Brennan asked if I would be satisfied if the Court simply acquitted my client. I told him that I thought that the Court had to address the constitutional issue. This made him mad.

"You are anxious to get a constitutional proceeding out of this, aren't you?"

If I'd had the experience of arguing just one appeal before this one, I would have said, "There's nothing I'd like more than for this Court to acquit Danny. But the only way to do that is to hold either that Danny wasn't wearing distinctive parts of the uniform, which is not true, or that he did not intend to discredit the military, which isn't true either. Respectfully, the only way this court can acquit Danny is to strike down the language prohibiting criticism of the military on First Amendment grounds."

But I had no such experience, so I answered, simply, "Yes"—which didn't make Justice Brennan any happier.

"You are not concerned to get your fellow off?"

"Yes, sir," I said, "we feel that a constitutional decision *would* get him off."

Then, as lawyers are taught to do when they've lost an appellate judge's favor, I changed the subject and looked directly at the fatherly Chief Justice Burger.

After the lunch break, I took Stu's advice and tried to make peace with Justice Brennan. I assured him that we would take any acquittal we could get and quickly moved on to other arguments. Despite committing the cardinal sin of stepping on some of their lines—I could hardly wait for Associate Justice John Marshall Harlan II to get his question out before assuring him that there'd been no violence at the protest—the justices were unmistakably inclined to side with Danny on the free speech issue. When I quoted Moose Hartman's vicious closing argument, some of the justices glanced at one another in disbelief, as if to say, "Kangaroo court."

Then, as Professor Wright suggested, I concluded by arguing that the Court made the rules and the Court could break them. Then I sat down and I could tell from Stu's face that we were doing all right.

The solicitor general argued so extensively—and brilliantly—that the Court had no power to relax its time limits for filing cert that he left himself only four minutes for the free speech issues raised by Danny's conviction, to me a pretty clear signal that he wasn't all that anxious to get there. But Chief Justice Burger extended Griswold's time—*and mine*, for rebuttal.

Griswold then argued that Danny's skit was not a theatrical performance because it wasn't on a stage, and it wasn't clear to observers that he wasn't actually a member of the armed forces. To this Justice Douglas barked, "And *what* was given in Houston, Texas?" (Meaning: Of course it was a theatrical production, nitwit.) And a bemused Justice Marshall remarked that he saw bums in the Bowery wearing parts of uniforms and didn't confuse them with army officers. When

Griswold said that had Danny removed the insignia, he might have avoided prosecution, Justice Stewart and I simultaneously mouthed "How?" at each another and smiled.

My rebuttal didn't last three minutes. I concluded with a brief statement that Danny's intent was to discredit the military and that the government had no compelling interest in stopping him because to do so impinged on freedom of expression. I didn't even get to the red light signaling the end; I just sat down. The chief justice smiled and said, "The case is submitted. Thank you, Mr. Berg and Mr. Solicitor General."

Mom taught me the Fluff Box rules. My debate coach taught me delivery. Alan taught me how to close. In retrospect, I don't know why I needed to go to law school.

I filched four quill pens from the counsel table, shoved them in my briefcase, and walked out.

And, because the gods do have fabulous senses of humor, Danny and Scout's seats on the flight home were only a couple of rows behind Judge Noel—whose trip to Washington may have included slipping into the Court to hear the argument. Danny and Scout made it a point to laugh loudly all the way to Houston. As they got off, Judge Noel smiled and said that he knew why Danny was in DC. I must admit I was disappointed to hear that he was so pleasant.

On May 25, 1970, less than two months later, a *New York Times* reporter called to tell me that the Supreme Court had unanimously reversed Danny's conviction. First, the Court held that it could relax its own rules for filing and, generously omitting the basis of its decision, that the delay was out of Danny's control. Then, exactly as we had argued, it held that the skit was a theatrical production within the meaning of the statute and that the words "if the portrayal does not tend to discredit that armed force" violated the First Amendment and had to be stricken from the law. So guerrilla theater was legitimized and Danny was free. The story ran on the front page of the *Times*, although the otherwise admirable reporter failed to mention my name, so I cannot remember his.

And now, with *Schacht* behind me, I could no longer ignore a deeply troubling fact:

Charles Harrelson had hired Percy Foreman.

# 10

Two months before Harrelson's murder trial, Harriet spotted Foreman on a street corner in downtown Houston. With his massive height, outsized head, and sweaty hair that hung pasted to his forehead, he was an unmistakable presence. "Mr. Foreman," Harriet said, walking right up to him, "I'm Alan Berg's widow. Please don't tear my husband up."

Foreman removed his fedora, leaned down, and replied,

"Nature has already done that, Mrs. Berg. I never would."

But I had been in practice long enough to hold a different view of our hometown hero: I told Harriet that he was lying. Foreman had a two-step formula for winning that he repeated in every case: the first, common among defense lawyers, was to put the victim on trial, argue that lots of people had a motive to kill him, and besides, the son of a bitch had it coming. The difference with Foreman was that he made most of it up—turned trials into a viciously inhumane assault on the dead man's character. Four years earlier, he'd pulled this off spectacularly in *State of Florida v. Candace Mossler and Melvin Lane Powers*. Powers was Candace's lover (and nephew) and the two of them had been accused of conspiring to murder Candace's husband, Jacques Mossler, a wealthy financier. In his opening statement, Foreman called Jacques a "sexual deviate" with no shortage of people who wanted to kill him:

If each one of the 39 knife wounds had been inflicted by a different person, there still would be many times that number of people left with real or imaginary justification.

Both defendants were acquitted. (Later, when Candace sued Percy for the return of hundreds of thousands of dollars in real estate and jewelry she'd given him as collateral, Foreman testified that he was entitled to every penny and more because "both of them were guilty." Percy won that trial, too.)

Foreman's second step was not just backup: it was bulletproof. In case character assassination alone might fail, he reached into his stable of "reserve witnesses," as he called them: former clients and others who repaid his favors by swearing to have been with his defendant at the time of the crime. It wasn't just opposing prosecutors who knew that Foreman operated this way: his colleagues and even attentive laymen understood that he would do anything, no matter how dishonest, to win a trial.

Perhaps the only person in all of Texas capable of underestimating the ruthlessness of Percy Foreman was Ogden Bass, the thirty-five-year-old, first-term district attorney of Brazoria County, whose job it was to prosecute Harrelson for Alan's murder. By now, Sandra Sue Attaway had agreed to testify against her former lover, in exchange for having her own case dismissed. Bass, having been in office just a little more than two years and lacking serious jury trial experience, assured my father that Sandra Sue's testimony would make quick work of Harrelson, Foreman or no—and said it often enough that

Dad panicked. "He doesn't seem to know the facts and he never asks me anything about Alan," Dad told me one day. I had to hand it to my father. He'd intuited the indispensable rule for trial lawyers, the one I'd learned from Racehorse Haynes: All knowledge is potentially useful in a courtroom, especially about your client. If Bass wanted a conviction, his client would not just be the State of Texas but also my brother.

Dad's personal lawyer, Jim Cowan, the one who had met him and Claude Harrelson at the Avalon, raised a possible solution. Under Texas law, the victim's family can retain a special prosecutor: in our case, a lawyer of Dad's choosing—either to assist Bass or even take over the prosecution entirely—subject to Bass's agreement. Dad phoned F. Lee Bailey, the criminal lawyer famous for freeing Dr. Sam Sheppard (on whose story *The Fugitive* is based), to see if he was available. But Dad hung up, disappointed. "All he talked about was the fee." The same day, Dad met with Haynes, who not only agreed to take the case but also told my cash-strapped father to carpet his one-story office building and they'd be even on fees. I was thrilled when I heard and immediately called Haynes to say that I thought he was the only lawyer alive who could beat Foreman. "I don't know if that's true," Haynes said, "but I do know how Percy thinks, so I've got as good a chance as any. Still, it's going to be tough. He likes *every* advantage."

Haynes had a meeting with Bass set for the following day and he was already strategizing. Months before deciding to cooperate with prosecutors, Sandra Sue had called Haynes and asked him to represent her. She'd told him that one night before he killed Alan, Harrelson "went nuts" and fired his pistol in their apartment, this time lodging a bullet in the wall instead of his leg. "We should get a search warrant," Haynes told me, "and dig it out." Sandra Sue had also told Haynes that Harrelson had tossed his pistol in Galveston Bay. "It's a long shot,"

Haynes admitted, "but maybe we could dredge it, and if we find it, match it to the slug in the wall." Haynes also confirmed Dad's worries. "Ogden can't rely just on Sandra Sue. Percy is going to tear her up—and then you don't have a case. We need another witness or two and more hard evidence to back up her testimony."

When I hung up, I felt more hopeful about a conviction than I'd ever been. But the next day, when Haynes called to report on his meeting with Bass, he sounded disappointed.

"I've got some tough news, brother. Bass don't want me in the case. He said if I'm in it they won't write about him. He wants the press for himself."

"Are you kidding? Is there some way to change his mind?"

"Not any I could think of. I wasted two hours talking to that jack-ass. He thinks the case is open and shut. But nothing is ever open and shut with Percy."

~

At least one of those potential witnesses Haynes said we needed was down in South Texas, preparing to take the stand as the chief wit-ness against Pete Scamardo in the Sam Degelia murder-for-hire case. Jerry Watkins, who had accompanied Harrelson to McAllen when he shot and killed Degelia, had agreed to testify against Scamardo and Harrelson in exchange for immunity from prosecution. As in the case in Brazoria County against Harrelson and DiMaria, Foreman repre-sented the accused murderer *and* the man who was alleged to have hired him—in this case, Pete Scamardo, who did not remain "alleged" for too long. On March 31, 1970, Hidalgo County's veteran DA, Oscar McInnis, obtained a conviction against Scamardo for being an accom-plice to the murder—an astonishing victory for any prosecutor fac-ing Foreman. But Percy Foreman never stayed beaten for long: during the punishment phase, Foreman introduced evidence of Scamardo's otherwise clean record and his devotion to church and family—and convinced the jury to probate every day of his seven-year sentence.

Probation for murder! Thank you, Percy.

Still, despite the sentence, Watkins had survived Foreman's cross-examination and emerged a credible witness whose testimony helped convict Scamardo—which made all the more compelling the need for him to testify against Harrelson in the Angleton case. He had powerful evidence to offer: not only had Harrelson confessed Alan's murder to him but also, as the investigation intensified in October 1968, Harrelson had ordered Watkins to retrieve the shovel he'd used to try to dig Alan's grave from Crawford Booth—and to dispose of it. While it is unclear whether Watkins entered into a formal agreement to testify against Harrelson in the Angleton case, it seems inescapable that he had. Since the two DAs were cooperating, and Sandra Sue had agreed to testify against Harrelson in the Degelia murder case, it is reasonable to conclude that Watkins had agreed to testify against him in Alan's. And, indeed, two weeks after Scamardo's conviction, Bass finally returned to the grand jury for an indictment against DiMaria as an accomplice to murder. Thus it was that at 1 a.m. on the morning of April 15, 1970, a groggy, underwear-clad DiMaria answered the doorbell at his modest home in southwest Houston to find four uninvited guests with their revolvers drawn: the lead Brazoria County investigator, two HPD homicide detectives, and a Department of Public Safety intelligence officer. They arrested DiMaria and trundled him off to Angleton, where bond was set at $60,000 and he was put in a cell at a quarter to four that morning. He stayed there for six days and nights, even though his wife had retained Foreman and given him bail money the day of her husband's arrest—which would seem odd, unless you knew Foreman. He did things at his own pace, on his own terms, and for his own reasons, always.

It is an axiom of criminal law that delay works for defendants.

Witnesses disappear. Evidence is lost. It had been two years since Alan's murder, eighteen months since Harrelson's indictment, and the district attorney responsible for the case did not appear to be doing much. Justice for my brother seemed to be slipping away. And then suddenly there was movement: Jerry Watkins looked set to back up Sandra Sue Attaway's testimony. DiMaria was indicted and in jail. And the judge in Angleton refused any more continuances and set the trial for July 27, just three months away.

During this time, I was busier than ever with my own cases. I had become legal chairman of the ACLU, and on a bright March morning of that year I led some ragtag antiwar protesters whom the City Council had denied a parade permit into federal court and persuaded the judge not only to allow them to march down Main Street but also to compel the city to provide police protection. That afternoon, as I walked past the old Texas Commerce Bank Building, I spotted the bulldog edition of the *Chronicle* and was thrilled to see that my case was the headline story. I looked at my reflection in the bank's darkened window and felt something I had never felt before: singular.

I dropped a quarter into the newspaper dispenser, pulled out a copy, and folded it under my arm so that no one passing within fifteen feet could have missed the headline. Then I headed for the Inns of Court, where lawyers on both sides of the aisle gathered for drinks at the end of the day. Joe Jamail, already famous for large personal injury awards (although still two decades away from winning his record-setting $11.3 billion verdict in *Pennzoil v. Texaco*), was standing at the bar in a khaki suit, blue shirt, and striped rep tie. He was with a group of lawyers watching a television perched above the shelves of liquor. My case led the evening news. I couldn't make out what the lawyers were saying—but I didn't need to. Their outraged faces said it all.

Joe, a former marine, slammed down his glass, silencing the group.

"Let the motherfuckers march, you dumb sons of bitches. It's their right."

No one disagreed with him. I had heard no one ever did.

Joe, whom I'd met just once, saw me inching toward the bartender. "Are you the motherfucker who got that permit?"

I nodded.

"Let me buy you a drink," he said, loud enough for everyone else to hear. "I want to talk to someone with balls, not these dumb motherfuckers." The words resounded throughout the Inns, washing over me like a papal blessing.

A few months after that, when I walked in late to a seminar where Haynes was speaking, he paused to gesture toward me and say, "Congratulations, lawyer Berg!" Then he informed his audience of about a hundred attorneys, "He just won a case in the United States Supreme Court." That triggered applause, which I found flattering and embarrassing, although not so much that I would have raised my hands to stop it.

So I was off to a spectacular start in my practice—yet for every newspaper or TV story about a case I'd won, there were many more about the brother I'd lost. The headlines about Alan were sordid, and embarrassed me. I wanted to be known as the motherfucker who won impossible cases, not as the rookie lawyer whose reckless brother had gotten himself killed. And—I don't know why—the press seemed to be doing all it could to tip the scales in Harrelson's favor. In the *Houston Post* he was described affectionately by denizens of Lucky Pierre's as a "pretty boy" and "big spender." "He was a good tipper," one waitress swooned. "He would always leave the change." Another woman said, "Even if he did kill somebody, I still like him."

# 11

Many courthouses in Texas are arresting, with their creamy limestone exteriors and gilded cupolas, but Angleton's is not one of them. The architecture is awkward and the materials cheap. Every time I walk into it, I imagine it was designed by the county judge's brother-in-law.

Angleton the town was a dismal place, too: an isolated community of rice farmers and ranchers hardened by the sun and cut off from the rest of the country except by what they saw on TV or at the theater in nearby Lake Jackson (where two main streets intersect at the corner of "This Way" and "That Way"). Predictably, when the Harrelson trial starring Percy Foreman finally started up, it was the hottest ticket in town. On day one, the line of people waiting to enter the courtroom snaked all the way down four flights of stairs. When they opened the doors, it was like Black Friday at Wal-Mart. Men and women climbed over the benches for an up-close look at the famous criminal lawyer. "It is an honor to have you in my court, Mr. Foreman," Judge G. P. "Jeep" Hardy said. "Your client must be a wealthy man." "He *was*,"

Foreman replied. The judge and packed gallery, including potential jurors, roared.

Now Bass and Foreman began the trial's critical first step: voir dire, the legal term for jury selection. To recap: a lawyer's main goals in voir dire are (1) to identify the panelists he does *not* want on the jury; (2) to get rid of as many of those as possible; and (3) to prime the remaining candidates to think his way about the case. As for getting a panelist dismissed, this is done by one of two means: (a) by demonstrating that the panelist has "a fixed mind" about some significant aspect of the case, such as a defendant's guilt or innocence, and therefore should be disqualified by the judge "for cause"; or (b) by exercising one of a limited number of peremptory strikes (between three and twelve, in my experience, depending on the gravity of the crime and publicity generated by the case) granted to each side. "Peremptories" allow lawyers to disqualify panelists for any reason—including, in the late sixties, race, gender, religion, and, where applicable, lips the size of a chicken's asshole.

The term "voir dire" is derived from the Latin *verum dicere*, to "say the truth," and in order to encourage potential jurors to be candid in answering the lawyers' questions, judges across the country repeat some version of that definition to panelists daily. Foreman did not need the help. He seemed to have a preternatural gift for getting panelists to say exactly what he wanted, which inevitably created a large number of successful challenges "for cause."

Most of the time, judges bring in thirty to forty panelists, but in this case, anticipating that many would arrive with their minds already made up, Judge Hardy summoned *four hundred* of them— and that still wasn't enough. Foreman was so effective that he "busted the panel," eliminating so many of his unwanted jurors that the judge was forced to summon a hundred more. Each time the judge sent panelists packing at Foreman's request, it spared his having to use one of his precious few "peremptories" and left the remaining panel increasingly pro-defense. Striking a lopsided panel like that is not unlike shooting big game in a zoo, and it showed when, two weeks later, the sides finally selected a jury. All twelve of them were white males, some of them farmers and ranchers, and many of them Christian fundamentalists. As Linda put it, "I doubt any of them had ever met a Jew."

Still, Bass had an advantage, too: the jury came from a pool of voters who had elected him district attorney only eighteen months before. By now, with his hawkish prosecutor's demeanor, he was one of the most respected figures in the county—destined, everyone said, for a higher office, maybe even governor.

The next morning, August 12—Alan's birthday—Judge Hardy swore in the jury and both sides announced "ready." Unexpectedly, Foreman whispered something to Bass and together they approached the bench. After hearing them out, Judge Hardy announced a fifteen-minute recess. The two lawyers then disappeared into the DA's office, along with Bass's aggressive young assistant, J. E. "Buster" Brown, and a fourth participant, Charles Harrelson. That's where they remained for three hours, arguing about a plea deal.

I don't know where the bidding began, but I do know where it hit an impasse: Bass was down to a fifteen-year offer while Alan's killer demanded probation. Given the rules of the Texas Parole Board, with good behavior, Harrelson would serve only a third of his sentence— five years at most. That wasn't much jail time, but there was an obvious advantage for us, too, had Harrelson accepted: almost certainly he would then testify against DiMaria in order to reduce his sentence even further. He'd done something similar at least once before. In 1960, awaiting trial on charges of armed robbery in California, Harrelson had agreed to wear a wire and secretly record his cellmate confessing to whatever crime he was in for. Harrelson got the man to tell all, and, in exchange, the prosecutor arranged for Harrelson to receive a five-year probated sentence for robbing an eighty-year-old doctor at gunpoint, while his cellmate served a lengthy prison sentence. You could be forgiven for assuming that Harrelson would have turned on his own mother, never mind Frank DiMaria, to avoid serving one extra day in the brutal Texas Department of Corrections. On the other hand, if Harrelson were acquitted—and Foreman had not built his reputation on losing—DiMaria's case would automatically be dismissed as well, because the indictment against him relied entirely on his having hired Harrelson to do the job.

Foreman was not afraid to try any case, but he was also content to plead out a client if it meant avoiding the death penalty, which he adamantly opposed. Just a year earlier, he had done this with his famous client James Earl Ray, Dr. King's assassin. At Foreman's urging, Ray copped a plea in exchange for a life sentence instead of death. So, by comparison or any measure, Bass's offer was a great deal for Harrelson and fit tribute to the famous lawyer's reputation. "Take it," Foreman told his client.

Yet, even facing a possible death penalty, Harrelson remained adamant that he wouldn't serve hard time. "I've got Percy Foreman and God on my side," he said. Even Foreman was skeptical. "I've talked to God," he said, "and He told me to tell you to take the offer." But even He failed to change Harrelson's mind.

Bass told Dad where things stood. "Five years in jail for murdering my boy!" Dad said, and the matter was resolved. Bass, certain about his open-and-shut case, rushed back into the courtroom. "No deal," he barked at the assembled reporters. "We're going to trial."

Harrelson sank in his chair. That morning, he'd looked happy and relaxed, but no longer. Now he looked sullen and tense.

With the jury seated, Judge Hardy asked the defendant to please rise, read the indictment aloud, and asked, "Charles Harrelson, to the charge of the murder of Alan Berg, how do you plead?" Without hesitation, Harrelson responded, "Your Honor, I am not guilty!"

"Mr. Bass," the judge continued, "you may open for the state."

At last, the trial was under way.

Despite having tried just a handful of jury cases, I knew how critical this moment was. Jurors are impressed most by what they see and hear first and last—the psychological principle of primacy and recency. But "recency" alone is not enough: if you aren't persuasive from the start, it won't matter much if you finish your closing argument with the revelation of an Eleventh Commandment—it'll be too late. Jurors make up their minds quickly.

This was our family's moment, and Bass's golden opportunity to present my brother as a good and generous man, a husband and father, brother and son, a patriot who had volunteered to serve his country. And to preempt Foreman's predictable assault on his character and to mollify the fundamentalists on that jury—to concede that, yes, Alan Berg was a sinner, like all of us, that he'd let himself down and failed those who loved him most, but nothing in his life, not a single moment, justified a bullet to his brain. This was the crucial message, and now was the exact moment to deliver it.

Bass rose from the prosecution table, faced Judge Hardy, and said, inexplicably, "The state waives opening statement, Your Honor."

By the time Foreman finished his an hour later, he had destroyed whatever of my brother that nature had not.

"Alan Berg," Foreman began, "could have been killed by any one of eleven people who had the means and motive." His opening salvo resonated throughout the courtroom and compelled everyone to listen, much as a great first sentence compels you to continue reading a book. According to Foreman, Alan and Dad had employed "ex-convicts, some of them convicted murderers, as salesmen. Eleven of them complained of being cheated on their commissions during the eight months before Berg's death, and the defense hopes to show that any one of the eleven could have killed him."

His strategy was predictable: turn the spotlight away from Charles Harrelson and focus it on Alan Berg. You can't fault a defense lawyer for that—nor for outlining evidence that he believes in good faith exists. But you *can* fault him for stating things that are patently untrue.

"Alan," Foreman continued, "despite his marriage, fathered an illegitimate child who was born the day he died and . . . both the mother of the child and her husband had reason to kill Berg."

What?

As for the betting: "Alan Berg, the evidence will show, was a compulsive gambler and not just on football." He "fronted for a gambling ship, became a messenger carrying money from Las Vegas to Texas and every point in between, and let it be known he could fix basketball games. . . . Berg bet someone else's money on one of his trips to Las Vegas—making one enemy—and led another gambler to bet $109,000 on a basketball team that lost—making another enemy."

And so on. Foreman plunged ahead, writing his own script on the blank slate that Bass had handed him. When he sat down, he was light-years ahead. There was no denying that many of the basic facts of Alan's life, like his gambling or his business, were enough by themselves to turn those jurors against him and in favor of good ole Chuck, who tipped big and whose people lived up the highway just a ways. What really disgusted me was the shit I felt certain Foreman had made up, like the allegation about the secret child and the trips as a messenger between Houston and Las Vegas. And yet even I wondered: Was there more to my brother than I knew?

Early the next morning, before the jury arrived, Judge Hardy signed an order granting Sandra Sue immunity from prosecution.

Freed from the prospect of jail, she left the courtroom and entered Bass's reception area, where Linda and Harriet happened to be seated. They were startled by her being there, as well as by what she said:

"I know you can't forgive me, but I want you to know how sorry I am that I was part of this and for your loss."

"I thanked her for bringing Alan home," Linda said when she told me about the confrontation. Then she added, with that gullible lilt that always amazes me: "And she sounded sincere."

"*Sincere?*" I said. "Are we supposed to be *grateful*? Fuck her."

I had heard that Sandra Sue was beautiful. The slobbering *Post* reporter described her as "alluring." The *Chronicle* went with "shapely brunette." In my sister's opinion (somewhat redeeming of her earlier comment), "She had a really big mouth and from where I was sitting you could see all the way up her nose, even the septum." At any rate, Sandra Sue walked evenly to the witness chair, took her seat in the box, slipped on her oversized glasses with octagonal frames that matched her brunette hair, and said good morning to the men on the jury. For the remainder of that day and most of the next, she and Bass put on a riveting show, with him guiding her through the events that led up to Alan's murder, beginning with her suggestive phone call to Imperial Carpet. Sandra Sue told the jury about how she had told Alan that he was attractive and about how she had lured him with the promise of a blow job; then she told them about kidnapping Alan outside the Brass Jug and about dumping his body in the marshes on Surfside.

"Do you know who it was who asked for Alan's death?" Bass asked her.

Sandra Sue stared right at Harrelson and said, "Yes, Frank DiMaria." So far, so good.

"How did you know it was DiMaria?"

"Chuck told me from the start. He said DiMaria wanted Chuck to collect a gambling debt. And when he finished dumping Alan's body, he came back carrying his watch. He said he had to have evidence to show DiMaria that he'd done the job."

*Gambling debt?* This was new, and puzzling: within two days of finding Alan's remains, the authorities had ruled out gambling as a motive and said that Alan had been murdered for revenge. Worse, this version of the motive would give Foreman fodder for his cross-examination: Sandra Sue had not mentioned a gambling debt in her written statement—just a debt. Then she added something else to her story: A week after dumping Alan's body, Harrelson had returned to Surfside, so that he could retrieve the blanket in which he'd wrapped it and the bullet he'd shot into his skull. But when he got there, Harrelson had chickened out: "He was scared of snakes," she said.

At that, Harrelson laughed out loud, and the jury turned and glowered at him. This was a good sign for our side: after all, it isn't just testimony from the stand that counts. But I felt too sick to gloat over our sudden advantage. All I could think of was: *My brother's bones were picked clean by sage rattlers.*

The second day, Bass concluded his questioning of Sandra Sue and passed her to Foreman for cross, the single most critical point for a witness in any jury trial. If Sandra Sue were to change her demeanor from cooperative and direct with Bass to hostile and evasive with Foreman, the jury would hate her.

Foreman rose from his chair and launched his defense with an angle everyone else in that courtroom had overlooked.

"Do you still have the engagement ring Charles Harrelson gave you?"

"It was not an engagement ring and it's in my desk drawer where I keep all my junk."

"Then, to you, a wedding ring is junk."

"That wasn't a wedding ring. That was to show I was his woman, not his wife."

Not even Haynes had seen this one coming—and certainly not me. Foreman intended to prove that Sandra Sue and Harrelson had a common-law marriage. If he were successful, then, under Texas law, the jury would be instructed that a husband or wife cannot testify against the other (unless one had committed a crime against the other). If they decided that Sandra Sue Attaway was actually Mrs. Charles Harrelson, they would have to disregard her entire testimony—the linchpin of Bass's case. To accomplish that, Foreman would have to show three things: (1) that they had agreed to marry, (2) that they had held themselves out as husband and wife, and (3) that they had lived together in Texas. The last condition was not in dispute—but Foreman would have to prove the first two elements of the legal definition and, as always, he was prepared. Holding a stack of manila folders, Foreman asked Sandra Sue if it was true that, at Harrelson family reunions, Charles had introduced her as his wife. "Yes, he did, several times," she answered—and then added, "but each time he did I told them I was not his wife." She was off to a good start. Although unprepared for this line of questioning, she stayed calm and was not giving Foreman any easy shots at impeaching her.

Foreman then asked Sandra Sue if she and Dennis Weadock were married. After responding that they were not, Sandra Sue took her answer a step too far. She explained that they were waiting until after the trial because of the common-law-marriage question—and Foreman pounced: "If you don't consider yourself to be Harrelson's wife, why are you and Weadock waiting to get married?" Then he asked her whether she'd consulted an attorney about getting a divorce from Harrelson. Sandra Sue admitted that she had. Finally, he pulled out her application for her waitressing job at the Cork Club. In the blank for "Husband's Name," she'd put "Charles S. Stoughtenborough"—the alias that Harrelson used most often.

So much for a good start.

The next day, Foreman reminded jurors that Sandra Sue had not only participated in Alan's murder but also capitalized on it, sharing the reward with Weadock. She had already testified that they spent the entire $10,000 in a five-month period on "liquor, parties, and gambling," because "it was dirty money and we wanted to get rid of it." At that, Foreman asked another good question, one my family and I had wondered about, too:

"If it was dirty, why did you take it?"

"I was surprised when the deputies gave it to us."

Foreman waved Sandra Sue's statement at her. "*Surprised?* Didn't you state in your sworn statement that you and Weadock discussed the reward before he came to Houston to claim it?"

Sandra Sue was forced to admit she had. Foreman kept plowing.

"Did you consider flushing it down the commode?"

"That's what we were doing at the horse races," she said quietly.

Then she began to cry.

The weekend came and went and Sandra Sue, looking anything but refreshed, got back on the stand and waited for the jury to be brought in. It was then, while the lawyers were huddled around the bench visiting with the judge, that Harrelson first drew his thumb across his neck and mouthed at her, "Fucking cunt." Terrified, she said nothing and struggled to remain calm—but couldn't—and Foreman could tell. When the jury returned, he began by reminding Sandra Sue that she'd told the jury that Harrelson murdered Alan over a gambling debt and then demanded she show him where she'd said "anything like that" in her typed statement—and, of course, it was not there, not specifically. These are moments trial lawyers wait for: his witness undone, desperate to get off the stand, Foreman demanded Sandra Sue tell the jury the truth, that Harrelson never said anything about a gambling debt—or surely something that significant would be in her statement. But instead of simply reverting to what she'd written, she offered a slightly different version: that the $7,000 was a business debt, and that both Alan *and* Dad owed DiMaria the money.

"Do you know who Ananias is, Mrs. Stoutenborough?!!"

Sandra Sue said nothing.

*"Ananias is the biggest liar in the Bible!* He took an oath to God and lied—just like you!"

Then he accused her of "reconsidering and rearranging" her testimony because someone "behind" her had learned that "Frank DiMaria doesn't gamble." He meant Ogden Bass, of course, and his opportunistic claim that DiMaria wasn't a gambler was for the benefit of the fundamentalists on the jury. Foreman seemed destined to tear Sandra Sue's entire testimony into shreds—but then she recovered some of her credibility with a simple and spontaneous explanation for her waffling:

"It didn't matter, Mr. Foreman. It was all a lie anyway. You see, Chuck Harrelson told me different stories at different times. Charles Harrelson told me he was going to collect a gambling debt from Alan Berg. After he was killed, I asked him why he did it and he said it was because Frank DiMaria was cheated by the Bergs on some carpet."

Then Foreman took his final shot, the one he'd been planning all along: he suggested that "Dennis the Menace," as he'd taken to calling Dennis Weadock, knew where Alan's body was because *he* was the one who'd killed him.

Sandra Sue paled. For a moment it seemed to Linda as though she was about to confess that Foreman was right. Instead, she shook her head and turned to face the jury. "*I* told him where we left the boy. I couldn't stand it on my conscience anymore. I was about to have a nervous breakdown."

Finally, Foreman's cross ended: Sandra Sue stepped down.

Being involved in any trial creates enormous anxiety. Your hopes and fears rise and fall with each judge's ruling, each juror's grimace, each prolonged moment of suspense over what's coming next. For those of us who loved Alan, the roller coaster was almost unendurable. That night, the first of several spent seated around Dad and Dot's kitchen table, cigarettes snuffed out in half-empty cups of coffee, we tried to analyze what had happened and to anticipate the next round. I felt a duty to reassure everyone that things were progressing as well as could be expected, but in truth I was very concerned about the common-law-marriage defense, which I was certain had caught Bass by surprise, too. Linda was more optimistic.

"I was watching those jurors. They thought Foreman was too rough on Attaway. And no matter what she said about the debt, no one could make up those details."

The next day, Bass called Dad's investigator, Bob Leonard, to the stand. As soon as he'd sat down, folded his hands, and turned to face the jury, it was clear he'd done this before. Bass interrupted only rarely to ask questions, allowing Leonard to lead the spellbound jurors through his entire involvement in the case, from his initial conversation with my father to the discovery of the murder scene in Fort Bend, meeting with Weadock, and the search for Alan's remains. When he described finding our brother's skull, Linda ran sobbing from the courtroom.

Bass passed Leonard in less than an hour. Foreman began with some over-the-top questioning that underscored his allegations about Weadock being the real killer: "In other words," Foreman said, "he delivered two bodies for $10,000—a body for $5,000 and another body for the prosecution for another $5,000?" Or: $5,000 for Alan's remains and $5,000 for Harrelson's scalp. "That's one way of putting it," Leonard agreed.

Then Foreman asked Leonard if Dad had offered $10,000 to Harrelson to implicate "someone else," and Leonard seemed to know what Foreman was talking about. "I might have heard Nathan Berg say that," he replied. When Foreman asked if he could be more specific, Leonard shocked everyone in the courtroom.

"Berg has made so many wild comments at all times, I just can't recall."

*Berg? Wild comments? This was Dad's investigator?*

Foreman pressed Leonard, who explained that a woman he'd known for several years only as "Diane" turned out to be Harrelson's ex-wife and mother of their three sons, and that he'd told Dad about them. Leonard had contacted Diane and learned that she was planning to visit her ex-husband in the Angleton jail. Upon hearing this, Dad asked Leonard to ask her to pass a message to Harrelson: if he implicated others in the murder, Dad would put $10,000 into a trust fund for his three boys. Leonard said that he passed on the message and never heard back. Obviously, Foreman had.

The inference, of course, was that Dad had paid that same $10,000 to Weadock and Sandra Sue to make up a story implicating Harrelson and thus DiMaria as well.

Then Foreman produced the Houston police missing persons report on Alan. What happened next seemed to leave even Stan Redding, the *Chronicle*'s veteran crime reporter, stunned.

"Leading off with such nice phrases as 'Have you heard?' or 'Isn't it true?,'" Redding wrote, "Foreman elicited from Leonard, *without objection from Bass,* statements made to Houston police officers by Berg's mother, wife and father."

The italics are mine.

As Redding described what happened next:

Leonard testified that he had never talked to the mother, divorced from Nat Berg . . . but admitted he had information, had heard about, or had learned from informants that the mother had stated to police:

That her son was "mentally ill" from constant conflict with his father in business and personal dealings.

That Alan wanted to be a millionaire by age forty and if he had to gamble to do it, he would. He never made it.

That Alan Berg was "insecure" but delighted in his contact with thieves, gamblers, ex-cons, con men, and bunko artists, and made comments to the effect that he "could not be hurt by anyone," as he could have people killed for him.

That Berg, in the recent weeks before his death, had lost $19,100 to Las Vegas gamblers, and had access through his friends to LSD and marijuana and put himself before his wife and children.

Leonard testified that he had heard all of these things and that they were "substantially correct."

By now, there was no question: Leonard had sold us out. I couldn't say why. Maybe he was currying favor from Foreman, who he thought would throw him some business, or maybe Foreman had something on him. Maybe Leonard was terrified of Harrelson. Plenty of people were. But none of this mattered as much as the fact that Bass said nothing when he could have objected that every word my mother said was classic hearsay and would have been inadmissible, even had Leonard spoken to her, which he hadn't, not once. In fact, his testimony was hearsay on hearsay, because Mom's comments had been written down by yet another person Leonard had never spoken to: the policeman who took her statement.

The effect was devastating. By his failure to object, Bass had allowed an even more degenerate version of Alan, straight out of his mother's mouth, to pervade that courtroom. Outraged, I called my mother and told her that her shit-stirring complaints about Alan and Dad had come out at the trial.

"This was not an opportunity to get even with Dad!" I shouted. "Your big mouth is going to cost us this trial!"

"Well, honey, I only told the truth. I always tell the truth."

"And how in God's name can you say that Alan put himself before his wife and family? He supported you! He sent you money he didn't have. Couldn't you keep quiet just out of gratitude?"

"Darling, I had that money coming."

The next day, Leonard's third and final on the stand, began with Foreman asking him to summarize what he'd learned about Alan's character. Again, Bass failed to object while Leonard repeated Dad's statements that my brother was an "academic gypsy" and "a small man with a Napoleonic complex."

Throughout his testimony, Leonard had picked up his investigatory files to refresh his memory. Here was another sign that Foreman had gotten to him. If a witness uses notes that way, before or while on the stand, the witness must turn them over to the opposing counsel—which Leonard did when Foreman demanded them. No witness still in control of his senses and certainly not a seasoned investigator like Leonard would ever bring his notes into a courtroom, especially not when they were filled with potentially game-changing hearsay about his client's son. For the next several hours, Foreman read Leonard's notes aloud, and, after each unfavorable statement about Alan, Leonard confirmed that it had come from Nathan Berg.

By the end of that day, Foreman had provided the *Post* with bullet points as dispiriting as those that had appeared in the *Chronicle*:

Alan Berg "booked" bets for other students while attending San Jacinto High School.

He operated a "floating crap game" on a ship when he was in the Coast Guard.

A "con man" who swindled $150,000 from a Dallas widow was a pal of Berg's when he lived in Dallas.

Berg left Dallas owing $3,500 in worthless checks.

He borrowed money to go to Las Vegas the summer after he left his pregnant wife and had graduated from the University of Houston. He gambled there and ran his borrowed bankroll to $3,500 and later to $9,500.

Berg once lost $3,000 on a University of Houston basketball game. He and another man lost $4,500 betting on another game.

He married a girl named Smith a year after divorcing his first wife. The marriage was annulled after one day.

He and a Las Vegas gambler had a mutual interest in a gambling ship that attempted to operate off the Texas Gulf Coast in 1966.

Berg had a "big fight" with an employee the day he disappeared.

Another employee "came at Berg with a pair of scissors a few weeks before he disappeared."

He had told his father he was in desperate need of money to pay a debt and tried to borrow $7,100 from an uncle three days before he disappeared. He called other relatives and tried to borrow $10,000, telling them it was for a friend.

Some of what Leonard had written and the *Chronicle* published was out-and-out wrong, including that Alan served in the coast guard and had married a thirteen-year-old girl when he was seventeen and divorced her just before receiving his college degree. (It was, I guess, a reference to "Sarah," the woman Alan had divorced after learning she'd had an abortion, but if so the story had been thoroughly garbled.) One other "fact" actually made Dad and me laugh, despite ourselves. That was that, after leaving the navy, Alan had been a short-order cook. Alan could do a lot of things, like juggle three pairs of socks, twirl a glass of Coke around without spilling a drop, and fart when his son pulled his finger. Cooking was not one of them.

If it was in Leonard's notes that my brother served a two-year tour of duty in the navy and received an honorable discharge, it was never mentioned. Nor did the jury learn that the "academic gypsy" had worked hard and been accepted to medical school, even if he did not attend.

A day later, Foreman finally passed Leonard to Bass for redirect— and the prosecutor very nearly blew the case wide open. Prior to trial, the judge had granted Foreman's motion to preclude any mention of Claude Harrelson's involvement in the case, but Foreman's questioning about the notes had opened that door—a huge mistake. This time— high time—it was Bass who did the attacking. Pointing to an entry in Leonard's notes, Bass asked Leonard whether he and Foreman had neglected to mention a name that appeared there. Leonard said yes. Bass paused and in that moment, there was a gripping silence.

"Read that name."

"Harrelson."

"You wrote that name?"

"Yes, sir."

"Now read what's right under it."

Leonard began reading in such a quiet monotone that Bass snapped, "Read it loud enough so that last juror over there can hear you."

Leonard did. " 'The tip on the body: has a two-color, gold wrist-watch.' "

"Whose body?"

"Alan Berg's."

"Whose watch?"

"Alan Berg's."

"And who did that tip come from?"

"Claude Harrelson."

"And who is he to the defendant, Charles Harrelson?"

"My understanding is that they are brothers."

"Your *understanding*?"

"They are brothers," Leonard conceded.

At last. Given Foreman's blunder, Bass was now free to expose all he could about Claude, the investigator who'd "solved" Alan's murder within three days of being retained by my father and then, for enough money, was willing to disclose the whereabouts of the body—oh, yes: *and* who happened to be the accused killer's brother. Naturally, the next thing to do was to tie that information into the trial, and all that would require was a short series of pointed questions: "Isn't it true, Mr. Leonard, that during your own investigation, Mr. Berg told you—it's right there in your notes—that Claude Harrelson informed him that his son had been murdered?" And then: "That upon being paid three thousand dollars, he'd tell him where Alan was buried?" And after that—before Foreman could shout his objection: "Now, Mr. Leonard, where on earth do you suppose Charles Harrelson's brother got *that* information?" But Bass didn't ask anything like that. Nor did he recall Sandra Sue to the stand, this time to good purpose: to offer testimony directly from her statement about the scheme that the Harrelson brothers and Watkins had cooked up to extort the reward from my father. *Nor* did he call in Watkins, who would have confirmed the scheme and that Harrelson confessed to him that he'd murdered Alan. Instead—presumably still convinced the case was "open and shut"— Bass dropped the matter of Claude Harrelson altogether. And by the time Leonard stepped down from the witness stand, Foreman had demonized my brother beyond recognition. If it was a disadvantage in that courtroom that the murder victim had been Jewish, then it was even worse that his own parents had such terrible things to say about their son. One or two jurors, whenever they caught Harrelson's attention, were even smiling in his direction.

By the afternoon of August 19, after nearly seven days of testimony and only two witnesses, Bass asked for an early adjournment to "reorder his witnesses." He must have hoped that everyone would take this to mean "Maybe we can speed this up," but what I took it to mean was "I better get my shit together."

The next morning, Bass recalled Sandra Sue, to elaborate on her earlier testimony that Harrelson had shown her $1,500 cash and told her that it came from DiMaria—and that Harrelson had blown it all in less than seven days. This, of course, was crucial information that Bass had neglected to elicit while Sandra Sue was on the stand before, and her return needlessly gave Foreman another shot at her on cross.

But when Bass passed Sandra Sue, Foreman asked some lame questions about the discrepancy between the $2,000 she testified that Harrelson said he was going to be paid and the $1,500 she said he received. Then he committed a serious rookie mistake: he asked an open-ended question when he had no idea how Sandra Sue was going to respond. Referring to a $50 check that Harrelson's sister had sent him ten days after the alleged murder, Foreman asked Sandra Sue, angrily:

"Does it make any sense at all that a man who'd received $1,500 in cash only a week and a half earlier could need an additional $50 so badly—could have spent it all that fast?"

Sandra Sue calmly hit it out of the park:

"It made sense to me, Mr. Foreman. I watched him gamble away some and drink up the rest."

Finally, after three days on the stand, she stepped down for good.

The next day, a picture in the *Post* showed a much relieved Sandra Sue and Dennis Weadock leaving the courthouse for a flight to California, where both would be on call. Weadock, Bass had said, was not going to testify.

Bass called eleven more witnesses before resting his case. The first was Fort Bend deputy sheriff Roy Schmidt, the officer who'd been looking for car strippers back on May 29 and stumbled upon a possible murder scene. He said that he found "blood and drag marks and a partial excavation," which was consistent with Sandra Sue's testimony about what had happened there.

Deputy Sheriff Schmidt was followed by Edgar Chesshire, then a former Fort Bend deputy, who testified that he'd met Schmidt at the location that morning and removed a blood sample from a cow track— which a chemist testified came from a human. Then Harris County's medical examiner testified that Alan died of a gunshot wound to the head and that he could not resolve the issue of strangulation because Alan's hyoid bone was missing from his throat.

None of this was particularly helpful in incriminating Harrelson because it did not tie him to the murder scene. That was supposed to come next. But for pure unreconstructed nitwittery, nothing topped the testimony of the state's chemist. Just before he took the stand, Crawford "Big Man" Booth testified that he'd loaned a Sharpshooter-brand shovel to Harrelson about a week before Harrelson returned it on May 29, the day after Alan disappeared. The chemist then testified that he'd "eyeballed" dirt samples from the shovel and from the scene in Fort Bend and found that they matched. "Do you agree with me," Foreman then asked, "that you would probably find the identical samples of ashes and leaves and dirt on the shovel with the same colors in all 254 counties in Texas?" And when the chemist answered "Yes," there was very little physical evidence tying Charles Harrelson to the crime scene.

Ex-con Rudolph "Jabo" Jones, Bass's next witness, testified that his friend Charles Harrelson offered him $20 to clean out some "blood and stuff" from the trunk of his car on May 29. Jabo explained that he hadn't repeated what Harrelson said to anyone until after Alan's remains were found and he "began to piece things together." On cross, Foreman demanded to know how Jabo could possibly remember the precise date of their so-called conversation after remaining silent about it for more than six months. Jabo had a good answer: he remembered because he was worried about getting off work the next day, which was Memorial Day. Undaunted, Foreman offered a different reason—the motive for this monstrous lie. He accused *Jabo* of teaming up with Weadock and another man to murder Alan.

That night, Dad said to me: "If the bailiff takes the stand, he'll be the murderer, too."

On Friday, August 28, Bass rested the state's case. He'd put on a total of thirteen witnesses in thirteen trial days—but not one of them the victim's widow. That was incredible to me. Harriet would not have had much to say, but at least would have let the jurors see that Alan had a wife who loved him and had left three young fatherless children at home. What juror could be unmoved by that?

$\sim$

The following Monday, Foreman called the first defense witness, a former customer of Imperial, who testified that on May 28, 1968, he called to complain about a carpet he'd purchased. He said that he and Alan got into a screaming match over the phone and Alan "started talking about shooting me." But on cross, Bass forced him to admit that he'd actually "exchanged threats" with Alan—as Foreman himself had said in his opening statement. And while the witness could remember almost verbatim what my brother had said to him ("Any more threats and I'll put a hole in your head"), he couldn't remember a single word of his own. That's a tall order for a jury: to accept testimony from a man with a self-serving memory. By the time he stepped down, Bass left the unhappy customer looking like he had been exaggerating or even making the whole story up.

Foreman's second witness was one of Dad's earlier private investigators, who didn't make much of an impression either. But the third one did: she was a nurse's aide named Ruby Jean, who was so incredibly stupid that Foreman repeatedly demanded that she tell the story the way she had "coming down here in my car this morning." Inviting some doubt about her actual vocation, Ruby Jean stated that she was "enticed" by two men into a car late on the evening of May 28 and saw, in the backseat, a bloodied, unconscious man whose description matched Alan's. Foreman then showed her two glossy black-and-white photographs for her to identify—the very men, he announced, "Who murdered Alan Berg." But when he showed her "Jabo" Jones's photograph, Ruby Jean demurred: "I wouldn't swear to it," she said. Then Foreman shoved Dennis Weadock's picture inches from her face, and this time she didn't respond directly, just shook her head no and testified, "I tole you, Mr. Foreman, they was a Frenchman and a white." From the look on Foreman's face, that was not at all what she'd said in the car on the way down that morning. When Ogden got his turn, he asked the witness where she'd gotten the brand-new nurse's uniform she was wearing. "Mr. Foreman," she replied. Everyone but the defense team laughed, and Bass threw up his hands and let her go.

Burned by Ruby Jean, Foreman returned to his common-law-marriage defense. To bolster it, he put on twelve witnesses, including a very impressive couple: an assistant US attorney and his wife who testified that while living in Houston they had met and befriended another couple they knew as Charles and Suzanne Stoutenborough, Harrelson's now familiar alias. Then Foreman put on numerous members of the Harrelson clan who testified about family reunions where Charles introduced Sandra Sue as his wife—although one of the cousins backfired, admitting under cross that at least twice Sandra Sue had corrected Charles to insist that she was his girlfriend and not his wife.

Nonetheless content with this line of inquiry, Foreman moved on to forensics. He called another state chemist, the one who'd inspected Harrelson's convertible after his arrest but had found no hair or blood anywhere in it, not even the trunk. However, he did find carpet fibers "identical" to those found at the scene in Fort Bend, which also were identical to those sold by Imperial Carpet. On that point, Foreman got him to admit that the material was the same as that found in many GM cars—but, the chemist insisted, "not the color." Unwittingly, Foreman had elicited the most persuasive physical evidence thus far that Alan's body had been in Harrelson's car, thereby reminding the jurors why they were in that courtroom.

Then Foreman called Nathan Berg to the stand.

It was late in the afternoon on Thursday, September 4. As always, Dad was dressed well, but his auburn hair had recently gone gray and his cobalt-blue eyes sank into the black circles under them. Still, he did well during his initial exchanges with Foreman—although that was like someone hitting the daily double the first time he visits the track and wondering why he hadn't come sooner.

Foreman held Bob Leonard's notebook—the weapon he would use against my father—and should never have obtained.

"Was it in Dallas that your son associated with a confidence man who bilked a widow out of a hundred and fifty thousand dollars?"

Dad scowled. "Would you like to rephrase that question, Mr. Foreman?"

"Just answer the question."

"My son was butchered once. I don't think it's necessary to assassinate him a second time."

"I'm only using your words that you gave to the Houston Police Department, and you're the one who assassinated your son's character. Didn't you make that exact remark to Houston police?"

Dad acknowledged that he had but added, "Read further in those notes. I told Leonard that Alan didn't know that the man was a confidence man until a year after he met him." Then Dad looked squarely at Foreman. "Any more questions?"

Foreman continued to torture Dad with his own words, forcing him to admit one by one the disparaging things he'd said about Alan to Leonard. Dad insisted that he'd been misquoted on some items, but he had to acknowledge that a lot of what the investigator had written down was accurate. Then, uncharacteristically, Dad put aside his ego and his anger and answered from his heart, one father speaking to all the others in that courtroom: "Mr. Foreman, you try to tell them everything that might explain Al's disappearance and help find my boy." With that, Dad reached into his back pocket, retrieved a handkerchief, and wept.

Judge Hardy looked at my father for a moment and then announced that the trial would shut down for the day.

The next morning, the *Post* reported favorably about Dad's testimony: "Berg, of 3310 Durness Way, spoke in explicit, restrained tones and appeared to be angered by only one question by defense attorney Percy Foreman." I was proud of Dad; he'd mostly kept calm and emerged well and I had not expected that. I called before he left for the courthouse and told him that I thought he'd held his own and that as long as he kept calm, he'd be fine. But the article had emboldened Dad, who ignored my advice and decided to "get" Foreman: to take every opportunity to remind the jury that Alan was "an angel" or "the best sales manager in the nation, bar none" or some such accolade designed to resurrect his boy for the jury.

Foreman was ready for him.

"Do you have judgments against you for debts you have failed to pay?"

Embarrassed, Dad lied.

"I do not."

"Let me show you this document. Do you recognize it?"

"I do."

"It is a judgment, is it not, signed on April 22, 1964, by Judge Ben Moorhead, of the 11th Judicial District Court of Harris County, Texas, for $7,584.51 for ads you ran in the *Houston Chronicle*?"

"That's a business debt, not mine personally."

"Who owns the business?"

"I do."

"You guaranteed the payment, didn't you?"

"Yes."

"That's why the judgment is against the business *and* you personally, is it not?"

"I thought that had been taken care of."

With that, Foreman pulled out several judgments and mechanics' liens, money Dad owed for various carpet and upholstery-related purchases and services. Dad resisted every last claim, arguing over the justness of the debt and blustering to explain why it hadn't been paid.

Then Foreman asked Dad about the balance on his $50,000 small-business loan and established that he had paid it off with the proceeds of the "key man" policy on Alan's life. Foreman ended this line of questioning with a smug smile and a long pause, giving the jurors plenty of time for the implication to sink in.

During a break, Bass tried to calm Dad down and encourage him to be more cooperative. By now, however, neither man respected the other. Ever since Harrelson's indictment, Dad had driven Bass crazy with frequently angry phone calls about what was and wasn't being done. Relations between them had degenerated so badly that Dad instinctively refused Bass's advice to cool it—leading Bass to scream so loudly at him that he could be heard at the other end of the hall.

The upshot was three full days of ludicrous testimony, with Dad glaring at Harrelson, lying to no end, and being beaten into admissions that inspired newly humiliating headlines, each of them true. Foreman asked, "Didn't the two of you have violent quarrels, hang up on the phone, scream at each other, throw things at each other, and make threats?" Dad admitted the arguments but denied any violence and countered, "He always came to me for a shoulder to cry on."

"Berg Says He Quarreled Often with Son, Alan," read one headline. Another, far more damaging, reported: "Employee Threat to Kill Son Told by Berg."

Dad testified that he was not present when the threat was made. Again, a hearsay objection would have put an end to his answer, but Bass remained silent as a sphinx. (I was beginning to wonder whether he even knew the rule.) Then Dad repeated what he'd been told by yet another employee. "He threatened to kill Alan. He threw a carpet sample completely across the room when Alan told him he was fired."

When Foreman asked Dad if he knew that his son had replied to the threat by saying "I'll put a bullet in your head," Dad snapped, "That would have been the most unusual thing Al said in his entire thirty years. I would take my oath that Al never said that to anyone. Al was not a violent man. In fact, what he did was say that boy was troubled. He offered to get him some help."

But it didn't matter. For Foreman, getting Dad to admit that someone other than Harrelson or DiMaria had reason to kill Alan and had even threatened to do so was more than enough. The shame of it was that not one word was admissible evidence.

As devastating as that headline had been, the next one was even worse:

## Recording Links Berg Death to Gambling Debt

As promised during his opening statement, Foreman offered evidence of his claim that Alan had been murdered because of his gambling. The article stated that

> Alan Berg was killed by "out-of-town" mobsters to make an example of him for not paying a $109,000 gambling debt, according to the transcript of a tape recording introduced Thursday.
>
> The recorded conversation was between Mrs. Jenna Coy Huddleston, a Houston nightclub singer, and . . . a former employee of Imperial Carpet.

There was only one way Foreman got that tape of Huddleston: from Leonard, who'd gotten it from Dad, and it was admissible because Dad listened in on the call. It was also disastrous. Foreman proved that Jenna Coy Huddleston, the nightclub singer who'd said she'd heard that Alan had gone on "a long trip" and wasn't coming back, damning by itself, was in fact Jenna Coy *Weadock*: Dennis Weadock's ex-wife. This left everyone, including the Berg family, stunned and wondering whether the man Foreman had coined "Dennis the Menace" was more involved than we'd thought. Even if he wasn't—even if his ex-wife's cameo was mere coincidence and her motive simply to try to con Dad out of the reward—in that moment, the mere idea only supported Foreman's case.

By the time Dad stepped down from the stand three days later, my family's secrets lay smeared across the newspapers like a gutted fish. Even worse, Foreman's cross-examination—most of it right out of Leonard's raw notes—had killed us. I was certain that we were going to lose, that nothing could be more powerful than a victim's own father offering evidence of others who might have killed his son.

Still, even sharply lopsided trials can shift suddenly, especially if the lead lawyer makes a significant mistake, as Foreman did again when he needlessly called his next witness: Jim Cowan, Dad's private attorney. He wanted to know "everything" Cowan knew about the investigation and, by asking the question so broadly, opened the door to the state's best day.

Ironically, just the day before, Dad had gotten in trouble with the judge when Foreman asked him if it was true that an ex-employee had told him that Alan's body had been pushed through a meat grinder. Dad blurted out the testimony about Claude Harrelson that Bass should have elicited from Leonard when he had the chance: "Yes, sir. But Mr. Harrelson's brother also told me I could buy a body for three thousand dollars." Foreman leaped up and demanded a mistrial, arguing that Dad had violated the judge's prior ruling prohibiting any mention of Claude's involvement. The judge—veins bulging in his neck—excused the jury and denied the motion, citing Foreman's own questions of Leonard, which had made Claude fair game. But he also loudly admonished Dad to answer only the questions asked and not to volunteer anything else. Dad apologized and said he hadn't meant to do something that wasn't permitted. Then the judge brought the jury back in and told them that Dad's comments had been stricken from the record and that they were not to consider them for any purpose.

Still, that sort of testimony, which we call the "skunk in the jury box," doesn't just disappear. The jury's interest had been piqued about Claude Harrelson—and when Foreman passed Cowan to Bass, the prosecutor soon had the jurors leaning forward in their seats, eager to hear whether Dad's personal attorney had anything to say about the Harrelson brothers "coincidence." And Cowan—who had the kind of earnest good looks both women and men appreciate and trust—was leaning toward the jury in return. Indeed, he had plenty to say.

First Bass asked Cowan to describe his initial meeting with Dad, which was in June 1968.

"As a result of that conversation with Mr. Berg, did you have conversations with Claude Harrelson, the defendant's brother?"

"Yes."

"And did Mr. Berg later give you a $3,000 check, payable to you, and ask you to give it to Claude Harrelson if, in your judgment, it became necessary?"

"That is correct."

"And when would it become necessary?"

"Objection!" shouted Foreman. But the judge overruled him—and the next day the *Chronicle* trumpeted the damage Foreman had done to his own case:

"Witness Bares $3,000 Offer to Find Berg's Body," read the headline. Then, in the very first paragraph, the reporter summarized Cowan's testimony in a single sentence that vindicated Dad:

> Claude Harrelson, brother of Charles V. Harrelson, accused killer of Alan Berg, offered to locate Berg's body if Berg's father would pay him $3,000, a witness tacitly testified today.

*Tacitly?* The reporter had it dead wrong—the testimony was clear and damaging—and finally, Harrelson's case was in real trouble. It was at last beginning to look as though he might be convicted. Foreman must have thought so, too, because now he *really* started living up to his reputation.

He called Harriet to the stand. Seated within a few feet of the man who had murdered her husband, she became terrified, and froze—which made her look almost indifferent. Wisely, Foreman avoided stirring her up and questioned her gingerly, lest he create sympathy among the jurors. In fact, Foreman told Harriet that he was sorry for what she'd gone through. Harriet thanked him curtly and then acknowledged in response to one of the questions that Alan had lost $7,500 on the UH basketball game and had to repay "the gangster Ted Lewin" (Foreman's words) at a rate of $1,000 a week. So he had established yet another person with a motive to kill Alan. That was all he wanted from Harriet, and he passed her to Bass.

Bass picked up Alan's weather-worn billfold—everything in it discolored and wrinkled from long months under water in the ditch where his remains were found. Going through its contents with Harriet so that she could identify the wallet as her husband's, Bass removed a still recognizable color photograph of Alan, Harriet, and the kids playing on the beach in Galveston, evidence he intended to offset Foreman's portrait of Alan as a carouser. Even better for the prosecution, when Bass handed her the photo, Harriet finally broke down crying. While she gathered herself, Bass, as the rules require, handed the wallet to Foreman to allow him to inspect it and lodge any objection he might have to its admissibility. Then he turned back to Harriet.

At this point, Bass's assistant Buster Brown saw Foreman palm the family photo and *slide it into his coat pocket*. Astonished, Brown whispered to Bass what he'd seen. But Bass didn't believe him. "Percy wouldn't do that," he insisted. Later, when Harriet had finished her testimony and the judge broke for lunch, Linda told Bass that she'd seen the same thing—and Bass *still* refused to believe it. "Percy wouldn't do that!" he snapped again. "That's illegal."

Frustrated, Brown ran from the courtroom and called Harriet, who was already at home in Houston, to ask if she had a copy of the photo. She did but protested it wouldn't look anything like the faded one she'd identified that morning from the stand. Still, at Brown's insistence, Harriet raced back to the courthouse with the photo and Brown slipped it back into the wallet before lunch was over. After the break, when Bass formally offered several pieces of previously identified evidence into the record, including the billfold, Foreman announced that he had no objection. But Brown cautioned Foreman that he "ought to take another look through the wallet." Foreman followed his suggestion, found the picture, grinned at the young prosecutor—and announced again that he had no objection.

The next morning, Bass, finally convinced, requested an in-chambers conference, where he told the judge, "I have reason to believe from a very reliable source that a member of the defense team—to wit, Mr. Foreman—took a picture out of the wallet."

Foreman slammed his fist down on Judge Hardy's desk. "*No! No! No!* That's a damnable lie! I'd never do such a thing!"

But Bass refused to proceed until the matter was resolved and said that he was prepared to put people under oath. He even had a witness, he said (although he would not name names for reasons of "safety"), who'd seen Foreman tear something up in the bathroom.

"You've already got another picture!" Foreman barked. "Leave it in! I don't give a damn."

Judge Hardy leaned back in his chair, thought for a moment, sprung back, and told everyone to return to the courtroom. There he announced to the jury that a picture of Alan and his family had "inadvertently" been left out of the wallet, and that another one had been substituted.

*Inadvertently?* Whose side was *he* on?

For weeks, Bass had heard rumors that county judge J. V. Price and his brother, Leon, of Trinity, Texas—longtime friends and business associates of Charles Harrelson's father, Voyde—were coming to testify. About what, no one knew. Wiley Thomas, the Angleton lawyer who provided that tip, had been raised in deep East Texas, in

Groveton, close to the Harrelson and Price homesteads, and he knew and feared both their clans. When Bass asked Thomas to return to his hometown to ferret out whatever he could about the Prices' testimony, Thomas refused to go unless Bass assigned two armed deputies to accompany him. Bass agreed, and Thomas spent a week with the deputies at his side, trying to flush out what the Price brothers were up to, but returned empty-handed.

On Friday, September 11, Bass found out. One after another, Voyde Harrelson and the Price brothers took the stand, and in combination supplied an alibi for Charles, putting him in Trinity at sundown on May 28, a hundred miles from Houston, at the precise time and day when Alan was abducted.

Harrelson's father testified that just after dark that evening, his son and Leon Price had pulled into his ranch outside Lovelady and loaded a horse into a trailer. The horse was a sorrel with "four white socks" that Charles had sold to Price. Then Leon Price testified that he was indeed a "rancher and horse trader" and that he'd been horse-trading with Charles Harrelson on May 28 about "good dusk dark." (During Sandra Sue's testimony, Foreman had her repeat half a dozen times that she and Harrelson abducted Alan "around dusk.") Leon also explained that he'd tried to buy the horse once before but that Chuck had turned down a price of $600. This time, however, "Harrelson told me he had quit his job. He give me a pretty good hard-luck story. I saw that I had him." Leon claimed that he'd bought the horse for $400, and then he produced a bill of sale dated May 28, 1968.

"When did you first retrieve that bill of sale?" asked Bass.

"Someone from Mr. Foreman's office called me and asked me to look for it. Took me three days to find it."

"And when was that?"

"December 1968."

"Eighteen months ago?"

"Yes, sir."

"And you and Mr. Foreman knew about it? What about Voyde Harrelson?"

"Yes. He knew, too."

"So the three of you sat on this thing for eighteen months while Voyde Harrelson's son sat in jail accused of murder?"

"I didn't want to get involved."

"So you decided to get involved on the last day of the trial?"

Bass made his point well, but he couldn't make the bill of sale go away. And when Foreman called J. V. Price to the stand, his powerful position as Trinity County judge lent the alibi the heft and credibility of his office. What was more, Judge Price was wearing a sport coat, tight jeans, and a bolo tie, an outfit that in courtrooms in other states would have been clownish, but in this case was strategic: the prominent judge was one of them, right down to his boots.

Price verified that he had notarized the bill of sale, including the date and time, which he had penciled in as 8:15 p.m. In fact, the *entire* bill of sale was written in pencil, which meant, unlike documents in ink, that it couldn't be dated by any scientific testing—and could have been forged the night before the trial. Under Bass's questioning, Judge Price admitted that he had failed to enter the bill of sale into the log he was legally required to keep of every document he notarized. Bass also asked all three witnesses where the horse was now, or at any time since the "sale," and none of them seemed to know, not even the "buyer." Of course, Foreman had anticipated the problem of the ghost sorrel: his next witness, Rex Cauble, owner of the world champion cutting horse Cutter Bill, raved about the horse with four white socks—although he, too, could not say exactly where it was now. Still, when Cauble stepped down, the essence of the alibi remained intact.

Four weeks and six days after Sandra Sue first took the stand, Foreman rested his case. Over the weekend before the trial ended, Bass subpoenaed Harrelson's telephone records, introduced them as rebuttal evidence, but left the explanation of their significance to closing arguments and rested the state's case. There had been fifty-five witnesses in all, including forty-two for the defense.

Before closing arguments came the charge conference, which is when lawyers from each side submit instructions on the law that they want the jury to hear. Foreman prevailed on the two points that mattered to him most: if the jury believed that there was a common-law marriage, then according to Judge Hardy's instruction they were obliged to disregard Sandra Sue's testimony altogether, which would leave insufficient evidence to convict. And if the jurors believed that Harrelson was trading horses in Trinity at the time Alan was kidnapped in Houston, they were obligated to acquit. Judge Hardy did the right thing: with significant evidence of common-law marriage *and* an alibi, an appellate court would reverse a conviction if he had failed to instruct the jury on either issue.

And if the alibi were perjured? That was up to the jury to decide.

When Judge Hardy finished reading the charges, closing arguments began.

The universal protocol of closing arguments allows the state to go first and last, separated by the defense argument in between. Buster Brown opened for the state, recapping Sandra Sue's testimony and arguing that she had "bared her soul." He implored the jury to "look beyond her testimony and then look at the other evidence brought into this case by other witnesses. You gentlemen know that she did not tell anything but the truth regarding this act." Brown pointed out that Harrelson's phone records showed that the last call from his number on May 28, the day Alan disappeared, ended at 6:45 p.m., and was placed to Pete Scamardo, the man the jury knew as Harrelson's friend. If the jurors believed the caller was Harrelson, they could not also believe that Harrelson then drove one hundred miles to Trinity, negotiated the horse trade, and had the bill of sale notarized by 8:15, the time stamped on it by Judge Price. With that, Brown sat down and left the rest for Bass.

Now it was time for the defense, beginning with Foreman's local counsel, who spoke for the next hour and a half. Surprisingly, the youngest of them all, Sam Lee (brought into the case by his father, Sam Lee Sr.), made the most powerful argument of all and did it in just ten minutes. "The prosecution," Lee said, "does not have as strong a case against Harrelson as Mr. Foreman does against Weadock." Then he held up a piece of the suit that Alan had been wearing when he died and that was now tattered and discolored. In his other hand, Lee held up the quilt that Leonard had found with Alan's body, which had retained its bright colors. "I submit that this quilt was not even present the same length of time."

Lee argued that the quilt was thrown there by someone else so that Alan's body could be found and the reward collected—and that that someone else was Dennis Weadock. After all, Sandra Sue Attaway had testified that she hadn't seen where Harrelson threw the quilt, yet Weadock knew exactly where it was: hanging off a low bush near Alan's body. "If all Weadock knew was what he was told by Attaway," Lee said, "how did he know something she didn't?"

Then it was Foreman's turn. This was the reason Angleton's shops had been shut down and farms and ranches had been left untended.

Foreman spoke for four hours and twenty-seven minutes, breaking when court adjourned for the night and continuing the next day through a brief recess and lunch. He was at his Chautauqua circuit best.

"Chuck had high hopes for Sandra Sue," he began. "But she turned out to be a slitch—a combination of a 'bitch and a slut.'" The jurors chuckled with him. Then, for the greater part of three hours, Foreman pounded home the common-law-marriage defense, knowing perfectly well that if his client had a *bona fide* Get Out of Jail Free card, this was it. By the time he was through, the only thing he hadn't done was play Mendelssohn's "Wedding March." "Once you agree that they were married," Foreman reminded them, "you must acquit Charles Harrelson. The state's case collapses like a balloon."

Then Foreman took aim at Sandra Sue's motive "for lying." "I say that the evidence of Sandra Sue Attaway was bought, paid for, and purchased before she ever testified in this court. It was bought by Nat Berg's $10,000." Not only Dad but also Ogden Bass had bought her testimony—giving Sandra Sue her freedom in exchange for lying about Charles Harrelson. The case, he said, was "a legal assassination."

Waving the state's subpoena for Dennis Weadock in the air, Foreman asked why Bass hadn't put him on the stand. Good question. Then he proffered his own answer. "I'll tell you why. Ogden Bass was astute in not putting Dennis Weadock on the stand. Because Weadock would have had to have called Sandra Sue Attaway on fifty different lies or admit he had signed fifty different lies himself." Foreman accused "Dennis the Menace" Weadock once more of being in on the murder with Jabo: "I believe the killing occurred in a motel room in Houston."

Picking up Harrelson's phone records, Foreman said that they obviously weren't that important, since the prosecution hadn't bothered to subpoena them until the end of the trial. I couldn't have agreed more: whether they ultimately proved valuable or not, those records should have been subpoenaed the day Bass opened his file in November 1968. Then Foreman pointed out what everyone had to have been thinking: the only thing those records proved was that Harrelson had a phone in his apartment.

After recapping my father's dubious testimony, Foreman triumphantly added one more suspect to the list of people who had reason to kill Alan: his own father. The motivation? An insurance payment.

"After all, he had this fifty-thousand-dollar debt hanging over him and there was one certain way to get it paid off: Alan's death." At that, Dad sagged against Dot and quietly wept.

During his entire argument, for reasons known only to Foreman, he failed to mention the alibi witnesses, except in passing to call the county judge "an honorable man."

Foreman was sixty-eight years old. He told the jury—as he had told many jurors before, and would tell others—that this would be his last trial, that it would "soon be a half century since I began coming to Brazoria County. I began trying cases in the old courthouse here and it is proper that one of the last long cases I shall probably ever try is in this courthouse." In other words, *Dear jurors, I am but a humble old trial lawyer who may never pass your way again. Just give me one last victory before I die.*

At 3:08 p.m. Foreman urged the jurors to return the only verdict "imaginable": "Not guilty."

At which point Bass stood up and, according to the docket sheet, argued for fifty-nine minutes.

Relative brevity was not the problem. I knew firsthand from my Supreme Court rebuttal, which lasted less than three minutes, that sometimes short and sweet is best. Foreman's youngest cocounsel, Sam Lee, had also demonstrated that. But if you're going to be brief, you'd better have the goods.

Instead, Bass walked to the jury box, turned to the *defense* table, and asked, "Is it hot in here, or is it me?" Then he anxiously loosened his tie, marshaled his remaining energy, and finally spoke: "If the state has any case at all, it can't be here in argument. It has to be from the witness stand."

Bass argued that the alibi didn't make sense: that Harrelson's own father, Foreman, and the Price brothers had waited two years to come forward with their story, when, if they were telling the truth, they could have cleared Harrelson long ago. He also reminded the jury that the bill of sale had been written in pencil and therefore conveniently was undatable—and that it was not credible that a county judge would fail to log this document as legally required, as he admitted he'd always done.

Finally, Bass turned to the telephone records and, after repeating the argument that Harrelson could not have made it to Trinity by "good dusk dark" if he'd been on the call to Scamardo, made a far more compelling point: that in the month following Alan's murder several calls from Harrelson's phone had been made to Frank DiMaria. While this didn't prove the essential elements of the case, it did make clear that Sandra Sue wasn't lying when she testified that Harrelson knew DiMaria, the man Harrelson told her had paid him to kill Alan.

And then Bass was done, having made no mention of Claude, just a plea to the jury for a verdict of guilty.

On paper, Bass's argument might appear fairly strong—especially about the alibi—but in person he was pitiful. Afterward, Dot told me that she'd turned to the woman seated next to her and said, " 'He sounds so stupid I'd like to turn him upside down and shake some sense out of him.' The lady knew him and she still agreed."

At four-thirty that afternoon, the jury retired and deliberated until six. Then, sequestered for the night, they were sent to the Tarpon Inn Motel on Highway 322, but not before Judge Hardy assured some anxious jurors, "There will be no deliberations this weekend. Saturday is the first day of duck-hunting season." Foreman didn't show up the next morning, bedridden with a bad back. The jury resumed deliberations at 8:12 a.m. and, less than three hours later, at 10:55, the buzzer announcing a verdict sounded and the lawyers and Harrelson were summoned back into the courtroom.

The jurors filed into the box and the judge asked the questions ritually asked in courtrooms every day in this country since its birth:

"Have you reached a verdict, Mr. Foreman?"

The foreman, one G. L. Pousson, answered:

"We have, Your Honor."

"Will the defendant please stand?"

Everyone at Harrelson's counsel table stood. The Lees put their arms around their client.

"Read the verdict, Mr. Foreman."

"We find the defendant not guilty."

# 12

Hell, if I had been on that jury, *I* would have acquitted Harrelson, too.

I'd have had to, even if I thought his sorrel-trading "alibi" was horseshit and that Harrelson really did murder that nogood Jew bastard from Houston. To me, Foreman had proven the common-law marriage beyond almost any doubt, and Bass's failure to present any other witnesses to implicate Harrelson, followed by the judge's instructions on the law, left the jury no option but a not-guilty verdict. Juror ten, Harold D. Moore, a machinist from Pearland, agrees. Forty years after he served on that panel, he still remembers why he voted as he did: "The judge done that. He said we had to ignore Attaway's testimony if we believed they was married. And I did."

And without Sandra Sue's testimony, that jury could not have convicted Harrelson of jaywalking.

Still, Mr. Moore and I would have been in the minority on that panel. Almost everyone else acquitted Harrelson because of the "alibi." Not only that, two of Foreman's cocounsel—Sam Lee's father and Neil Caldwell—interviewed several jurors after the verdict and they said that prior to the alibi testimony, they would have voted to *convict*, common-law marriage or no.

So Harrelson returned to jail, acquitted of one murder, to await trial for another, for killing Sam Degelia. Although it took until December 1971 for Foreman to make room in his schedule—by then Harrelson had been in jail for thirty-seven consecutive months—he finally faced off again against Hidalgo County's DA Oscar McInnis in the Edinburg courthouse, where he'd won probation for Pete Scamardo.

McInnis knew that it was felony stupid to try a one-witness case against Percy Foreman. The deal he cut with Jerry Watkins—prosecutorial immunity for his testimony—would leave his star witness susceptible to powerful cross-examination. So at trial, McInnis led off with Watkins but followed up with Sandra Sue, who—terrified that if Harrelson got out of jail he would kill her—was happy to comply with his subpoena and substantiated Watkins's testimony with words right out of Harrelson's mouth.

Then McInnis called Texas Ranger Tol Dawson, who had led a road crew combing South Second Street in McAllen, where, according to Watkins, Harrelson had disassembled his gun and discarded it. And not only did Dawson's team find the pistol, but they also traced it through a purchase form signed by Harrelson to Bob's Sportsman's and Appliance Center in Vernal, Utah, in the mountains where, according to Sandra Sue, Charles had sung to her and bought a gun. The judge admitted the pistol into evidence. McInnis introduced ballistics tests that matched bullets fired from Harrelson's gun to those found in Degelia's body, and rested his case.

Foreman countered with none other than Pete Scamardo, now on seven years' probation for his role in Sam Degelia's murder. Scamardo agreed to testify, as he magnanimously told the jury, because "I know how it feels to have been falsely accused and falsely convicted and I am here because I don't want to see this happen to anyone else." Or, stated another way, he agreed to testify because he was scared shitless that if he didn't, Harrelson would get out of jail and kill *him*, too.

Scamardo told a convincing story to counter the prosecution's theory that he had Degelia killed to collect $50,000 in life insurance proceeds. Scamardo testified that he and Sam, partners in Cotton Marketing, a brokerage company, had obtained a $50,000 business loan from First State Bank of Bryan—but, as a condition, each was required to obtain a $25,000 life insurance policy, with the bank as the beneficiary (coincidentally, terms and amounts very similar to Dad's small-business loan). Scamardo explained that because of the double-indemnity provision, each policy was worth $50,000 in the event that either of them was murdered—but that money went directly to the bank to pay off the debt. Besides, even if all that money *were* payable to him, Cotton Marketing still owed another $125,000 to various business creditors. "If the $50,000 in insurance proceeds wasn't even payable to you and would have paid off less than a third of Sam's and your total debts," Foreman asked, "then what earthly reason would you have for killing your closest friend since the first grade?"

In the process of detailing their many business debts, Scamardo listed a jarring bill: $2,200 owed to Charles Harrelson, which he claimed represented Harrelson's 25 percent share of money that he'd collected chasing down customers who'd written bad checks to Cotton Marketing and getting them replaced with good funds. Each year, according to Scamardo, he and Degelia turned over approximately fifteen bad checks to Harrelson, and to date Harrelson had not been paid his 25 percent share of $8,800 in replacement checks he'd collected—a total of $2,200.

On cross-examination, McInnis immediately turned to the

Harrelson-as-debt-collector defense, a story invented to explain why, in the days following the Degelia murder, Scamardo had begun writing personal checks for the first time ever to Charles Harrelson:

"As a matter of fact, you didn't get any bad checks in your business to amount to anything, did you?"

"Yes, sir, we got a number of checks that did not clear the bank."

"All right, sir. Then, can you give me a list of the people that he collected bad checks from for you and Sam?"

"No, sir, I cannot at this time."

"Well, can you name just one person that he ever collected a check for, for you or Sam?"

"I don't recall at this time, no, sir."

"So out of forty-five checks over the past three years, you can't tell the jury just a name of one of those people so that we can get him down here and see whether or not this man collected a check from him?"

"I'm sure I could check and find out."

"Well, think about it a little right now. Can you give us one right now?"

"No, sir, not that I can recall."

Now, that is what I call an A+ cross-examination—and I am a tough grader.

McInnis also was up to speed on the insurance policies. He knew that Scamardo was telling the truth about his and Degelia's total business debt, but also that he was flat-out lying about the amount of insurance proceeds that he, Scamardo, expected to receive. First, he got Scamardo to agree that in April 1968, three months before the killing, he and Degelia decided to double the amount of insurance they carried—with the same double-indemnity provision covering murder.

"And this required you to take a physical again; did it not?"

"Yes, sir, it did."

"And, you actually went and took your physical and your policy went into effect?"

"Yes, sir, that is correct."

"And Sam didn't take his physical? He had not taken it up to the time of this death; you know that, do you not?"

"Yes, sir."

"You know it now; right?"

"Yes, sir, I knew it then."

"Come on, Mr. Scamardo. You thought that you had $50,000 total insurance on the life of Sam Degelia Jr., and $100,000 in case of accidental death; is that right?"

"No, sir, that is not correct."

"In fact, did you not, on the eighth day of July 1968, before Sam's body was found on the eleventh day of July, make the statement to Tol Dawson, a Texas Ranger, and in the presence of Chief of Police A. C. Gonzalez, Edinburg, Texas, at the police station here in Edinburg, before you left to go back to Hearne, that in the event Sam turned up dead that you had two $25,000 policies on his life?"

"No, sir, I don't recall making such a statement."

But the two law enforcement officers did—and instead of putting them on the stand during the state's case in chief, the wily district attorney had waited, allowed Foreman to elicit Scamardo's lie about the amount of insurance proceeds he thought he'd receive, *before* putting Ranger Dawson and Chief Gonzalez on the stand in rebuttal, to quote Scamardo saying he had expected to receive $100,000. Foreman knew that when those two very credible men testified, the intricate web of lies that he and Scamardo had created would collapse. The King of the Sandbag had been sandbagged, and, judging from his next step, Foreman knew it. He called Charles Harrelson to the stand.

Of all the decisions a criminal lawyer has to make during a trial, the riskiest is to let the client testify, not only because taking the stand opens the door to all kinds of incriminating evidence that would otherwise have remained inadmissible, but also because no amount of charm can overcome the difficulty of explaining away criminal conduct when you're guilty. But Foreman was desperate, so Charles Harrelson climbed into the box and told the jurors a story so cockamamie that it would make your eyes glaze over. In short: Harrelson said that Jerry Watkins did it with Harrelson's gun, which Harrelson had loaned him. The details included an anti-Castro group called Alpha Sixty-Six, a man referred to as El Tigerino, and a conveniently timed alibi dinner with a nightclub singer named Louise.

There is a simple way to undo this kind of far-fetched testimony: don't give the story any credibility by cross-examining on every point. Instead, demonstrate that the witness is a habitual liar and thus untrustworthy across the board. Which is exactly what McInnis did:

"Mr. Harrelson, you are a person that will tell a lie under oath if your own personal welfare is concerned; are you not?"

"No, sir."

"All right. You have done so in the past; haven't you?"

"Not from the witness stand."

McInnis handed Harrelson his own driver's license, confiscated at the Brazoria County jail, and gave him the opportunity to lie right then and there. First he had Harrelson agree that the picture on the license was his, but the name, Steven Stoughtenborough, was not. Then he handed Harrelson his license application, which McInnis had subpoenaed from the Department of Public Safety and on which Harrelson had sworn that Steven Stoughtenborough was his "true and only" name—and that he did not own any other driver's license in any other state. Confronted with this, Harrelson attempted to outsmart McInnis, with about as much success as Dad had had with Foreman:

"Mr. McInnis, Steven Stoughtenborough had never had a license in another state."

"Well, *you* had, hadn't you?"

"As Charles Harrelson, yes, sir."

"And so, whenever they asked you in there if you had ever had a license in this state, did you interpret that to mean that you had never had a license in this state under a fictitious name?"

"I beg your pardon?"

Ah, yes, the old "I beg your pardon" defense. Very persuasive.

Finally, when McInnis asked Harrelson for the name of just one person who would testify that Harrelson had even known his supposed employer Sam Degelia before the night of his murder, Harrelson answered, "Pete Scamardo," and could not come up with another soul.

Another A+ cross. His credibility in smithereens, Harrelson at last looked headed for the electric chair—until Foreman called his last witness.

She was Louise Scott Gannon, the nightclub singer with whom Harrelson had claimed to be having dinner at the McAllen Holiday Inn near Edinburg at the time Watkins had testified Sam Degelia was killed. She verified the dinner date, down to what they ate and drank, and testified that, afterward in the lounge, she had entertained an audience containing Harrelson for much of the night.

As in the Angleton trial, the judge instructed the jury on the law of alibi. If the jurors believed that Harrelson was somewhere other than at the scene of the murder at the time it was committed, or if they had reasonable doubt that he was there, then they should find him not guilty. The jury deliberated for three days and finally sent out a note saying they were deadlocked—with one holdout for acquittal. The judge declared a mistrial—hardly a victory for the prosecution, but still preferable to a not-guilty verdict. Harrelson was returned to his cell to await retrial, and by the time Foreman got around to defending him in court again, in July 1973, his client had spent almost five consecutive years in jail. It is small consolation to me that what the law could not extract as punishment, Foreman did instead.

∼

Following the mistrial, McInnis assembled a team of investigators headed by the outraged Texas Rangers who tracked down evidence that Louise Scott Gannon was lying—and charged her with perjury. (I haven't been able to confirm the basis of her indictment, but other witnesses had to have put her somewhere other than in McAllen the night of Degelia's murder.) During the retrial, an officer sat in the gallery holding her arrest warrant—and made no secret of the fact. Ms. Gannon never showed, choosing instead to vacation in Aruba until well after August 12, the day when Harrelson finally was convicted of murder (and, like the start of the Angleton trial, Alan's birthday).

Citing Harrelson's lies from the witness stand and his heinous crime, McInnis asked the jury to assess the death penalty. Instead, they sentenced him to fifteen years in the Texas Department of Corrections. Maybe they'd been prejudiced by the news of Scamardo's probated sentence or Watkins's free pass. Or maybe, just maybe, they'd been strong-armed, psychologically or otherwise, by Foreman—who, when it came to conditioning jurors to see things his way, worked in mysterious ways.

Still, McInnis got his conviction, and Harrelson would be off the streets for at least five more years before he'd be eligible for parole. Had Ogden Bass employed the McInnis Overkill Theory—or what we lawyers like to call "preparation"—he, too, would have had a very good chance of convicting Harrelson. If Claude, especially, had been indicted with his brother and Watkins for attempted extortion and agreed to testify against his brother to avoid a lengthy prison sentence, the odds are good that Charles would have accepted a plea bargain to avoid the electric chair—and almost certainly, given his history as a jailhouse snitch, he would have testified against DiMaria. And if not—had Charles Harrelson insisted on a trial—he would have faced testimony of biblical proportions: brother against brother, with Claude detailing the plot that would have allowed his brother to profit again from the murder he'd committed—and admitted. Taken in combination with the testimony of Sandra Sue, Jerry Watkins, Jim Cowan, my father, and me, *and* those damning fibers found in Harrelson's trunk and at the scene of the murder, identical in chemical composition and color to that of carpet sold by Alan, Bass might actually have had his "open-and-shut" case. Even Percy Foreman and a team of his "reserve witnesses" would have found that evidence difficult to overcome.

Also, Bass could have made that opening argument that would have made all the difference in the world. When Judge Hardy said, "Mr. Bass, you may open for the state," Bass could have risen, walked confidently to the lectern, and said,

"Gentlemen, good morning.

"It's August 12, Alan Berg's birthday. He would have been thirty-four today, and he would have celebrated his birthday with his three children and this woman . . ."

Here, Bass would walk to Harriet, positioned in the front row of the gallery. He would put his hand on her shoulder (to establish a physical and psychological connection) and ask her to stand. "Good morning," Harriet would say to the jury, with a sad smile and what warmth she could muster. Now the prosecutor would walk back to the jury box, but this time he would remain *in front* of the lectern, to remove that physical barrier between the jurors and himself. Then he would go on,

"Alan and Harriet have three children. Two of them were under five when their father was murdered, and the third, a little girl named

Allison, after her dad, was born exactly one week after his remains were discovered where they had been dumped [*pause*] in *our* county and—as an eyewitness will testify from the stand—had been dumped there by *that* man, Charles Harrelson. And, as that same eyewitness will tell you, earlier that same night, May 28, 1968, Charles Harrelson fired a bullet through Alan's brain and then, when Alan wouldn't die, strangled him with a sash cord. Here's something else you will learn: Charles Harrelson had no beef with Alan. He didn't even *know* him. He murdered this young husband and father, as the evidence will show, for money: fifteen hundred dollars paid by a man named Frank DiMaria, a business competitor who sought revenge against Alan's father. The state does not deny it: DiMaria got his revenge. Alan is dead and his father, as you will see, is half mad with grief."

Next, the prosecutor might promise the jury that in addition to the "pretty young woman" providing the eyewitness testimony, there would be "corroborating testimony from *at least* one other witness who will testify that Harrelson bragged to him about murdering Alan."

Then it would be time to deflate Foreman's onslaught against every aspect of my brother's life and at least to try to neutralize the anti-Semitism on that jury:

"Now, Alan was not perfect. As I understand it, the last perfect man died two thousand years ago. Alan, like the rest of us, could be tempted. Despite his great love for his wife and children, and despite his never before having been known to stray outside his marriage, you're going to hear that Sandra Sue Attaway, at her boyfriend Charles Harrelson's direction, lured Alan into his own kidnapping with the promise of sexual favor."

"Objection!" Foreman would thunder. "Charles Harrelson is her *husband*, not her boyfriend, and he did no such thing!"

"You'll have your turn, Mr. Foreman," the judge would say without actually ruling.

After detailing the evidence found in Sandra Sue's typed confession, the prosecutor would lower his voice to bring the jurors closer in and then reveal to the World War II veterans among them, especially those under the impression that Jews never enlisted, that:

"Alan Berg was a good man, a patriotic man, who enlisted and served a two-year hitch in the United States Navy as a gunner's mate aboard the USS *Leyte* and received an honorable discharge. And here's what else the evidence will show: he worked hard when he got out of the navy and was accepted to the University of Texas medical school over in Galveston. But he wasn't sure that he wanted to be a doctor. It was what his dad wanted for him, but he wasn't sure it was what he wanted for himself. We all know how that is. So he did not attend, and that is more the pity. If he had become Dr. Alan Berg instead of carpet salesman Alan Berg, he'd be in Houston right now, treating patients and spending evenings with his young family, not lying in an early grave.

"Gentlemen, you are the voice of this community. We value life in this community, even a sinner's life, especially when he's a funny, good-hearted, generous sinner like Alan Berg. When the evidence is in, once the state has met its burden to prove Charles Harrelson's guilt beyond a reasonable doubt—a burden I proudly accept—I will ask you to return a verdict of guilty: guilty of the murder of Alan Berg."

Then it would be Foreman's turn. And even after a strong opening from the prosecution, it wouldn't be pretty. But when Foreman finishes, there would be nothing to stop the prosecutor from sidling over to Witt Wade, the court reporter, and asking, loudly enough for the jury to hear, "Witt, how soon can you type up Mr. Foreman's remarks? I'm going to need 'em for closing argument."

Then, during closing argument, Bass could have said, "You probably remember me asking Witt Wade to type up Mr. Foreman's opening statement. Now I'll show you why. I took the liberty of blowing up a couple things Mr. Foreman said he *hoped to prove about Alan Berg*—those were his exact words—and I blew 'em up bigger than Dallas so no one could help but see. And after I show you *what* he said, I'm going to tell you *why* he said them in the first place.

"Let's look at the first one: 'Alan, despite his marriage, fathered an illegitimate child who was born the day he died and . . . both the mother of the child and her husband had reason to kill Berg.' Gentlemen, if this were actually true, don't you think Mr. Foreman would have subpoenaed these two people into this courtroom and let you hear that story and maybe see the date on that birth certificate? But he didn't."

"OBJECTION!" Foreman would shout. "The burden of proof is on the state, not on Mr. Harrelson and his defense lawyers."

"Your Honor," the prosecutor would snap, "I am well aware that I have the burden of proof—but those were *his* promises. He invited that argument or I would not have made it."

"Move it along," the judge would say.

"Now let's look at another thing Mr. Foreman told you he *hoped* to prove. 'Alan Berg could have been killed by any one of twenty people who had the means and motive.' The Bergs 'employed ex-convicts, some of them convicted murderers, as salesmen. Eleven of them complained of being cheated on their commissions during the eight months before Berg's death and the defense *hopes* to show that any one of the eleven could have killed him.' But, gentlemen, you heard Alan's father testify that only *two* of their employees had criminal records, one of them, it is true, for murder, but also that Alan and Nat Berg believed in giving people a second chance. That's two men out of *one hundred* employees over a three-year period.

"Now, recall the evidence Mr. Foreman actually offered on this point: Mr. Berg testified that he had *heard about*—he wasn't even there—an employee getting angry and threatening Alan after Alan had fired him. Folks, I made a terrible mistake when I didn't jump up and object to that hearsay, and I owe you and this court and the Berg family over there an apology for that. I must have been asleep at the wheel. Hearsay should not be among the evidence, but it is, so let's review it now: What did Alan Berg do to the man who threatened him? Did he turn him in to the police? No. Nat Berg's uncontroverted testimony is that Alan thought the boy had problems and *offered to get him some counseling.* Alan gave him the benefit of the doubt, which is more than I can say for Charles Harrelson and Frank DiMaria, who gave Alan no benefit at all. And while we're at it, that's only *one* of the *eleven* salesmen Mr. Foreman said had the 'means and motive' to kill Alan because they'd been cheated out of commission. Who and where are those men? Let me point out: not one salesman took the stand to say anything about the Bergs cheating them in any way. It was all smoke. It was all mirrors.

Then, before Foreman would have a chance to bellow his objection to the prosecutor impugning his good name, Bass could have bellowed himself: "Why would Mr. Foreman make promises he knew he could not keep? Because Percy Foreman is like one of those sleight-of-hand artists who tell you to look up here [*points skyward*] while he's picking your pockets down here [*waggles hand in pocket*]. He wants to try Alan and take your minds off Charles Harrelson, because he knows that there is an ocean of evidence that Charles Harrelson mercilessly murdered that young man in cold blood. And for what? Fifteen hundred dollars—so another man he barely knew, Frank DiMaria, could have his revenge against another man Harrelson did not know: Alan's father."

But to have made arguments such as these would have required that the prosecutor learn enough about Alan to humanize him, which Bass had not.

~

It is not just because of Sandra Sue's testimony or even because of Foreman's "reserve witnesses," or just common sense that I believe the sorrel alibi was 100 percent fiction. It is also because of something Sam Lee, the impressive young lawyer who helped Foreman get Harrelson acquitted, told me in 2009.

I first met Sam in his office on Locust Street, right across from the Brazoria County courthouse, where he still practices in the same small, white-frame house in which his father practiced before him. He is a tall man, muscular and fit, with close-cropped brownish hair that is just beginning to thin. He still plays competitive softball, and one of the first things he told me was about how impressed his teammates are with his hitting and fielding, given that he is now in his sixties. We had lunch, and, although he was initially reticent, Sam in time revealed a number of critical details—including that only one of Harrelson's lawyers knew about the alibi witnesses, and that was Percy Foreman. The other three (Neil Caldwell; Sam Lee; and his father, Sam Sr.) listened to the sorrel-sale testimony in astonishment—as did a fourth man sitting at their table: Harrelson himself. When the testimony was over, Harrelson turned to young Sam Lee, grinned, and said in a low voice, "You know, I had forgotten *all* about that."

Lee also told me how he would talk to Harrelson every day during the trial because "I was more or less in charge of keeping him occupied." But they never discussed Alan. "Mr. Foreman told me not to talk to Chuck about the case because he did not want Chuck to 'confess anything' to me." So they talked about movies, and music ("He liked Merle Haggard")—and, however briefly, about ties:

> Chuck did not have any ties. He may have had one. I don't recall. I gave him enough ties so that he would have five. I

didn't have very many myself. Actually, I think I got a couple of my dad's old ties also. I told Chuck that they all came from me because that seemed to make him feel better.

At the beginning of the trial, Lee said, he did not have an opinion as to whether Harrelson was guilty or innocent. By the end of the state's case, however, he had been "personally persuaded" by Sandra Sue's testimony because of its "specificity." "I thought it would be hard for her to make up those details if she had not actually been present," he wrote to me. Often it is seemingly irrelevant details that help persuade jurors the witness is telling the truth, like "and then some mayonnaise dripped off his sandwich" or, in Sandra Sue's case, Harrelson "had given me a watch to hold which changed colors in the map light of the car. It was a very expensive watch with a very flexible band but was so small that I could not see the brand name."

Lee also wrote:

> Before the trial my dad told me that Ogden was going to try to use a "guilty" verdict in this trial as a stepping stone to run for governor. A few weeks after the trial my dad and I were talking about Ogden's alleged political aspirations and I commented something like, "I doubt that very many folks ever got ahead by trying to use Percy Foreman as a stepping stone." Dad agreed.

Later, Lee even explained how Bass could have rebutted the Price brothers' testimony about the bill of sale for the horse—and admitted that the defense team worried that he'd figure it out. "If Bass puts the oldest notary in the county on the stand and asks him if he has ever, *even once*, time-stamped or handwritten the time on any document he has notarized—the answer is going to be 'no.' Then Ogden asks him if he has ever seen a time entered on *any* notarized document, and again the notary says 'no.' And finally, Ogden asks if any provision in the law requires a notary to enter the time of day when he notarizes a document; the old man answers 'no,' and Ogden argues that it was written in deliberately to create an alibi. Ogden then circulates the bill of sale to the jury and lets them see for themselves. If he'd done that, I think it would have all been over.

"My impression," Lee added, "was that the alibi witnesses just stunned Bass and Brown and they never recovered."

In 2012, I also spoke to Buster Brown, Bass's old assistant. He told me about seeing Foreman swipe the family photo out of Alan's wallet, among other details—including that the county judge claiming to have notarized the bill of sale owed Foreman a favor. ("We did some research and found that Foreman represented [him] on some kind of embezzlement charge that got dismissed.") Brown also described for me Foreman's voir dire strategy. Since Harrelson's was a death penalty case, the lawyers questioned individual panelists in the courtroom, while the others waited outside. Brown said that whenever Foreman didn't want a certain person on his jury ("the hard-liners, the Dow Chemical engineers from over in Freeport, the conservatives, the hang-'em-high types") Foreman posed the same hypothetical and question: "I have a client here. The state is going to try to show you he took Alan Berg to a remote area. Put him on his knees. Shot him in the head and killed him. Now the judge is going to tell you that if you find him guilty the law says you can give him five years probation to life. So my question is, if you believe that my client did that, can you give him five years probation?" Not wanting to seem weak, the "hang-'em-high" types would answer, "No," "Of course not," and "Not under any circumstances"—which, to their amazement, allowed Foreman to get rid of them, arguing that a refusal to consider probation amounted to a refusal to consider the full range of punishment under Texas law. That alone, Foreman insisted to the judge, disqualified a panelist from jury duty because that person's mind was made up about an important aspect of the case (probation) before the trial had even begun. Almost every time Foreman made this argument, the judge agreed and sent the potential juror packing. Still, there was an obvious method for stopping the purge of all those "hang-'em-high" types the prosecution needed on the jury—and from the start, Brown urged his boss to employ it. Bass could have explained to every panelist that the judge was going to give them a range of punishments—anywhere from five years to life in prison, with the possibility of probation up to ten years. Then Bass could have explained, "You only have to *consider* that range of punishment. Not necessarily *give* it." "But," as Brown said to me, in a tone that suggested Bass disregarded his advice, "we didn't do that."

There's an old Texas saying about trial lawyers that goes, "You can't lose 'em if you ain't tryin' 'em." That is true of all of us—including Racehorse Haynes. So when I criticize Ogden Bass for what he did and didn't do forty-plus years ago, I am mindful of the fact that even Race would have had trouble convicting Harrelson with Foreman on the other side. But Bass made some truly egregious mistakes, not the least of which was allowing his ego and ambition to block Racehorse from helping him out. And if I know anything at all about Richard Haynes, it is this: had he been in charge, that jury pool would never have been pared down to twelve Foreman fans and those three alibi witnesses would have been left looking like the Three Stooges. Above all, no matter how it came out, my friend *never* would have quit fighting for a conviction. When I suggested to juror ten that Bass seemed to give up after the alibi witnesses, Mr. Moore replied, "Give up? He didn't even try."

In 2008, when I began writing this book, my son Gabe told me that ten years earlier, curious about his uncle Alan, he'd obtained the court files from the Harrelson trial but found so little remaining that he'd then written a letter to Bass to ask him if he could fill in some of the blanks. Bass wrote a four-page letter in response—on yellow lined paper and handwritten in all caps:

HOWDY:

I AM A SENIOR JUDGE, RETIRED OF THE 300TH JUDICIAL DISTRICT COURT, BRAZORIA COUNTY, TEXAS. I REMAIN A JUDICIAL OFFICER OF TEXAS, SUBJECT TO ASSIGNMENT. IN ADDITION, I AM A SUPERANNUATED CRIMINAL DISTRICT ATTORNEY, RETIRED.

BY THIS WRITING ATTEMPT WILL BE MADE TO FURNISH ADDITIONAL INFORMATION SURROUNDING THE MURDER OF ALAN BERG, AND THE TRIAL OF CHARLES V. HARRELSON. . . .

The rest of the letter outlines Bass's view of the acquittal, which he attributes to a pro-defense jury instruction on common-law marriage plus an alibi that hinged on a trade for a nonexistent horse. Despite the "Howdy" and being handwritten, the letter has a businesslike, matter-of-fact tone—a tone in keeping with the way he ran his court but at odds with the Ogden Bass I met at my request in his son's law office in Angleton in 2010. I sat down opposite Bass, who had peeled off his maroon Texas A&M Windbreaker and hung it on a hook on the wall. We had not been talking five minutes before he said, looking out the window behind me, "I'm sorry I lost your brother's case." Then he thought a moment and said, "Maybe lost is not the right term. I'm not sure what I could have done better. I believed then and I believe now Harrelson killed your brother. Just not able to convince the jury."

He sounded so sincere that I could not help but try to make him feel better. "You don't owe me an apology," I said. "I just want to gather as many of the facts as I can." After the meeting, over a pleasant barbecue lunch with Bass's son and a couple of their friends, Bass reached back for his only good memory of the trial. "The *Chronicle* reporter, Stan Redding—I don't know if he's still with us but he wrote a magazine article about it. He said, 'The prosecutor was like a cavalry officer with his sword drawn.' " To that, I smiled and said nothing. We all have our selective memories—and our private fears. After that day, Judge Bass refused to return my calls or respond to the letter I wrote asking for his response to my questions about his trial strategy and failure to bring other indictments.

"That trial broke Ogden's heart," Sam Lee said to me not long afterward. "He brought his A game and it wasn't good enough. I don't think he tried another criminal case after that, or at least not a serious one. He turned them over to his assistants."

On the other hand, at least Ogden Bass is law-abiding—which is more than we can say for Brother McInnis. In 1980, Oscar McInnis was convicted of perjury for lying to the grand jury about a failed plot to lure his lover's husband across the border into Mexico, where the husband would be killed by a police chief whom McInnis had hired (through a dope dealer McInnis had freed from Hidalgo County jail explicitly for that purpose). God love Texas.

∼

When Harrelson pled guilty to the federal weapons charges in Kansas City, the judge agreed to run his state and federal convictions concurrently. That allowed Harrelson to serve most of his time in the federal penitentiary at Leavenworth, Kansas. There, Foreman was quoted as saying, Harrelson enjoyed the "happiest time in his life." "He probably had more respect in Leavenworth than anywhere else he'd been," Foreman also said. "The hired killer has a certain aura about him. I'm sure he was happy in an environment where he was the upper crust of the establishment."

Five years later, in September 1978, it was announced that Harrelson was coming up for parole. The same month, Dot was alone in Alan Carpet & Fabrics, the retail store she and Dad opened after shutting down the boiler room once Alan's remains were found. A crazed-looking woman hurried into the showroom with a teenage boy in tow and, on the brink of tears, said, "I'm Sandra Sue Attaway's mother. This is her son. Charles Harrelson is getting out! He is going to kill my daughter!"

Dot glared at her.

"Mrs. Berg, your husband needs to do something to keep him from getting out!"

"Your daughter killed our son. Why would Nat do anything for you?"

With that, Dot pushed the woman and boy out the door, locked it behind them, and called Dad to tell him what had happened. Dad said the same thing he used to say when I handed him one of my disappointing report cards: "*Jesus H. Christ!* You have *got* to be kidding!"

Sandra Sue wasn't the only one worried about getting killed. Foreman had taken Voyde Harrelson's eighty-eight-acre ranch as part of his fee and Sam Lee told me, "Chuck wanted his father's ranch back. He thought Percy overcharged him." (DiMaria paid Foreman and another Houston lawyer an additional $400,000 for the murder case and an IRS investigation.) When Lee confessed to Foreman that he was scared of Harrelson, Foreman replied, "I wouldn't ride from here to Houston with him." (He said it in Angleton, less than an hour away.)

"*Percy Foreman* was afraid of Harrelson?" I said.

"Well, goddamn, David, we all knew what he did for a living."

Within a year of getting out of Leavenworth—a year spent hustling pool, playing blackjack, and sending a good deal of the proceeds up his nose—Harrelson had his biggest payday yet. Jamiel "Jimmy" Chagra, an El Paso drug dealer, paid him $250,000 in cash to murder US District Judge John "Maximum John" Wood, in whose court Chagra faced a certain life sentence if convicted of drug-trafficking charges pending there. On May 29, 1979, Harrelson waited outside Judge Wood's San Antonio home and shot him with a high-powered rifle point-blank in the back of his head, then stole quietly away—and remained at large for two years. He was finally apprehended in West Texas on I10 near Van Horn, where I had represented my criminal law professor's nephew years before. He was high on cocaine when he pulled over to check his engine and somehow shot out the Corvette's rear tire. Local authorities found him holding a gun to his head, ranting about injustice—and confessing to the murder of Judge Wood *and* JFK. For several hours he held the officers at bay by threatening suicide before he surrendered. On a notepad retrieved from his motel room, Harrelson had written: "God, it's been a tough way I'm sorry Not for me but for the pain I've caused others, both those who've loved me and those who've loved the people I've killed But I've never killed a person undeserving of it."

In 1982, Harrelson was convicted of Judge Wood's murder and sentenced to two consecutive life terms. By then, one of his three sons, Woody Harrelson, had attained stardom playing Woody, the dimwitted bartender in *Cheers,* and since has gone on to major roles in many other movies, including *Natural Born Killers,* in which he plays a cold-blooded murderer enthusiastically embraced by the media. I have read that Oliver Stone, who directed the film, instructed Harrelson more than once to do it "more like your father."

In 1997, Woody Harrelson assembled a superb legal team, including Professor Alan Dershowitz of Harvard, to argue on a writ of habeas corpus that his father had not received a fair trial for the Judge Wood killing—an argument that I did not dismiss out of hand, nor would Alan have. The government outspent Harrelson's defense lawyer, Tom Sharpe, by millions of dollars to his $7,000 or so in a trial conducted in the John H. Wood Jr. Courthouse and presided over by a judge who had been a pallbearer at Wood's funeral. But Woody also implied that he believed his father was innocent. "A judge was killed in Texas," he said in a December 1996 interview in *George* magazine. "They don't know who did it. My dad had already been convicted of murder for hire, and he was in the area." There he lost me. (Incidentally, the younger Harrelson was also quoted as saying, on the subject of evil in general: "We want to demonize people. We want to make Charles Manson the devil, yet if you listen to the guy, you'll find that this guy speaks a lot of truth.")

During the writ hearing, US District Judge Fred Biery, a distinguished jurist from the San Antonio Division, appeared to be sympathetic to Harrelson's argument. Then, one evening after court, the judge played several one-on-one games of pickup basketball with Woody Harrelson in a hotel gym. When prosecutors found out and a controversy erupted in the national press, Judge Biery was forced to take himself off the case, citing the appearance of impropriety. A second judge conducted another hearing, in 2000, and denied the writ in 2003.

In 1995, prior to filing his writ, Charles Harrelson had tried to win his freedom by escaping from the federal penitentiary in Atlanta. Caught before he got out, Harrelson was transferred to a supermax: ADX Florence, in Fremont County, Colorado. Like the mobster John Gotti, Unabomber Ted Kaczynski, and Oklahoma City terrorist Timothy McVeigh imprisoned there, Harrelson spent twenty-three hours of each day in a windowless cell with concrete furniture, receiving his meals through a narrow slot in the door. The twenty-fourth hour he was allowed to exercise alone in an outdoor cage. After ten years of that, on March 14, 2007, at age sixty-nine, Harrelson was found dead in his cell of a heart attack.

# 13

In 2009, with the help of a very resourceful former FBI special agent named Mike Wilson, I located Sandra Sue Attaway, who was living under her married name in a tiny West Texas town. Wilson also managed to find, buried in the online archives of the Texas Department of Public Safety, the twelve-page single-spaced statement Sandra Sue had typed in a Brazoria County jail cell forty years earlier. I was in my study when he forwarded the scanned document to me, and I immediately printed it out, slid my keyboard aside, and read it with a lawyer's eyes and—I don't know how else to say this—a brother's heart. I took notes, filled in gaps, and held my breath as I absorbed some of the details of Alan's death, like how hard it was to kill him.

At first when I called Sandra Sue, she did not recognize my name. When I identified myself as Alan's brother, however, she paused. "I thought about calling you every time I read about a case of yours," she said. "I assumed you'd want to know everything." Still, she claimed to remember very little about what she called "the event." And when I asked her to start from the beginning, with the phone call she made to Alan, she denied that she ever spoke to my brother. "Chuck went inside the Brass Jug and came out with Alan," she began. When I stopped her and said that I had her signed statement in front of me, and that it said that she had called Alan and he'd agreed to meet her there, and that then she and Harrelson had kidnapped my brother together, she said, in a deflated voice, "Well, if that's what it says, then that's the truth."

One thing about our conversation was stunning: despite all that he had done to her, Sandra Sue Attaway was not done with Charles Harrelson. She told me, "The sick thing is that there were qualities about him. He was a fabulous man. He was an extremely bright guy and I was real happy to be with him. I was in love with him." In the end, I learned only one significant detail I hadn't already known or imagined. When I asked her if she remembered anything specific that Alan had said, Sandra Sue told me that Alan had promised Harrelson that if he let him go, Dad would pay Harrelson a million dollars. "Your daddy doesn't have a million dollars," Harrelson replied. He was right.

Even before speaking to Sandra Sue, I had interviewed Dennis Weadock. Linda somehow remembered the name of Weadock's lawyer from the time of the trial—Oliver Kitzman, the former DA of Madison County, north of Houston—tracked him down, and discovered that he was still in touch with his former client. When Linda explained the reason I wanted to talk to Weadock, the lawyer said he'd be happy to pass along my cell number but insisted that Weadock would never call me back, that that was a period in Dennis's life he wanted to forget. But Weadock did call—the next day. He emphasized, sounding sad and respectful, that Alan had been "a nice boss"—the same words he'd used with Dad forty years before—and he said that Sandra Sue had told him that there were "a lot of religious slurs said by Harrelson" in the car when Alan was kidnapped. He was still protecting Sandra Sue, telling me that Harrelson had told her he only wanted to talk to Alan because he'd been unable to get an interview and wanted to go to work for him. Weadock was almost eighty but he boasted about "stealing Chuck's girlfriend" with a "great body if you know what I mean," like a teenager bragging to his friends.

I tried to reach Weadock again to verify a couple of things he'd told me, but this time I got only as far as Kitzman. "Dennis wants to put that behind him," Kitzman told me. "Turning on Harrelson ruined his life." Ruined his life? Weadock walked away with "Chuck's girlfriend" *and* the $10,000 reward, which had to have been more money than he'd ever seen. Harrelson spent ten consecutive years, from 1968 to 1978, in jail, and then, two years later, went back to prison for killing Judge Wood and never came out. How had Weadock's life been ruined? Or, as I had always wondered, was Weadock more involved somehow? Was his real regret that he failed to warn his "nice boss" about the card-carrying hit man? About midway through the notes of my conversation with Weadock, I typed this comment: "Coincidences" thus far: "Chuck" is DW's drinking buddy; DW hears DiMaria say "I'd like to kill that Jew bastard" with CH "at the gin table." And, not entirely surprising, "I was working for Alan and your Dad when CH murdered him." Add to this Sandra Sue's statement where she quoted Weadock as saying he was going to Houston to borrow $500 from Crawford Booth—Harrelson's friend, who had loaned him the Sharpshooter shovel—and the suspicion only grows.

I would have given my right arm to cross-examine Dennis Weadock.

About a year after my first conversation with Sandra Sue, I called her to confirm my notes and ask some additional questions, and she agreed. I told her that I wanted to know what Alan had said to her and Harrelson the night he died. I wanted to know about the anti-Semitic taunts. I wanted to know everything. "I sincerely do not remember anything but the event," she responded. I coaxed her to open up, assuring her that I would not use her married name or reveal where she lived; I even told her that I didn't want her to try to protect my feelings by withholding anything—but she insisted that she had already told me everything she could recall.

"I certainly understand your need to understand all this," she said. "The thing is, I couldn't have done anything about the event—well, I could have taken the gun and shot Harrelson, which is what I should have done, but I didn't. The thing I feel really bad about is that I didn't immediately go to the authorities and tell them the story and do whatever I had to do to keep you and your family from wasting all those nights worrying about your brother. See, that's what I've thought about—why in the world didn't I have the self-respect and conduct myself in an honorable manner as much as I could have after the event, and go to the authorities? I was just a stupid little girl. I mean, the worst thing that happened to me before that was my dad died in 1966. The rest of the time I'd been a young mother working as a typist."

I know about young mothers working as typists. I know about young mothers giving up sons. For a discomfiting moment, I forgave Sandra Sue: I told her that in a different life, we might have been friends. Almost immediately, I felt a wave of remorse. *She had been an accomplice to my brother's murder.* I heard my tone of voice turn cold as I told her that I appreciated what she'd said and that I knew my sister would, too. That much I could say without feeling as though I were betraying Alan.

Oh, yes, there was one more thing we discussed: I asked Sandra Sue about her son, the one she'd abandoned to her mother's care. Sandra Sue admitted that their relationship wasn't good. "He never forgave me for leaving him behind. He doesn't understand the threat I was under from Chuck," she explained. "He's almost fifty now. He's going to have to get over it or it's going to be too late."

"What does he do for a living?" I asked.

"He's a lawyer," she said, "who does nothing but argue cases before the Supreme Court."

～

In 2011, I found former Fort Bend deputy sheriff Ed Chesshire, who had testified briefly in the Angleton trial, recounting how he'd met Deputy Roy Schmidt at the murder scene the morning after Alan's disappearance—and now told me what else had happened. As soon as he arrived, Chesshire, who was a rookie, immediately started collecting evidence. But then Fort Bend sheriff R. L. "Tiny" Gaston showed up, and when Chesshire said that he and Schmidt thought they'd stumbled across a murder scene, Gaston said, "Leave it alone." Chesshire was taken aback. "I don't know, Tiny . . ."—but Tiny pushed back. "I don't know," Chesshire repeated until, finally, the sheriff got angry.

"Listen to me real goddamn good!" shouted Tiny (who, incidentally, is six seven and weighs about three hundred pounds). "There's only two kinds of deaths in Fort Bend County: natural or accidental. Somebody killed a deer. Now leave it alone!" (When I contacted Tiny Gaston, long since retired as sheriff, he said he might have said it but it didn't sound like him.)

When Tiny left, Chesshire said to Roy, "We're going to look like Ned and the First-Grade Reader. I'm going to draw up a crime scene and put it in the backseat of my car."

Then, he told me, he did the best he could.

"I didn't even know how to preserve blood. The crime scene guy would have known how to handle it. I had a vial in my car and I dipped it down into that cow track. The blood wasn't even coagulated. . . . I put a stopper in the vial and put it in my freezer. I took it to a woman I knew who worked in a hospital clinic. She [tested it and] told me that it came from a man about thirty-five and that she found a brown hair in it."

Alan was thirty-one and had brown hair.

But weeks passed and, thanks to Fort Bend's determination to preserve its peaceful reputation, this evidence was never properly examined, nor did the officers return to the scene to carefully search for the most critical evidence: the bullet that killed my brother, if in fact Harrelson hadn't gone back and retrieved it. And had the story about the crime scene broken when it was first discovered, Sandra Sue or Jabo might have come forward sooner, or maybe "Big Man" Booth would have tipped off law enforcement about the shovel he'd loaned Harrelson and gotten back the day after Alan's death. There might even have been a tip from some other source I know nothing about. But that didn't happen—and while our family was robbed of justice and whatever peace that brings, Charles Harrelson was able to spend his pay and kill at least twice again.

I also attempted to track down Claude Harrelson. I especially wanted to question him about his comments in the "Ironic Coincidence" story in the *Post*, where he stated that he "received only occasional phone calls" from his brother, "did not know where they came from," and "didn't know anything about him"—given that Sandra Sue's statement implicating him in the extortion plot contradicted his every word. Was that the real reason he had said facing my father "was the hardest thing" he ever had to do? But by the time I got around to finding him, there was yet another "ironic coincidence": Claude had been dead for two decades, shot and killed by a madman while working as a security guard at the county hospital where Harriet had worked when Alan disappeared—and where she forced herself to look at every male corpse they brought in to see if it might be Alan, because she did not know for six months what Claude had known for five.

With his coconspirator in my brother's death acquitted, Frank DiMaria could not be prosecuted because his conviction required that Harrelson be found guilty, and the accomplice-to-murder indictment against him was dismissed. This meant that the extent of DiMaria's punishment was to be left in a jail cell for the six days it took Foreman to get around to posting his bond. When DiMaria divorced in 1987, Dick DeGeurin and his law partner, Lewis Dickson, both friends of mine, represented his wife. Ironically, Dick, now a famed criminal lawyer himself, had gone to work for Percy Foreman shortly after the Harrelson acquittal and had researched and written the legal memo that convinced Ogden Bass that he had no choice but to dismiss the charges against DiMaria. During his deposition in the divorce case, DiMaria testified that he believed the reason Foreman left him in jail in Angleton for six days was that the defense lawyer had been busy sleeping with Mrs. DiMaria. "After I got out," said DiMaria, "she never wanted to touch me again." DiMaria may have been on to something. As Foreman once confided in Sam Lee, "You know what makes the practice of law so great? It's not just the money. It's all the pussy."

On June 17, Lewis Dickson selected a jury in the DiMaria divorce case in a Harris County courtroom. Among the documents remaining in the file is "Dickson Exhibit 1," a copy of Mrs. DiMaria's retainer agreement with the law firm. In it, Dickson explains one of the reasons he was charging such a stout fee (a nonrefundable retainer of $100,000 plus a 25 percent contingency interest in her share of the community assets): "One of the things we first talked about when you came to me was who your husband is and his reputation and propensity for violence. I knew that approximately nineteen (19) years ago your husband hired Charles Harrelson to kill his then business partner, Allen [sic] Berg, whose brother, David Berg, is a good friend of mine. Your husband had, unsuccessfully, attempted to intimidate me in this case and I believe that he is certainly capable of a repeat performance." Dickson was right: the repeat performance came one month later, just outside the courtroom before a pretrial hearing. In a lengthy memorandum that he copied to senior Harris County prosecutors, Dickson described the encounter and alerted them, "If anything happens to me . . . Mr. DiMaria should be the focus of your investigation." Then he detailed DiMaria's not-so oblique threat to kill him:

> Mr. DiMaria approached me in the presence of one of my witnesses. . . . Mr. DiMaria pointed his finger at me and stated that I was "playing dirty pool" and reminded me that he had "come from the streets" and, in a threatening manner, told me that he was going to take me "out to the streets" and show me where he came from. As Mr. DiMaria left to go into the courtroom, he added, "I think you know what I'm talking about." I certainly knew what Mr. DiMaria meant by that.

Quoting his fee agreement almost verbatim, Dickson again made clear that he had no doubt who was responsible for my brother's death:

> Approximately eighteen years ago, Mr. DiMaria hired Charles Harrelson to kill his business partner, Allen Berg. Both Harrelson and DiMaria were indicted, but because Harrelson went to trial first and was acquitted, the State was collaterally estopped [precluded] from convicting DiMaria for hiring Harrelson to kill Berg.

Dickson continued, describing in lurid detail how, during a break in the hearing, unconcerned that his own lawyer, the bailiff, and the court reporter were standing there,

> Mr. DiMaria then started telling me that . . . a former employee of his had made a big mistake coming to me and telling me about his (DiMaria's) business dealings. . . . On the same afternoon, March 5, Mr. DiMaria called the home of [the former employee] and spoke with [his] wife. Mr. DiMaria told

[her] that her husband had made a big mistake by talking to me and turning against him and stated, "I'm speaking to you as a Jewish mother—you know—you have your son . . . you know what I'm talking about."

Dickson had digressed:

Back to the courtroom on the morning of March 5. Mr. DiMaria continuously reminded me that, "When I say I'm going to do something, I do it—you know what I'm talking about, don't you, Lewis?" Mr. DiMaria also reminded me, "I have spent more time in court on this divorce case than I did on my murder case," again adding, "You know what I'm talking about, don't you, Lewis?"

Dickson recalls that when DiMaria took the stand during the trial of the case, he testified that he always put his family first. On cross-examination, Dickson's first question was, "Were you thinking about your family when you hired someone to kill Alan Berg?" DiMaria's lawyer moved for a mistrial, Judge Daggett granted it, decided the property issues himself, and soon thereafter entered a Final Decree of Divorce. So DiMaria never answered that question, at least not on the record.

During the four decades since Harrelson's trial, although we live in the same city, I have seen DiMaria only once, in 2010, when he shook hands with a lawyer friend of mine in front of the plate glass window at the Avalon Drug Store. DiMaria has remained in the carpet business he opened after Alan's murder—and he has done very well. If there were any chance he'd tell the truth, or if I were any less repulsed by the thought of talking to him, I'd ask him whether gambling had anything to do with Alan's murder after all. Since the authorities had dismissed gambling as a motive, I hadn't even considered that that might have been the reason until, in 2011, Sam Lee Jr. told me, "About two years after the trial was over, my father told me something I should have told you when we met a year ago. Foreman told him your brother was killed over a gambling debt. Some guy in Las Vegas hired DiMaria to hire someone to scare him. Not kill him, just get him to pay off his debt."

I asked if it was Ted Lewin and Sam immediately said, "Yes, that's it! That's what happened! Lewin hired DiMaria to get someone to scare Alan. Harrelson was supposed to take him out to that spot in the country, hand him the shovel, and tell him to dig his own grave. Then, after Alan dug for a good while, Harrelson was supposed to say, 'I'm not going to kill you, but if you don't pay off your debt by two weeks, I will.' When he handed Alan the shovel, however, he turned to say something to Attaway and Alan hit Harrelson with the shovel. Harrelson must have lost it because he wrestled Alan down and shot him."

Upon hearing this, my first reaction was an emotional one: it reminded me so much of my brother, and sounded so much like something he would do, that I wanted it to be the truth. But then I sat down with a flow sheet and put the story on one side and the rebuttal on the other and decided that it probably wasn't. For one thing, both Foreman and Harrelson were dishonest. Second, Harrelson would have had good reason to make up this "self-defense" version, which cast him in a more sympathetic light with his lawyer and his "alibi" witnesses, including his father. Third, bookies don't kill people who owe them money, especially not someone like Alan, who was paying it back. Fourth, Sandra Sue wrote in her statement and testified at trial that *first* she heard a shot, *then* she saw Alan facedown in the dirt, and that it was only *after* he killed Alan that Harrelson opened the trunk and took out the shovel—not the other way around. Nor does her statement make any mention of Harrelson having sustained any kind of injury that night, which would seem likely if he'd been hit at any point with a shovel. And finally, Sandra Sue never wrote or testified that Harrelson said, explicitly or otherwise, "I wasn't going to kill him until he hit me."

On the other hand, while Alan's gambling was widely known even before the *Houston Post* published the first article about his disappearance, the amount of his UH bet wasn't known at the time Sandra Sue typed up her statement, in which she wrote that Harrelson had told her that Alan had cheated DiMaria out of $7,000—which is close to the $7,500 he bet and lost. Nor have I ever put out of my mind her surprise testimony in the trial—that Harrelson said he'd been hired to beat up the boy "over a gambling debt." And then there's Weadock's ex-wife, Jenna Coy Huddleston, who also said that gamblers had had Alan killed. Perhaps Ted Lewin was involved, concerned Alan would end up testifying against him if he were indicted for interstate gambling. And it is not at all implausible that if Sam is right about Lewin hiring DiMaria, that Lewin had learned of DiMaria's feud with Dad and Alan from Alan himself. If that scenario is true, then it is an even greater waste that my brother died because Lewin dropped dead of a heart attack only months after Alan was murdered.

So maybe I'll never know the truth.

Could Alan have lived? I doubt it.

Did he hit Charles Harrelson with a shovel? I hope to God he did.

~

My path crossed Percy Foreman's a good many more times before he died in 1988 at age eighty-six. From 1970 to 1973, after I moved out of my first law office, we actually worked in the same building, although on different floors. I don't think I knew he rented there when I moved in, but even if I had, it wouldn't have made any difference. I felt no need to confront him personally and for several years, whether alone with him in the elevator or seated near him on the downtown bus to or from the courthouse, I never said a word to him and he never offered one to me. He did try to contact my sister-in-law about a year after Harrelson's acquittal. He left a message on her machine, asking her to call him. Harriet thought it "creepy" and, of course, didn't call him back.

There were, however, a few times when I was forced to speak to him, the first following the Jimmy Carter presidential campaign in 1976. Then governor Carter came to Houston and, along with two or three other political activists, I met with him in his room at the Hyatt. I was already a fan of the man who was putting a new face on the South, and when he quoted Dylan Thomas, I was sold. I joined his campaign and, after his election, moved to Washington as a member of the Justice Department transition team, where I stayed right up to the day of the inauguration—at which point I left town one step ahead of being fired. For a brief time I had been among the brightest stars in Carter's political firmament, assigned the task of drafting the pardon of Vietnam War resisters (known in less forgiving circles as "draft dodgers") and to make recommendations regarding the upgrade of those who actually fought in Vietnam but had received less than honorable discharges. Carter had pledged to pardon the resisters, so I wasn't worried about them. But as I learned more, I became very concerned about the men who had been in combat—most of them poor black or Hispanic kids for whom an upgrade would mean eligibility for GI Bill benefits such as college tuition and low-cost home loans. (When I picked up Charles Kirbo, Carter's closest adviser at the time, at Washington National Airport, he referred to this matter as primarily a "nigger problem," and I'm afraid it was not long after I failed to correct him that a front-page article ran in the *Washington Post* naming me as the person rumored to become the next White House counsel.) But when I flew down to the Carter peanut farm in Plains, Georgia, to present my recommendation to the president-elect, Carter looked unhappy. "I didn't learn anything from your memo," he snapped, "that I didn't hear from Father Ted [Hesburgh, the president of Notre Dame]. *He* wants a universal upgrade, too. So does Teddy Kennedy." Still, I persevered, first assuring him that those who received dishonorable discharges—mostly for violent crimes—would not be included. Then I explained, "I've met with several groups for and against the pardon and upgrade. A deputy general counsel of IBM came to one of the meetings, and when I asked him why he was there, he said: 'My son was a Marine, killed in a firefight in Vietnam. He would want me to tell you that if you don't upgrade the discharges, those guys aren't going to college. They're going to go to jail.' I agree with that and that is why I recommended a universal upgrade."

Looking incredulous, Carter was quiet for a moment and then blurted out, slapping his hands on his knees:

"Even the *HO-MO*-sexuals?!"

My mind went back to his acceptance speech at Madison Square Garden for the Democratic nomination when he addressed my "EYE-talian" friends. And that's when the piss fight began.

On the plane back to DC, Stu Eizenstat (Carter's chief domestic adviser, who'd been in the meeting, along with Vice President-Elect Walter Mondale) turned around in his seat to face me and Senator Ed Muskie, both of us deep into the sauce and talking about what an asshole Carter was. "David," Stu said, "you can't talk to Jimmah like that. I can."

He was correct. I left town faster than you could say "Best career move I ever made," but not before I received a call from Percy Foreman. He had been approached by a Delta Airlines stewardess who needed representation because she'd been accused of "making out" with a passenger while on duty. The passenger had been carrying a brown briefcase that had a Jimmy Carter campaign sticker on it, and Foreman suggested I was that person. I wouldn't put it past me, but in this case I was innocent: I didn't make out with any stewardess. I told Foreman that yes, I'd been on the flight, but that the rest of the allegation was false, and that was it.

The first two years back home were like starting over—and very difficult financially. Then I got the case in which I successfully defended Diana B., the woman who'd shot and dismembered her husband. Shortly after her acquittal I ran into Foreman on a street corner and he congratulated me on a "remarkable result." It had seemed that way to me, too, but suddenly my triumph had lost some of its luster. "Thanks," I mumbled, and walked on. It did not occur to me until much later that what I should have said was, "You're right. And I did it without suborning perjury. Imagine that."

In 1988, Foreman called Haynes and asked him to meet him at the old Capitol Club in the Rice Hotel, where Foreman customarily sat at a corner table, usually by himself, drinking and fielding calls from clients who knew where to find him. On this particular day it was ten in the morning and Percy was already drinking. Haynes pointed out that it was a little early.

"I don't have that much longer to live, so it doesn't make any difference. I wanted to tell you, Haynes, you need to do something else with your life besides practice law. The only three things I do are chase pussy, and I'm too old for that anymore; drink, and I'm doing that all the time now; and try cases, and I haven't done that for years."

"Well, Percy, I sail my boat every weekend. I play golf. I read a lot."

Three months later, Foreman was dead.

I don't pretend to understand Percy Foreman personally, but I do understand the ways in which he perverted justice. He was extremely smart and an incredibly talented performer, but he repeatedly put on fraudulent testimony—and worse: he didn't even need to. He just had to be willing to accept a loss every now and again. "I'm in a profession," Racehorse once said to me, "where I get high marks for batting .250." In truth, Racehorse Haynes's lifetime average was a hell of a lot higher than .250, and he earned it honestly.

Now that I think of it, there was one encounter with Percy Foreman that I *don't* regret.

In 1972, two years after Harrelson was acquitted, I got a call from the ACLU chairman, Jim Calaway, who was recently separated from his wife. He said that he'd come home from a sailing trip to discover that his art collection and jewelry were gone. He'd called the police.

"You don't need the police," I said. "I can tell you without knowing: Your wife hired Percy Foreman."

The next morning, Jim and I stood before Judge Andrew Jefferson, the first black state district judge in Texas's largest county and to whom Foreman readily admitted that he had arranged for an employee to back a truck up to Jim's house and remove virtually everything valuable, "for safekeeping."

"From what?" Judge Jefferson demanded, and ordered Foreman to have everything returned immediately.

Afterward, in the hallway just outside the courtroom, Foreman accused me of forum shopping for that "nigger judge," a characterization I felt duty-bound by my high office to pass on to the judge's best friend. Nor did it hurt when I put my client on the stand and asked him where he was while Foreman was "pilfering your art." ("Objection!" hollered Foreman. "Sustained," said the judge, harshly admonishing me please not to say that anymore.) In response, Jim informed the court that he had been sailing at the time—ironically, with the selfsame best friend of Judge Jefferson.

Jefferson awarded Jim everything except the car he'd given his wife prior to their brief marriage, which, while right on the law, still pisses me off. Then he awarded Foreman $350 in legal fees instead of the

$35,000 he had sought. When Foreman and I met the next morning in a conference room across from the courtroom to settle up, I handed Foreman the car title. He asked me if I had the check for his fees and asked, "Or are you going to Jew me down on that, too?" I took the check from my inside coat pocket and looked at him and then at Jim, who nodded and smiled as I tore it into parts as tiny as Daddy Joe's diced eggs. I left it in a little pile on the table. Then Jim and I walked out, pausing at the door long enough for me to say, "Paste it together, asshole."

Foreman followed me down the hall like a puppy dog, asking me to have Jim write another check. But Jim never did, and Foreman never took us back to court to get it. Small victory, true, but if it is not clear by now that I am a petty man, then when will it ever be?

# 14

Two years to the day after Alan's remains were discovered, two thugs broke into Harriet's town house and, while her three children slept in the next room, raped her at gunpoint. When it was over, one of the men held the gun to her head and ordered her out to their car. Entirely by coincidence, Harriet's cousin and a friend dropped by, and when Harriet came to the door they sensed something was wrong. After retrieving a pistol from their car, they rang the doorbell again. This time, the rapists ran out past them and took off.

Harriet called me from the hospital. I saw her from down a long hallway, illuminated in white light, standing in a hospital gown. She looked disbelieving, but she was not in shock. She did not cry. As always, she kept her suffering to herself.

The rapists were arrested and convicted and the jury assessed a ten-year jail sentence for one of the defendants and a ten-year *probated* sentence for the other, stunning and embarrassing the prosecutor. It's possible that the jurors were left unmoved by Harriet's testimony: steeling herself against the humiliation of a court, she again showed very little emotion on the stand. Not long after, I read a story in the *Chronicle*: the thug on probation abducted a woman in San Antonio, drove her to a deserted field, raped her, and shot her dead.

After Alan's murder, Harriet retreated into her own family. Eager to overcome their trauma, the Laviages did not welcome contact with the Bergs. Still, Dad and Dot took Alan's children on occasional Sundays. My nephew Jonathan says that those visits were "the only thing we had going for us," and yet they also frightened him sometimes because "Grandpa always talked about Alan and took us to his grave."

Three years after Alan's death, Harriet remarried and I drifted away from her and the children, which I regret still. Soon after I began writing this book, I asked her to help me fill in some blanks, and she agreed to meet me one morning at the Avalon Drug Store. In her early sixties now, she is still striking and her kind and patient demeanor still reminds me of Momma Hattie. Soon we were talking and laughing about Alan and about how I, the freeloading brother-in-law, was there the night they returned from their honeymoon. When I asked her why she and Alan let me live with them, Harriet's answer shocked me, although I don't suppose it should have. "Your brother was afraid you'd kill yourself," she said.

Lisa, their oldest child, cannot speak of her father. She was five years old when he died and she says that she has memories of him, but thinking about how his life ended gives her "the willies." Their third child, Allison, called me in 2002 to ask if we could discuss Alan. My conversations with her led me to make contact with her brother, Jonathan, too, by then a successful entrepreneur who lives with his wife and three boys, triplets, high atop a hill in California. Down below is a perfectly manicured, regulation-size, Little League baseball diamond that Jonathan built for his sons in violation of several local ordinances. When the city tried to force him to tear it down, he fought them and won. Wait until San Diego discovers the three stables next to the ball field.

Dayle and I divorced in '77—Alan's murder and her mom's death too much for our already tenuous marriage to survive. Years later, in the nineties, a reporter writing a profile of me asked her what happened to our marriage and Dayle said, "We were both jerks. He was a jerk. I was a jerk." This was a vastly overgenerous view of my culpability, but otherwise I think she got it right.

About a month after our divorce, Dayle asked to meet with me, and in the boardroom of the bank where I had offices—the clear night lit with bright streetlamps and a yellow Shell sign across the way—she spoke with determination, as if she'd rehearsed what she was going to ask. "Would you consider taking custody of the boys until I get on my feet?"

I accepted on the spot. Geoff and our second son, Gabe, were eight and six at the time and I moved them into my two-bedroom town house on Yoakum, in the museum district, where we lived for the next five years. I had racing stripes painted on their walls and drove them to school in the mornings—and, like my father driving me, often got them there on time. In the afternoons we carpooled, and if I was in court, another parent or our housekeeper would pick them up. One night I came home so exhausted from a trial that I pulled down the shades and moved all of the clocks ahead by two hours so that I could put the boys to bed at six instead of eight. Still, I wanted the job and I was made for it, if maybe a little too involved in everything from Little League to homework. Even now, when I commence to meddlin', Geoff calls me "Mom."

When our sons entered middle school, Dayle and I began to share custody. She and I are good friends now, a rapprochement attributable to time, our children, and a shared loathing for one of Gabe's girlfriends. Dayle has jogged my memory about what life was like for us when Alan disappeared and after we buried him. One of the first things I asked her was why she loved Alan so much. "Because he loved you," she said, "and your parents didn't."

It was a very long time before Dad could speak of Alan without crying. I heard this secondhand, from Linda, because from the early seventies on, my father and I spoke rarely and only once about Alan. In 1988, he wrote me a letter asking that we talk through "whatever our problems are," and I agreed to meet him but insisted that we discuss *everything,* and he agreed. I even mentioned the one subject I'd never raised with him before.

"Will you talk about getting expelled from medical school?"

Dad did not hesitate.

"Everything, son. Everything."

We met at Anthony's Restaurant on Montrose Boulevard, near where Luigi's had been and where Dad and Dot and I spent Thursday evenings eating chicken cacciatore and listening to the owner sing arias. Dad was in his seventies now, but he had a full head of silver hair, and in his silk suit and tie he looked well and happy to see me. We ordered lunch, put the menus to one side, and I lost no time asking him what had happened at medical school. Dad didn't answer. Instead, he turned red and laughed, the same embarrassed way he laughed when I asked him if my dick was ever going to grow. But I wasn't laughing. I put my hand on his arm and said, "Everybody cheats sometimes, Dad. I cheated off Rick Kaminsky in chemistry lab. He's still mad at me, and that was the eleventh grade. I just didn't get caught. You need to forgive yourself." With that, Dad grabbed his handkerchief, pretended to cover a sneeze, and bolted from the table. When he returned, his eyes were red and damp and we ate our lunch in silence.

Afterward, over coffee that Dad's shaking hand spilled into his saucer, I brought up something else:

"Do you remember when Alan and I talked to you about not bad-mouthing DiMaria?"

"I don't. What are you talking about?"

"You don't remember the three of us sitting down in the employ-ees' lunchroom at Imperial?"

"Honestly, I don't."

"Come on, Dad. Just tell the truth!"

"I am not lying!"

"Well, let me remind you: We begged you to back off from DiMaria. We told you he was dangerous and you got mad. You ignored us. That probably cost Alan his life!"

"That's not true. I wouldn't just ignore either of you."

"Dad, you should have listened to us. That's why I avoid you. That's why I'm angry. It might be why Alan is dead. You *never* listened to us."

With that, he reddened again, asked for the check, paid it, and left without saying another word.

Dot later told me that Dad came home from that meeting out-raged, saying that I had made up a "preposterous" story about how Alan and I had tried to warn him off DiMaria.

"He said you accused him of being responsible for Alan's murder."

"I did."

"Well, David, I don't understand that. Your father worshipped your brother."

It didn't really surprise me that our conversation about DiMaria had vanished from my father's mind. We often conspire with our memories to make things come out as we want, not as they did. And while most parents will find a way to blame themselves for a child's death, even a death from natural causes, my father was a master of self-deception, especially when it allowed him to disassociate from anyone's bad fate, including his own. The day after DiMaria's arrest, in 1970, the *Post* quoted Dad as saying that he knew DiMaria but "not very well. Alan was the one associated with him." I can understand my father's desire to distance himself from DiMaria. I can imagine how awful it must be to feel even a modicum of responsibility for the death of your child. But his self-deception—and my frustration over his denial—froze our relationship in place. All I wanted out of that lunch was one honest conversation with my father. Maybe I wouldn't have stayed so angry with him for so long. We might even have gotten closer toward the end. I think both of us would have liked that.

In his late seventies, my father slipped into dementia. He became paranoid, obsessive, and dangerous. Frequently he would show up at my office to rant about Dot, who he was convinced was having an affair with my cousin's husband, a good man twenty-five years younger than she. When Dot agreed to take a lie detector test and passed, Dad accused her of having sex with the polygraph operator. Then he bought a gun and threatened to kill her. When I heard that, I took Dot to court and got an order committing him to the Harris County Psychiatric Center. Dad stayed locked up for a month. Upon his release, thanks to thirty days' intensive therapy and psychotropic drugs, he was the father I remembered from my early days in Houston.

That was 1994, the year I'd married Kathryn Page, whom I'd met three years before. Soon after his release, Kathryn and I invited Dad and Dot to dinner at our home. Around a table set with candles that seemed to keep things calm, Dad told us what he had learned about himself in the psychiatric center. He told a story he unearthed during group therapy, about catching his mother in bed with the landlord. He told Dot that he was sorry; he knew she wasn't having an affair. And he said that he missed his mother and father—that their Yiddish accents had embarrassed him but that he would give anything to hear their voices again. He did not mention medical school. We did not mention Alan.

Thirty days later, Dad quit taking his medicine and slipped back into dementia. Within the year, his kidneys began to fail; his body was shutting down. He wore diapers and depended on Dot's care, which was generous and forthcoming. I was trying a case in Florida when Dot called my office to say that he was dying. The judge let me off that Friday and I flew home. Geoff and I went to his house and found Dad seated in the living room, his hands perched on a cane, dressed fastidiously and looking and acting nowhere near death or dementia. His speech was halting but understandable, and while the three of us sat together Dad and Geoff talked about Israel. My son said something to him in Hebrew and my father, straight-faced, said, "Did he just tell me to go fuck myself?" We laughed but it was an odd moment: for all his "goddamns," I'd never heard him once say "fuck."

When Geoff left the room, Dad sobered and, completely lucid, said, "I want you to tell Mother something. Tell her that the worst mistake I ever made was to leave her. I was a shit heel the way I treated her." He said he told Dot that he wanted to leave Mom his share of their property and Dot said that was fine, that it was his money. He didn't do that, maybe because he died before he had the chance to arrange it, but when I told Mom what he said, she was content. Dad always said, "Don't live a life of regret." I would never have imagined that his included my mother.

The next day, Dad woke up disoriented and unable to speak coherently. Dot took him to the hospital, and a few days later he was gone. Alone in the room with him, I brushed his silver hair back and kissed his forehead. He was already growing cold. "I am so sorry, Pop," I said, "I am so sorry."

Do I love my father? Yes, but that love is buried beneath a mile of resentment and grief. And I have felt enormous compassion for him, in particular when my sister tracked down his medical school transcript and I read the words "On April 9, 1936, Mr. Berg was expelled on account of failure in surgery and infraction of discipline—attempted bribery." Everyone fucks up big-time now and again. I don't fault my father for that. I fault him for allowing his failures to define his life—and my brother's. So yes, I love him, and I feel compassion for him, and I am grateful that he and Dot spent their last dime without cavil while looking for my brother. And I am aware—haunted, really—that Woody Harrelson was more comfort to his murderous father as he aged than I was to Dad. But most of all I feel sadness over who he was and who he could have been if only he had found a way to confront his past and extinguish his shame.

I once heard Johnny Carson ask the British psychologist Sir Ashley Montague how he would define the family. Sir Ashley did not hesitate: "The family unit is the institution for the systematic production of mental illness." Not wanting to fall victim to my own family's pattern—especially of unfulfilled promise—I have tried in many ways to live my life as the anti-Nat, failing in one respect: I am too quick to anger. But as a father, I have done all right with my two sons, Geoff and Gabe, and my daughter, Caitlin (from my second marriage). Obviously, being a good parent is not the same as being a perfect parent. We all have our moments. I do, however, believe firmly in a simple aphorism: Let the string get taut—but never let it break.

After Alan's death, Mom moved to Houston to be closer to her children and grandchildren. She kept the books for my practice and sent the invoices out before the end of the month so that mine would go right on top of the recipients' bill-paying stack, a practice my firm maintains to this day. But when my monthly income soared to $1,500, she began referring to me behind my back as one of those "goddamn rich Jews." And she was forever a shit-stirrer. Once, while babysitting my boys, she told them that their father had betrayed his own brother by representing a man accused of murder and getting him off. They were five and seven. When I confronted her, she said what she always said: "Well, honey, I just told them the truth."

Of all the fictions of self-made men, perhaps the most dubious is that of being self-made. I owe a lot to Alan and Racehorse, of course, but a great deal to Mom, too. I often think about how her work ethic, her belief that I could do whatever I set my mind to doing, and all those things she taught me that I wouldn't learn in school, like typing at age eight, speaking without fluffing, and especially how to respect money, were crucial support and examples that my brother didn't have. She could also be very funny, Mom. Toward the end of her life I was there in the nursing home with her when her oximeter dropped to potentially fatal levels, moving a doctor, two nurses, and some attendants to crowd around her bed. She motioned to me to come close and said in a stage whisper, "I am surrounded by a colony of Amazons. Get them *out* of here." Then she added, "Also, you need a haircut."

In 2000, as Mom lay close to death in her hospital bed, eyes closed, breathing labored and with an oxygen tube in her nose, I sat down beside her. I didn't know if she could hear me, but she looked terrified. "Now you'll see Alan again," I said. Her eyebrows shot up, her dark almond eyes opened wide, and she was smiling. I liked sending her off with that thought. I didn't really believe it, but she seemed to, and that was fine with me. A little while later, in the same room, Linda asked me in a whisper when I thought Mom would die. I told her that I didn't know but we could get a pool going. I hoped that our mother didn't hear me, or that if she did, she thought it was funny. Linda didn't.

My sister never recovered from Alan's death. She cannot shake the mourning, even now, although she once had a dream about Alan, fifteen years after his murder, in which he told her to quit worrying about him. For my part, I have never unraveled all the ways in which Alan's murder has affected me, or all the reasons I refused to mourn his death. I have, however, come to understand that the main reason that I cannot mourn Alan's death was Alan himself: I was angry at my brother, whose recklessness put him in the company of worthless, violent men and squarely in the bullet's path.

And on some profound level that I can neither reach nor erase—despite dental records and skeletal remains that long since confirmed my brother's demise—I cannot accept his death. I awoke just the other morning and murmured, "Run, Alan, run." And in 1983, when Klansmen murdered a Denver talk show host named Alan Berg, I actually thought it might be my brother. My mind raced with hope that he had, after all, run off and started a new life—and, irrationally, the news of this Alan Berg's death caused me to think: now that I've found him, he's been killed all over again.

In 1993, Kathryn and I were at a Nature Conservancy fund-raiser on Long Island and bid on two tickets to the "Concert of a Lifetime": the reunion of Simon and Garfunkel at Madison Square Garden. We won, and it was on the flight from Houston to New York for the concert that I proposed and she accepted. The first shock that night came as we approached the Garden and saw on the marquee that the "once in a lifetime" concert was actually going to run for thirty days. The second came when Woody Harrelson and his party sat down in the box next to ours. All evening, I could not concentrate on the music. The only thing I could focus on were the thin, outstretched legs of my brother's murderer's son. He was wearing jeans and tennis shoes and seemed to be enjoying himself. When he laughed, I wanted to leave, but I didn't.

So it was the concert of a lifetime after all.

In 2007, I read a *New York Times* interview with Woody Harrelson, who was quoted as saying about his father, "I would give anything, anything, just to have done with him what we are doing right now, which is to sit outside on a beautiful day having a meal." I put the paper down and wondered whether his father's other victims hated Woody for saying that, too. That same year, *No Country for Old Men* was released and I went because I never miss a Coen brothers movie. I'd had no idea that Woody Harrelson was in it, or I never would have gone. I had never been able to watch him in anything, and whenever he came on TV, I immediately switched channels. But I stayed, and at the moment in the film when the sadistic killer—again, suggestive of Charles Harrelson—levels his shotgun at Woody's character, I studied Woody's eyes and realized I'd been wrong when I caught a glimpse of them at the Garden: they looked nothing like his father's. And when his character asks the murderer "Do you realize how goddamn crazy you are?" I wondered if Woody had ever asked that of his father—and, if he had, what his father had said in return.

~

It was on the morning of September 18, 1970, that Harrelson was acquitted of Alan's murder, and late that afternoon I was seated alone at the Inns of Court, drinking coffee and trying to concentrate on a TV report about Jimi Hendrix, who'd died that same day. Racehorse Haynes came to my table. He stood there for a moment and then said, "I'm sorry about the verdict, brother." I responded, "It affirms my faith in the judicial system." I was being sarcastic, of course; in truth I felt the opposite. I am an idealist. I have enormous faith in jury trials; it is jury-fixing and perjury I despise.

In 1979, *Parade* magazine profiled me with the headline "Is He The Meanest Lawyer In Town?," but by then the question had become rhetorical. Of course I was mean. I was *angry*. It wouldn't take Freud to figure out that I'd found an outlet for my rage and that winning cases was my revenge. The more difficult the case, the more "indefensible" the client, even better. Still, I would be lying if I said that what my mother told my sons about betraying Alan didn't bother me (and not just because she said it). Long before, I was troubled by that thought. And more than once, most memorably following the acquittal of a genuinely terrifying murder defendant, I lay awake at night worrying whether he would kill again. I have also agonized over introducing evidence of a victim's bad character, as Foreman did to my brother—yet not so much that I didn't do it, provided, of course, that the evidence was true. So in 1991 I began converting my practice to civil trials, and that same year, represented the survivors of a family of an African-American woman killed at a railroad crossing in Brazoria County. The case was tried in a courthouse adjoining the one in which Harrelson was acquitted twenty-one years before. At mediation, the railroad's lawyer offered me a pittance to settle, and when I rejected it, he put his arm around my shoulder and told me he liked me and was trying to do me a favor, because no black family "would get any money from an Angleton jury." Still, I wondered if I had done the right thing—it was, after all, the setting of the worst injustice I'd ever known. But the trial went well for us, and just before closing argument, the lawyer quadrupled his earlier settlement offer. By then I'd practiced almost twenty-five years and could read jurors pretty well; I thought I detected in the twelve white folks on that panel a real change of attitude. I told my clients to reject the offer, which they did, and the all-white jury returned a record $12.25 million verdict—disabusing the railroad lawyer, one assumes, of his misconception about black folks and white juries in Angleton, Texas.

The more troubling issue, one I will never resolve, is how I could have put my ambition and reputation above showing up for Harrelson's trial. It's true, I wasn't there. I followed it obsessively, on television, in newspapers, and through daily reports from my sister, who bravely attended each day, and I have since reconstructed it here with the aid of court records, articles, interviews, and my own memory of what I learned back then. But at the time I could not bring myself to go. I did have one good reason. Had I gone, Foreman would have subpoenaed me, not because he intended to call me to the stand, but because he wouldn't have wanted my grieving face in the courtroom. Without agreement of the parties, no fact witness is ever allowed to listen to the testimony of others. (I have never understood why he didn't subpoena Linda for the same reason, except to guess that maybe he didn't know Alan had a sister.) So I didn't show up and didn't give Foreman that satisfaction. But that wasn't the only reason. It wasn't even the primary reason. The primary reason was that just as Harrelson's murder trial was getting under way, my career was taking off. At last, I was not *just another Berg*. I had won a case in the Supreme Court. I was the triumphant motherfucker who'd gotten the ragtag war protesters their parade permit. I did not want, simultaneously, to be dragged down by the sordid headlines about my family that were all over the local media. Forty years later, however, I am still racked with regret. I can understand my ambitious twenty-eight-year-old self running away from those headlines, and my family's past. But running away from Alan? Even under subpoena, I could have been present for opening and closing arguments, and the verdict, which would have been something of a testament to my brother's memory. I can only comfort myself with the tenuous hope that if he were here to weigh in on my absence, Alan would understand and forgive me. I can't.

# EPILOGUE

For years I ran along a strip of beach on the Atlantic listening to the rumble of waves as they gathered offshore. When they hit the beach on moonlit nights, white light burst across their rims like a fingernail snapped across the top of a phosphorus match. I would race the waves as far and as fast as I could, until I couldn't run anymore. Now my knee has given out, so I can no longer run, but I still walk very fast down the same corridors of sand, next to the same waters, often thinking of Alan. The pounding of the waves is a constant and a comfort in my life, as are the memories they evoke of my generous, wisecracking brother. Most often I remember him that day he returned from the navy, standing in the den, bathed in sunlight, wearing dark glasses.

I have visited Alan's grave three times since we buried his remains. I went for the first time after the *Schacht* decision, to brag. But after a couple minutes, I realized I was babbling about Erwin Griswold into empty space in the remotest part of a Houston cemetery, felt like an idiot—and bolted. The second time was thirty-five years later, when Alan's daughter Allison asked me to take her. We walked along the street and among the graves until we found his, which now is surrounded by others. I knew some of the names on those other gravestones, and the ones I recognized were not, after all, impious, suicidal, or criminal. Someone had planted a beautiful, evenly cut, horseshoe-shaped hedge around Alan's headstone and neither Allison nor I had any idea who had done that. While we sat at his graveside, Allison was speechless, riven by guilt because she had not been to her father's grave before, as if neglecting a mound of grass were a reflection of her character. She seemed relieved to know I hadn't been there but once myself.

The third time, I went alone, on a sweltering August day, when I was having difficulty finishing this book. I drove to the cemetery on a Saturday but found it closed for Shabbat, so I parked my car in the driveway and climbed over a chain-link fence papered with multiple warnings not to trespass. The fence was already bent, and as I climbed, slipping my fingers through one chain link and then another, it bowed all the way over as I reached the top and delivered me gently to the grass on the other side. I was filled with a sense of accomplishment: here I was sixty-eight and not only had I scaled the fortress walls, I had committed at least one misdemeanor to do so—maybe two, if you count the destruction of property. And now I'd made it and there was no one else around, not even a caretaker.

This time, I headed right for Alan's grave, where I focused on the headstone with its banal inscription, about his being a devoted husband, father, brother, and son. If his children agree, I have it in mind to replace it with one that says, "Here lies Alan Berg. He was very funny."

I stood there for a while, fidgeting, sweltering in the heat. Finally I sat down heavily, near where Alan's skull would have been buried. I *did* feel close to him. I spoke to him: "I did what you told me, man. I quit talking. I did things." Then I blurted out something that I have never said aloud to anyone, ever. "I also got rich." I had to laugh at myself, telling that to the dead earth when I would be embarrassed to say it even to my wife.

Not long ago I found a poem that captures in its angst something I believe to be true: nothing is more difficult than death out of order. The poem is two thousand years old, by the Roman poet Catullus, about whom little is known except that he wandered the discovered world until he found his warrior brother's grave and there left traditional gifts. I know it by heart. I love to say the title out loud in Latin, and that day, I did: *"Ave Atque Vale."* Then I recited it in English, for my brother:

> By ways remote and distant waters sped,
> Brother, to thy sad grave-side am I come,
> That I may give the last gifts to the dead,
> And vainly parley with thine ashes dumb;
> Since she who now bestows and now denies
> Hath taken thee, hapless brother, from mine eyes.
> But lo! these gifts, the heirlooms of past years,
> Are made sad things to grace thy coffin shell,
> Take them, all drenchèd with a brother's tears,
> And, brother, for all time, hail and farewell!

I repeated the last line in Latin, lingering over *frater*—brother. Finally I was crying, then sobbing—and couldn't stop. I don't know how long I sat there like that, addressing him, saying his name out loud for the first time in such a long time, but soon I was spent. And in the quiet of that afternoon, almost lulled to sleep by the heat and the steady drone of the cicadas, my mind wandered to that day in Galveston, so long ago, when Alan and I sat and stared from the unsullied shore into the Gulf of Mexico and envisioned our future together.

We would share everything, we said.

# ACKNOWLEDGMENTS

I am a writer who needs an editor, witness the first draft of this book, which weighed in at 335 pages. When I told a friend in publishing that cutting it down was like killing off my children, he immediately recommended Lisa Halliday, a writer herself, former agent, and gifted editor. Without her help—primarily convincing me that not every funny thing that ever happened to me was of interest to readers—this book would have remained a rather meandering history of the Jews of Arkansas.

Just before submitting the book to publishers, my dogged agent, David McCormick, suggested that I have a fresh set of eyes take one last look and that led me to his friend Jamie Malanowski, also an author and editor, who took a look from thirty thousand feet and suggested some structural changes that proved invaluable.

In 2012, four years after I began writing, I found an agent and my book a publisher. Colin Harrison at Scribner read the book and suggested that he and I meet for coffee at the Pig 'n' Whistle across from his offices, where he actually drank coffee and I did not as I nervously awaited his verdict. In fact, he loved my book, we got along famously, and within the week, on his recommendation, Scribner was my publisher—which is especially meaningful to English majors such as me who revere the writers of the twenties and thirties and the role that Scribner played. And if Maxwell Perkins has spiritual heirs, surely Colin, with seven novels of his own, is one of them, whose gentle suggestions I appreciate almost as much as I appreciate his refusal to mention my embarrassing grammatical errors.

Even before Lisa and Jamie came Diana Gallagher and Matthew Miranda, writers themselves, who, sitting around my kitchen table, took turns reading the book aloud—three days from start to finish—for me, an excellent way to edit, to make certain I had written the way I speak. I recently repeated the exercise when I received the galley proofs, this time with Devon Plachy, a young musician—not only to search out nits in the manuscript but also to test a nonwriter's reactions. And given that a fourth of the book had been off-loaded to the editing-room floor, we finished in just two days.

My sister, Linda Todar, researched much of this book, uncovering documents from across the country that gave a broader context to the story I had to tell—especially Dad's transcript from the University of Arkansas medical school. She has read every word of every draft of this book, has been unfailing in her support and praise of what I was doing—and for that, and the closeness this book created, I am very grateful.

Two friends in particular have gone out of their way to help spread the word about my book since reading the first draft: Lou Briskman, who spread the word by email, and Slavka Glaser, who spread the word by leaving that first draft on a BA flight to Turkey. My lifelong friends Paul Gerson, Gene Keilin (my high school debate partner), and Mark Paull reminded me of things germane to this book from decades ago, some about us, some about Alan, and some of it on these pages. I really owe my niece Vanessa Tucker something, not money, of course, but something, for sparing me the embarrassment of a glitch about dates that she caught and I would never have seen. My ninety-year-old clear-eyed uncle, Maurice Besser, provided extraordinary detail and insight into my family's early history, much of which fell under Lisa Halliday's ax, but what remained caused him to ask Linda if I always talked that dirty. I've also sent the manuscript in various incarnations to close relatives and friends. As they know who they are and as there are too many to thank individually, I thank them all in general, for their encouragement through the years.

I was able to continue practicing law while writing both this book and my first one because my indulgent and devoted law partner of thirty years, Joel Androphy, took up the slack at the firm. There's no way to thank him enough. There were others who willingly bore an extra burden because of my absences, including our business manager, Kathy Wagner, and my assistant, Jean Rivers.

Above all, I thank my former sister-in-law, Harriet Weisz, whom I love not only for reminding me of forgotten moments that are woven into this book but also for her four years with Alan. Her children, my nephew and nieces, Lisa, Jonathan, and Allison, deserved better than what they got and I hope that this book allows them to know better, as it is said, warts and all, their Gatsby-esque first father.

Writing this book has been something of a family affair and each member of it has, in different measure, provided me with comfort, suggestions, and when I needed it, isolation. My wife, Kathryn, my ideal reader, is the one person I don't have to pay to be totally candid about what she has read. She edited this book early and late and as thanks has had the singular honor of living with a man whose mood rises and falls in direct proportion to the quality of the last paragraph he wrote. My son Gabe really shocked me when he told me that he had

ACKNOWLEDGMENTS

retrieved the Harrelson trial file from the Brazoria County courthouse and corresponded with Judge Bass—all a decade before I learned about it. That material, and his great insight into writing, has been invaluable. My eldest son, Geoff, may not realize how relieved I was the day I wondered aloud what the reception would be to my book and he responded, "Who was it who told me you can't succeed at anything unless you are willing to make a complete asshole of yourself on the front page of the *New York Times*?" Apparently, he was listening. Thanks also to Caitlin, our fifteen-year-old daughter, already another wiseass Berg and an aspiring actor, for making room in the house during these past five years for my other child (my book). At last, I'm giving it up for adoption.

Finally, I want to acknowledge that the story of "Diana B." in the prologue and a smattering of other material are from my book *The Trial Lawyer: What It Takes to Win* and appear on these pages courtesy of the publisher, the American Bar Association. In addition, it was from Bryan Burrough's excellent book *The Big Rich: The Rise and Fall of the Greatest Texas Oil Fortunes* (© Penguin Books, 2009) that I learned of Hugh Roy Cullen's letter to the *Chronicle* opposing zoning.

# ABOUT THE AUTHOR

DAVID BERG is a writer and lawyer whose first essay, "If You Hate Lawyers, Read This," was published in the *New York Times* in 1979. Since then he has written dozens of political, personal, and legal essays and articles that have appeared in national newspapers and magazines. His first book, *The Trial Lawyer: What It Takes to Win,* remains essential reading for trial lawyers.

Berg is the founding partner of Berg & Androphy, with offices in Houston and New York. During his early years, he devoted himself to civil rights and criminal cases, and in 1970, at twenty-eight, argued and won a First Amendment case in the US Supreme Court. In 1981, he and his friend Morris Dees of the Southern Poverty Law Center represented Vietnamese fishermen in a lawsuit that ended the Ku Klux Klan's reign of terror along the Texas Gulf Coast. His practice later evolved to white-collar defense and commercial litigation as well as frequent pro bono service to the city of Houston.

David Berg is married to Kathryn and has two sons, Geoff and Gabe, and one daughter, Caitlin, who aspires to a Broadway career and who also attends high school.